Di questa sorte dal Asino nõ e grã tempo ch ne era uno in la
patria mia. il quale si e puoi abandonato p la morte del
padrone molti dicano cheghi'era un util mudo e che li
Colori si macinauano ottima mẽte ch nõ c'di poca impo
rtantia nel Arte

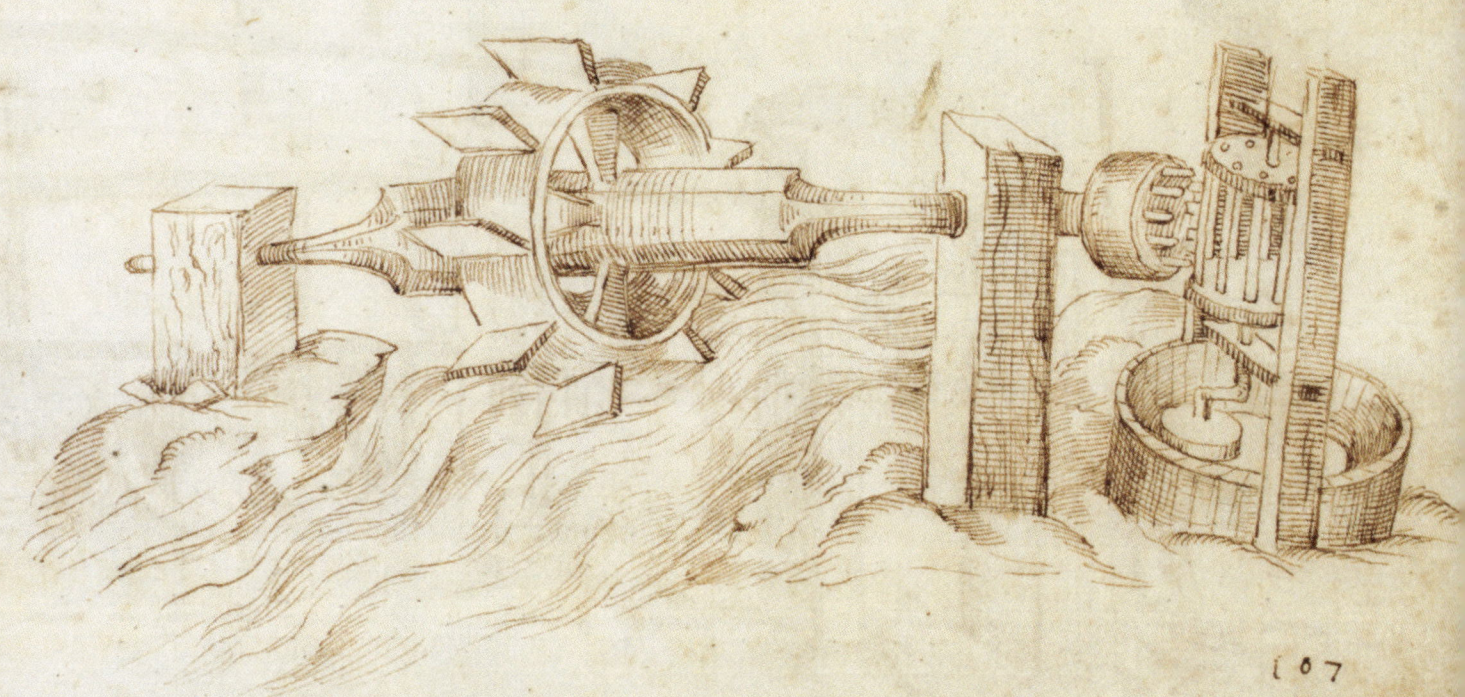

107

E come il mulin da laqua questo e molto mirabile in que
sto esercitio p ch egli stilla i Colori e quanto sono me
glio macinati tanto so di piu utile di piu sparagnio
e uengano di piu p fetione al fuoco! un quasi di que
sto andare hó ueduto io in Fuligni Cita di Roma.
ma di piu bello ingegnio cosa degnia di consideratione
impero ch un solo uccelletto macina doi Mulini che chi
la ua ben considerando il medesmo faria di 3 e di 4.

Stillare tolto da
colloro Et Lambican

MAIOLICA AND FAIENCE

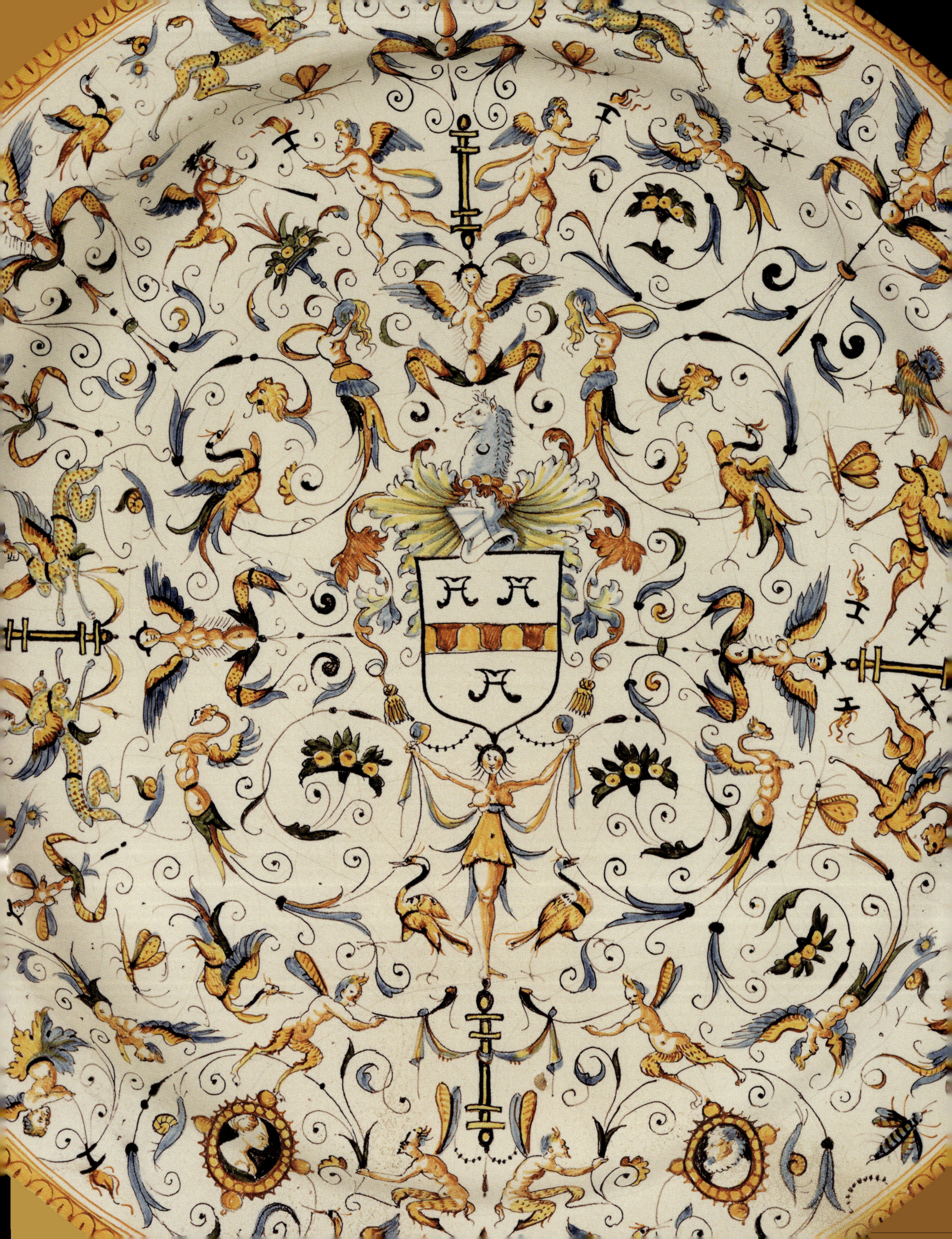

MAIOLICA AND FAIENCE

*

Acquisitions of European tin-glaze and related pottery for the Ashmolean Museum, 2017–25

*

Timothy Wilson
Matthew Winterbottom
Francesca Leoni

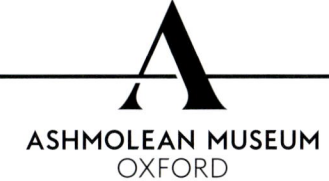

ASHMOLEAN MUSEUM
OXFORD

Dedicated to the memory of Martin Foley (1932–2025)
and published in association with the Oxford Ceramics Group

MAIOLICA AND FAIENCE

Copyright © Ashmolean Museum, University of Oxford 2025

Timothy Wilson, Matthew Winterbottom and Francesca Leoni have asserted their moral right to be identified as the authors of this work.

British Library Cataloguing in Publications Data

A catalogue record for this book is available from the British Library.

ISBN: 978-1-910807-73-6

Photography by Eleanor Atkins, Henrietta Clare and David Gowers

Edited by Lizzy Silverton

Designed by Stephen Hebron

Printed and bound in the UK by Gomer Press

Frontispiece: detail of no.**12**

Endpapers: drawings by Cipriano Piccolpasso from his *Three Books of the Potter's Art, c.*1557; front: three types of mills for grinding colours – human-powered, donkey-driven, and connected to a water wheel; back: water-powered double mill for grinding colours and a canalside grinding mill in Venice. © Victoria and Albert Museum, London

For further details of Ashmolean titles please visit:
www.ashmolean.org/shop

Published with the support of the Ceramica-Stiftung, Basel

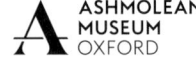 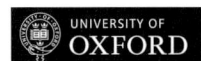

Contents

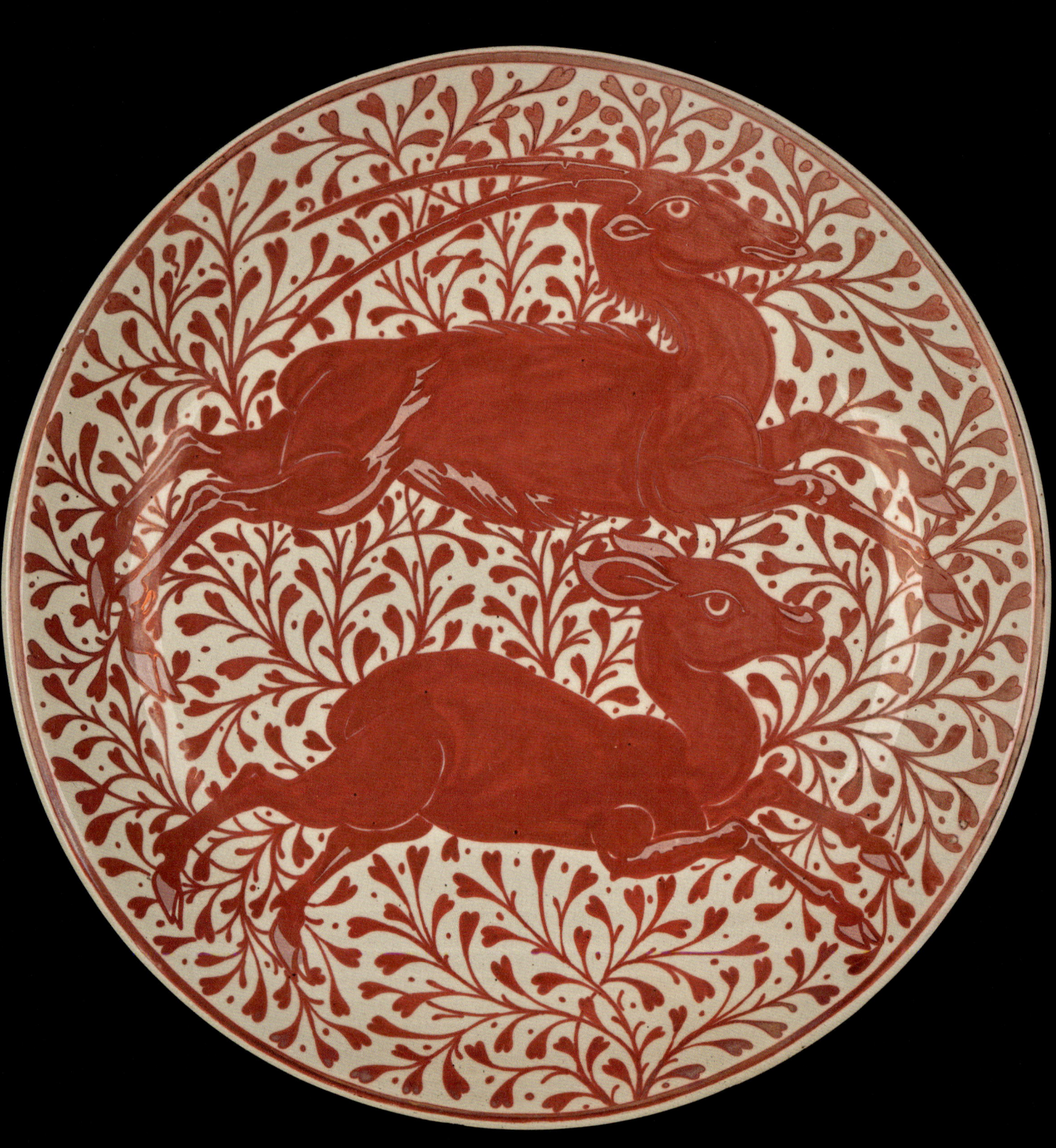

Introduction

Timothy Wilson's catalogue *Italian Maiolica and Europe* (2017), included the whole of the Ashmolean Museum's collections of post-Classical Italian pottery up to the date of publication. It also included an extensive selection of pieces from Spain, Portugal, France, Germany, the Low Countries, England, and Mexico to illustrate the spread of tin-glaze pottery in Europe from the fourteenth century onwards and the positive impact of skilled immigration on technology transfer and creativity. Nearly a third of the 287 items included had been acquired for the Museum since 1990.

Since 2017, the Museum has continued to enrich and extend its collections of Italian maiolica, French faience, and other wares related to the themes of the 2017 catalogue, mainly through the generosity of its friends and supporters and through the British Government's admirable system by which works of art can be accepted in lieu of inheritance tax.[1]

A particular theme has been in the post-Renaissance development of the technique of metallic lustre, culminating in the brilliant bowl by the contemporary Iranian potter Abbas Akbari and the work of three contemporary European exponents.[2]

The period has seen a dramatic growth in the Ashmolean's collections of nineteenth-century decorative arts, mainly, but not exclusively, English, in great part through the support of Barrie and Deedee Wigmore of New York City. In the context of the present publication, pride of place is taken by the work of William De Morgan, the multi-talented artist who single-handedly created a revival in England of the traditional technique of reduced-pigment lustre. At the time of writing, the Museum has on indefinite loan an extensive collection of De Morgan pottery from the De Morgan Foundation. Added to the collection, and included in this publication, are nine fine examples of De Morgan pottery (six of them lustred), two examples of the so-called 'faience' made at the Doulton Studio at Lambeth, and two pieces, in 'Persian' style, of the 'faience' produced by the Burmantofts Pottery in Leeds, as well as two tiles of the colossally successful 'majolica' developed by Minton's of Stoke-on-Trent around 1850.

The present publication describes 61 of these acquisitions and so constitutes a supplementary volume to the 2017 catalogue. Entries nos **14**, **18**, and **43–59** have been written by Matthew Winterbottom; no.**61** is by Francesca Leoni; the remainder are by Timothy Wilson.

In the same period, the Ashmolean collections have been enriched by other important acquisitions of European ceramics that fall outside the scope of the present publication. These include a uniquely magnificent example of Vauxhall porcelain accepted by H. M. Government in lieu of inheritance tax on the estate of Anthony Du Boulay, in accordance with his wishes;[3] and thirteen examples of early English salt-glazed stoneware from the collection of Jonathan Horne, accepted by H. M. Government in lieu of inheritance tax on the estate of Mrs Rachael Horne.[4] In both cases, the Museum enormously appreciates the good will of the collectors involved and their heirs and executors. Gifts of English porcelain in the same period include two rare and delightful saucers of the group marked *A*, which is perhaps the very earliest English porcelain but which, despite evident links to the Bow factory, remains in many respects mysterious, presented by John Mallet in memory of Robert Charleston;[5] and a Bow porcelain sauceboat of *c*.1750 imitating a contemporary London silver shape presented by Dinah Reynolds in memory of the Rev. John Reynolds.[6]

The present publication has been supported by a munificent grant from the Ceramica-Stiftung, Basel. We also warmly thank the late Martin Foley (Mexico City), Londa Weisman (New York City and Vermont), and a supporter who wishes to remain anonymous for sponsorship of printing. We are happy that it is supported by and published in association with the dynamic Oxford Ceramics Group.

Enlargeable images of all the pieces in this volume and the 2017 one are, or will be as soon as possible, on the Ashmolean website: https://ashmolean.org/collections-online. Addenda and corrigenda to the 2017 catalogue can be found on the web pages https://timothywilson.co.uk/publications.

Apart from those thanked in individual entries, we thank for help in various ways: Catherine Casley, Stephen Hebron, Carrie Hickman, Declan McCarthy, Dana Macmillan, Jody Wilkie, and Jane Wilson.

1 In managing these and numerous other acceptance in lieu (AIL) cases, the Museum has cause to be grateful over many years for the wisdom, pragmatism, and professionalism of two wonderful public servants working for Arts Council England, Gerry McQuillan and Anastasia Tennant, as well as their successors.

2 For the techniques and terminology of lustreware, see Caiger-Smith 1991, especially p.17.

3 Ashmolean Museum, WA2024.15; see *Cultural Gifts and Acceptance in Lieu Report 2024*, no.18; Massey 2024.

4 Ashmolean Museum, WA2025.15–27; see *Cultural Gifts and Acceptance in Lieu Report 2024*, no.29; Hildyard 2025.

5 Ashmolean Museum, WA2024.13 and 14; see Mallet 2024, pp.26–33.

6 Ashmolean Museum, WA2015.7; see *Oxford Ceramics Group Newsletter* 60 (October 2024), p.23, fig.3.

Opposite: no.**52**

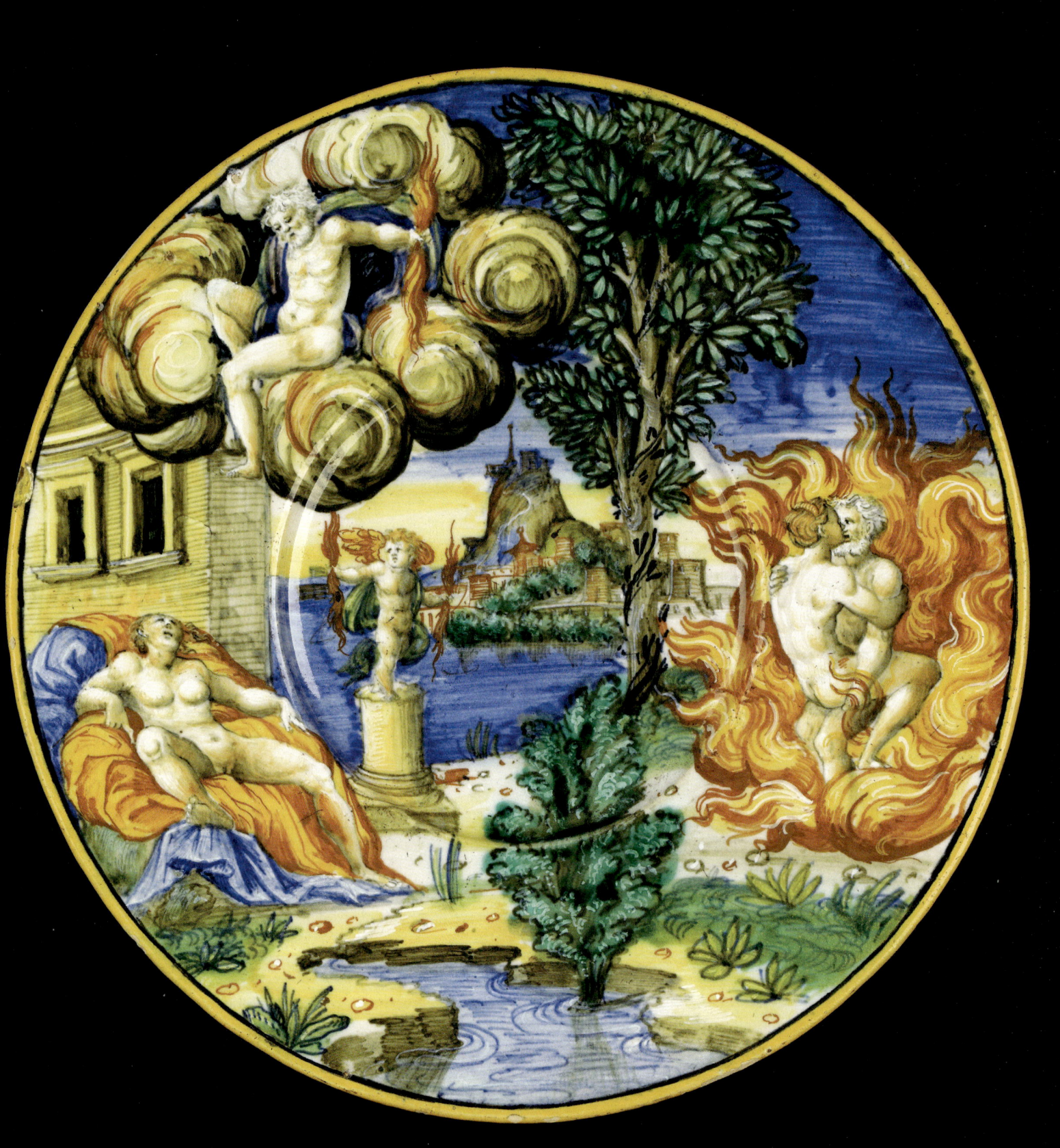

ITALY

Three pieces of Italian maiolica from the collection of the eminent Minoan archaeologist Sinclair Hood (1917–2021) were accepted by H. M. Government in lieu of inheritance tax in 2022 and allocated to the Ashmolean according to Mr Hood's wishes. They were already on loan to the Museum and were published (as promised acquisitions) in *Italian Maiolica and Europe*: a plate with Amphiaraus, Polynices, and Eriphyle by Francesco Xanto Avelli, cat.59 (now WA2022.700); a plate with Jupiter and Semele by Francesco Durantino, cat.65 (now WA2022.701, illustrated on the facing page); and a small Deruta or more probably Orvieto plate, cat.100 (now WA2022.702).[7] They are not described again here.

7 See *Cultural Gifts Scheme and Acceptance in Lieu Report* 2022, no.26; *Burlington Magazine* 166 (December 2024), pp.4–5, no.8.

Opposite: fig.1 *Jupiter and Semele* by Francesco Durantino, Urbino *c.*1542. Accepted by H.M. Government in lieu of inheritance tax from the estate of Sinclair Hood and allocated to the Ashmolean, WA2022.701

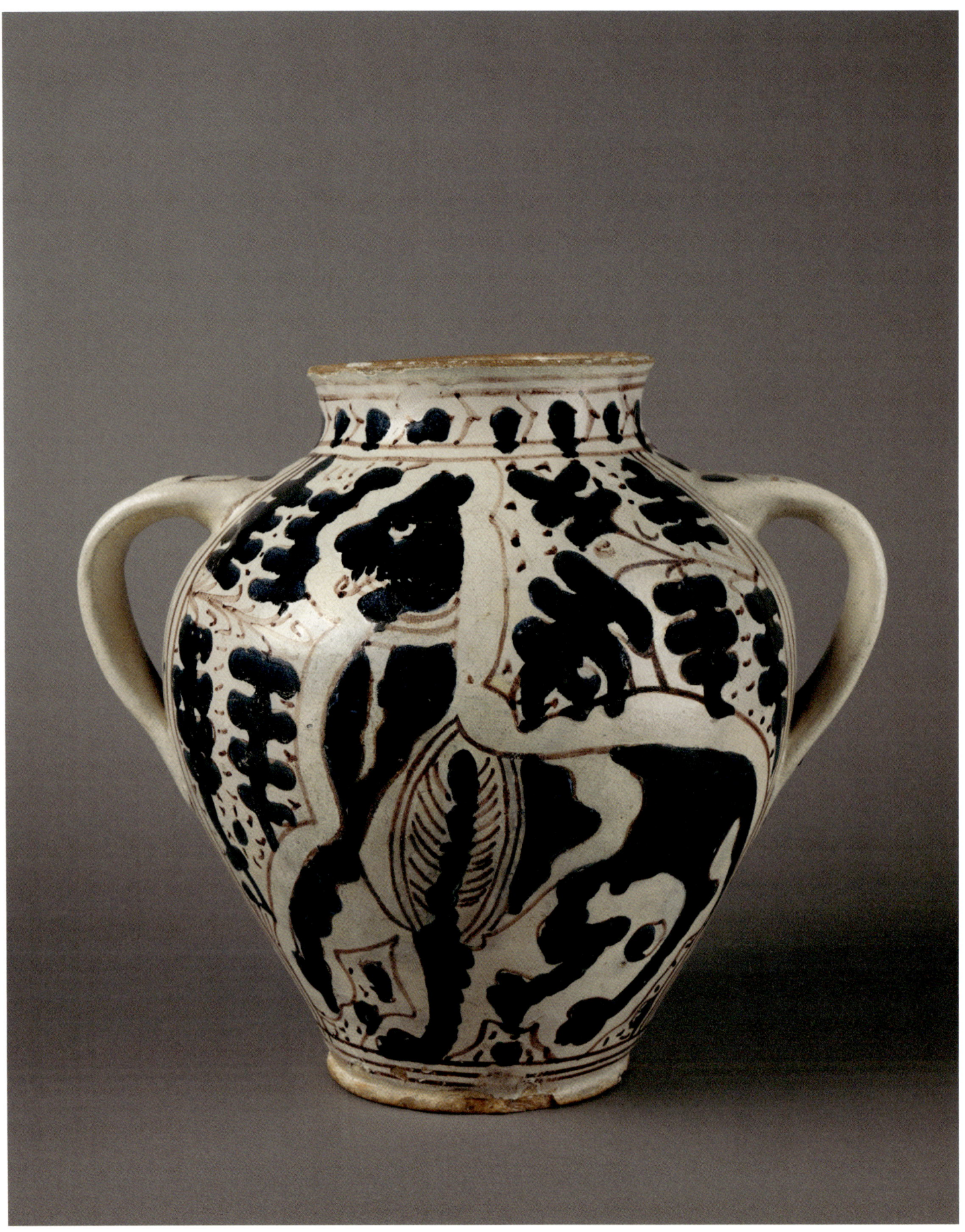

1

Pharmacy jar

Florence district, probably Montelupo, c.1420–40
Accepted under the Cultural Gifts Scheme by H. M. Government from Sam Fogg Ltd
and allocated in accordance with the condition of the gift to the Ashmolean, WA2025.49.

Reddish earthenware, covered on the outside with a white tin-glaze, crackled and of a greyish tint; the flat foot is unglazed; the glaze on the interior is severely degraded, presumably corroded by the drugs it once contained. The rim is slightly flanged allowing the jar to be closed with oilcloth, paper, or parchment tied round the neck.

Height: 27 cm

CONDITION: apparently intact, but with some flaking of glaze and retouching. The handles, which were missing when the jar was sold in 1902, are modern replacements, but a fair approximation of the handles the jar would have had.

PROVENANCE: Stefano Bardini, Florence; sold at the Bardini sale, Christie's, London; 26–30 May 1902, lot 239 (as Montelupo), bought by 'Guinot' for 25 guineas; perhaps private collection, Italy; Hampel Fine Art Auctions, Munich, 27 June 2013, lot 547 (as Siena); Sam Fogg, London.

BIBLIOGRAPHY: *Collection Bardini 27 Mai 1902* (a separately numbered photographic album produced in connection with the Christie's sale), pl.17, no.471; Sani et al. 2017, no.6; Luber 2023, no.34.

The bulbous jar is of a form favoured for pharmacies, and perhaps also for general storage use, in Tuscany from the fourteenth and through much of the fifteenth century. The surface is painted over a rapidly executed drawing in manganese purple, with a solid dark blue that stands out strongly in relief, known in Italian as *zaffera a rilievo*. On either side, set in a contour panel against a pattern of leaves (perhaps intended as oak leaves), is a creature striding to the left, *passant* in heraldic terminology. The collared animal has some resemblance to a dog, but is probably intended as a leopard (or panther).[8] Round the neck is a band of alternating horizontal chevrons in manganese and blobs of relief blue.

This is a larger than average and imposing example of the most iconic type of early Renaissance Italian maiolica,

named by the English artist-collector Henry Wallis (1830–1916), in an elegant, illustrated volume devoted to them in 1903, 'Oak-leaf jars'.[9] Among the surviving jars of this type are about twenty bearing the crutch mark of the Florentine hospital of Santa Maria Nuova, which can be connected with a document recording a

large order from the hospital in 1431 for a new pharmacy from the potter Giunta di Tugio, whose workshop near Porta Romana in Florence has recently been excavated.[10]

The ornament on jars of this type has strong echoes of the arts of the Islamic world. The solidly drawn animals and

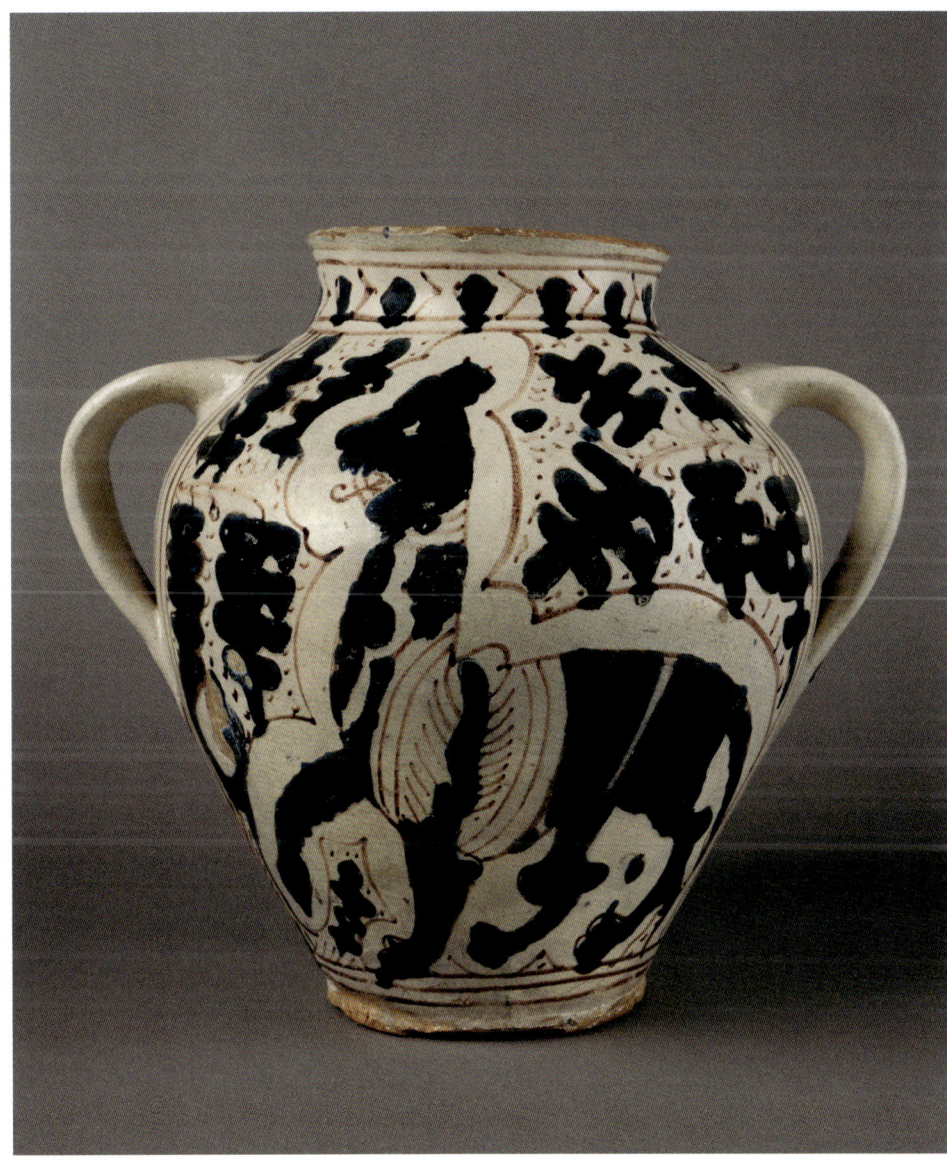

birds that appear on them derive from the lustreware made by Islamic potters around Valencia in eastern Spain (known to Italians at the time as 'maiolica'), which was a fashionable import into Tuscany in particular. The device of the 'contour panel', in which the main subject is separated out from a background of denser decoration by an outline following its overall shape, has its roots in earlier Middle Eastern pottery. The use of cobalt oxide, introduced into Italian pottery in the fourteenth century, and used thickly on jars of this type to produce a dominant dark blue, also has Islamic precedents and was sometimes known in Italy as *alla damaschina* (in the Damascus fashion).[11] The overall decorative conception has numerous parallels in Italian textiles, including Lucchese silks and the north-central Italian woven fabrics known as 'Perugia towels'.[12] These textiles were themselves heavily influenced by imports from the Middle East.

Beneath each handle, painted in manganese, is a small vertical ladder. This mark occurs on several examples of fifteenth-century Tuscan maiolica, which has led some Italian scholars to write of a *Bottega della scala*. Galeazzo Cora, from his vast knowledge of finds from many places in the Lower Arno valley, attributed pieces with this mark to a pottery working in the city of Florence.[13] Since then, several

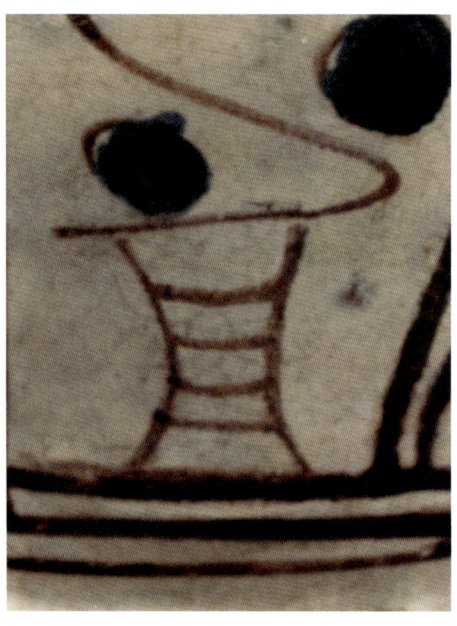

fragments bearing this mark, datable over much of the fifteenth century, have been found at Montelupo, about fifteen miles down the Arno from Florence, and were doubtless made there.[14] However, some of the potters who worked in Florence in the first half of the fifteenth century were from Montelupo, or from another nearby pottery village, Baccheretto, and there was much movement of potters between the city and these two rural centres, as well as collaboration and subcontracting. As such, the mark could have been used in workshops, perhaps belonging to a single family, in both Florence and Montelupo. An attribution of this jar to Montelupo, rather than Florence, looks probable, but not certain. In the second half of the fifteenth century, Montelupo developed production on a near-industrial scale, with national and international markets, and came to eclipse Florence as a pottery-producing centre.

Two other large jars painted with heraldically conceived leopards and bearing the ladder mark are recorded: one, with two animals rearing up to face each other (heraldically *affrontés*) is in the Victoria and Albert Museum, South Kensington, the other, with one leopard *passant*, as on this jar, was in the collection of the Spanish scholar-collector G. J. De Osma (1853–1922).[15] Both bear the ladder mark and may be by the same painter as the present jar. Smaller but similarly painted jars with leopards, but without the mark, can be found in the museums in Faenza and in Dublin.[16]

Aside from their sheer visual splendour, oak-leaf jars have claims to a pivotal role in the history of European ceramics.[17] They are the first class of Italian maiolica of which examples have survived above ground in quantity, rather than being excavated; thanks to the Santa Maria Nuova documentation, they are the first type that can be specifically connected with archival documents; and they are the first European pottery since Antiquity that regularly bears identifiable workshop or potters' marks.

Although J. C. Robinson (1824–1913) acquired a fine example for the museum

that was to become the V&A in 1856, pottery like this was, in general, of little or no interest to European collectors or museums until late in the nineteenth century. As such, collectors like the French and English Rothschilds, the collector-dealer Frédéric Spitzer (1815–1890), Sir Richard Wallace (1818–1890), and C. D. E. Fortnum (1820–1899) did not acquire examples.[18] It was from the 1870s and 1880s onwards that collectors and then museums began to take an interest.[19] Protagonists in this new taste for Quattrocento maiolica were two English artist-collectors (and periodically, especially Murray, dealers), Charles Fairfax Murray (1849–1919) and Henry Wallis, both of whom encouraged and helped the national museums in London to build their collections;[20] two curators, Wilhelm von Bode (1845–1929) of the Berlin Museums (the most active force in European museum collecting of Renaissance art for several decades) and Émile Molinier (1857–1906) of the Louvre;[21] and two Florentine dealers, both of whom had trained as painters, Stefano Bardini (1836–1922) and his one-time restorer turned dealer, Elia Volpi (1858–1938).[22] The new taste came to be high fashion with German collectors under the influence of Bode, such as Adolf von Beckerath (1834–1915) and Alfred Pringsheim (1850–1941), and was fully established by the time American mega-collectors like John Pierpont Morgan (1837–1913) and then Mortimer L. Schiff (1877–1931) crashed into the European market in the early years of the twentieth century.

Stefano Bardini, the dominant character in the Florentine art trade for many decades, both helped create the growing fashion for Quattrocento Florentine art and exploited it effectively. Not all that he sold was authentic, or in anything like original condition, and how much he deliberately diffused fakes is still a matter of debate. However, this is an issue in which Quattrocento sculpture and painting are at the centre, and not, in the main, maiolica.[23] The authenticity of the present jar is not in doubt. He sold

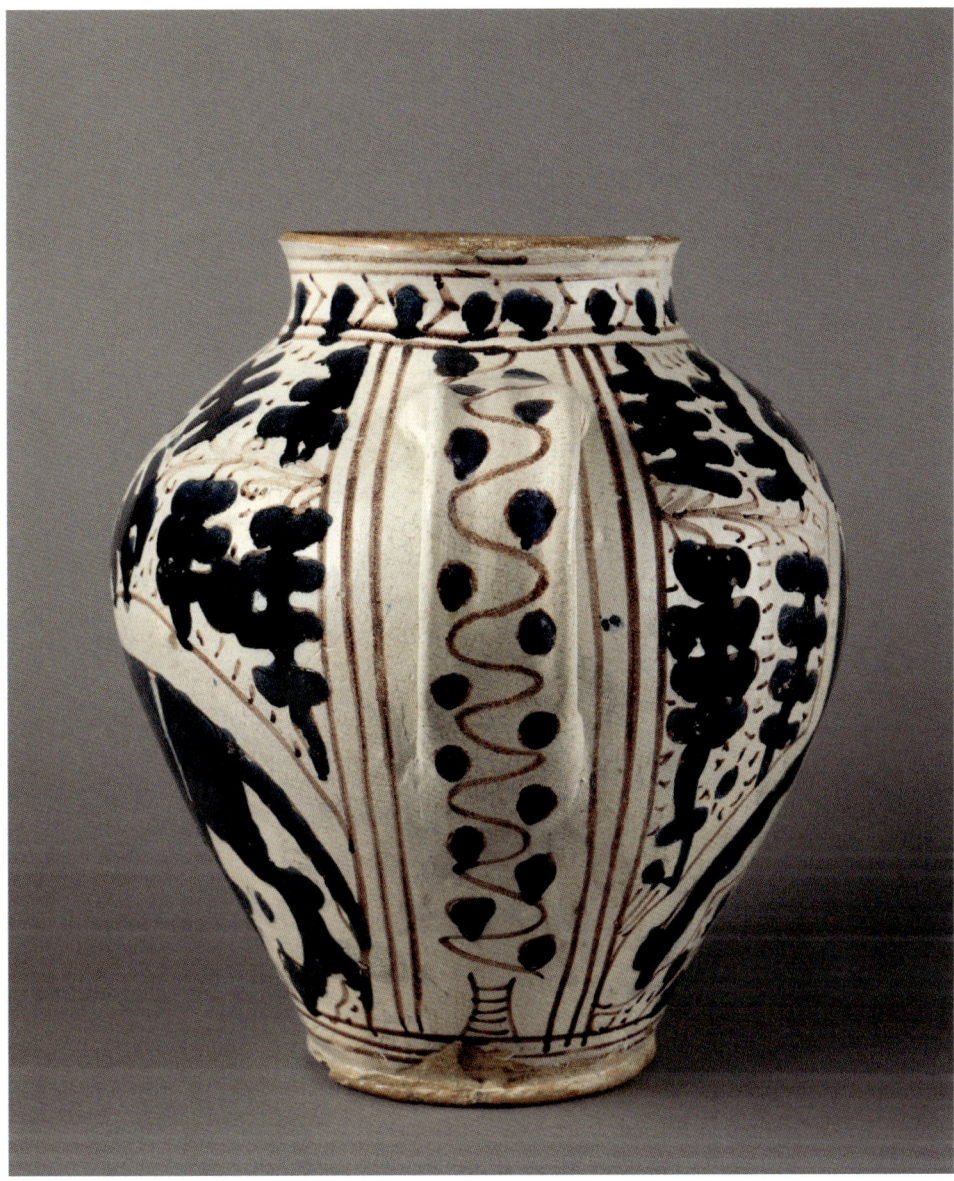

8   Moore Valeri 1984, p.484.
9   Wallis 1903.
10 See, most recently and with further references, Wilson 2018, no.1.
11 Cora 1973, I, pp.58, 86.
12 Moore Valeri 1984, pp.477–500; Sani et al. 2017, p.66.
13 Cora 1973, II, tav.73.
14 Berti 1997–2003, I, p.195; II, p.124; V, p.248. I am indebted to my friend Marino Marini for comments on this contentious issue. He points out that the archaeological evidence for the place of manufacture of the 'scala' group remains inconclusive, but he inclines towards a Montelupo origin for this jar.
15 V&A, 2562-1856; Cora 1973, II, tav.74a. Cora 1973, II, tav.72, 73a and c.
16 Ravanelli Guidotti 1990, no.5. National Museum of Ireland, 139-1890 (acquired from Fairfax Murray); Wallis 1903, fig.2. Cora 1973, II, tav.73b, illustrates another from a private collection in Florence; he attributes it to the 'Bottega Marca Scala', but does not specifically say it is marked.
17 An extensive anthology of examples, including ones with lions and other animals, birds, fishes, fleurs-de-lis, and human figures, is provided by Conti et al. 1991.
18 V&A, 2562-1856.
19 For a lucid overview, see J. Raccanello, 'On the Early Collecting of "Primitive" Maiolica', in Sani et al. 2017, pp.29–41; see also Thornton and Wilson 2009, pp.18–19.
20 Elliott 2000; Tucker 2002 and 2017; Wilson 2002.
21 Bode expanded his 1898 article, 'Altflorentiner Majoliken' into the monumental volume, *Die Anfänge der Majolikakunst in Toskana* (1911). See Bode 1898; Bode 1911. Molinier 1888.
22 Ferrazza 1994; Teodori and Celani 2017; Cappellini 2022.
23 For the extensive literature and various controversies about Bardini see Moskowitz 2015. For Bardini and maiolica see Marini 2024B and the studies cited in note 1 of that article.
24 Wainwright 2002; Niemeyer Chini 2009.
25 The two 1893 purchases are illustrated by Hollein et al. 2002, p.47.
26 The lack of an 'oak-leaf jar' was noted as a painful deficiency in the Ashmolean collection by Wilson 2017, p.38.

extensively to great European museums, like the South Kensington Museum, and above all to the Berlin museums led by Bode.[24] Among his private clients was Johann II, Prince of Liechtenstein (1840–1929), who bought from Bardini in 1885, 1890, and 1893 four substantial oak-leaf jars, which are still in the Princely Collections.[25]

Aiming, no doubt, to attract new clients among wealthy English collectors, Bardini consigned, in 1899 and again in 1902, batches of Renaissance art, including a large amount of maiolica, for sale at Christie's in London. The present jar was included in the second of these sales.

C. D. E. Fortnum, the Ashmolean benefactor whose taste was formed in the middle years of the century, had not responded to this new interest among younger collectors by the time of his death in 1899. The Ashmolean maiolica collection, though developed and enriched in recent decades, is still rooted in Fortnum's collection and documents his taste. For many years, a good example of an oak-leaf jar has been a prime desideratum for the Ashmolean, but no opportunity to make such an acquisition had presented itself.[26] This handsome example, with its wide cultural resonances across the Mediterranean, is an important addition to the Ashmolean's collection of Renaissance maiolica.

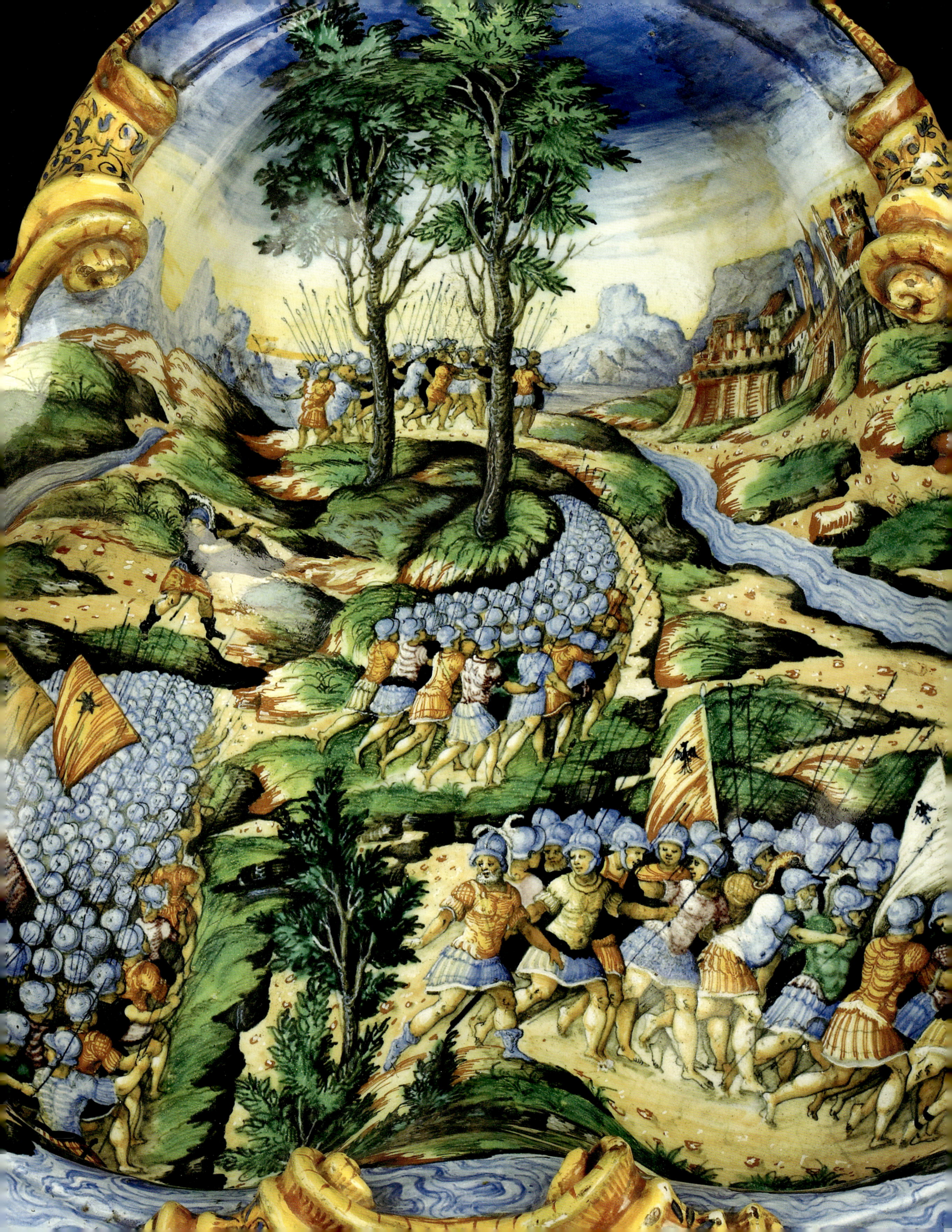

Nos 2–10: Italian maiolica from the collection of Airlie Holden-Hindley

I N 2022, NINE items of sixteenth-century maiolica from the collection of the late Airlie Holden-Hindley (1923–2021), of Edenhall, Cumbria, were accepted by H. M. Government in lieu of inheritance tax. The offer was made through the good will of the family, and the collection was allocated to the Ashmolean in accordance with Mr Holden-Hindley's wishes.[27]

As far as their provenance is known, these pieces were bought by Mrs Arthur Hindley (mother of Airlie Holden-Hindley) between 1933 and 1936. This was a time when the market for maiolica was in decline from a high point before the Wall Street Crash; this is reflected in the fall in price of the Diana dish, no.**2** (135 guineas at the Cook sale in 1925; 50 guineas at the Burns sale in 1935).[28]

Mrs Hindley's group of works represents both a clever exploitation of the falling market for maiolica of the 1930s as well as, in a longer perspective, a late flowering of a tradition of art collecting in which Britain had been pre-eminent since about 1850. Throughout the later Victorian period, sixteenth-century maiolica, particularly *istoriato*, had been, in Gerald Reitlinger's words, 'the mainstay of enlightened and scholarly nineteenth-century collecting' in Britain.[29] Examples reached spectacular heights in the market of the second half of the nineteenth century. A Gubbio roundel of 1525 was bought in 1861 by the collector Andrew Fountaine for £480; the same year, the National Gallery paid £241 for the great *Baptism of Christ* by Piero della Francesca.[30] Mrs Hindley's acquisitions are in this passionate Victorian tradition, being focused on Urbino *istoriato* of high quality and scholarly interest. They include items from two of the best of such assemblages in England, the Cook and De Zoete collections, and constituted one of the very few surviving maiolica collections in the UK in this tradition. The group constitutes the most substantial single addition to the Ashmolean's world-class collection of Italian Renaissance maiolica since the bequest from C. D. E. Fortnum (the 'second founder' of the Ashmolean Museum) in 1899.

27 See *Cultural Gifts Scheme and Acceptance in Lieu Report* 2022, no.28. Six early-seventeenth-century Augsburg *basse-taille* enamel plaques (WA2022.712–717) with scenes from the lives of Christ and Saint John the Baptist were accepted and allocated to the Ashmolean as part of the same AIL offer. Our thanks to Mark Holden-Hindley for arranging the AIL and providing documentation from his father's files.
28 On the market at this time, see Wilson 1994. As far as the Museum has been able to ascertain, none of the objects has a provenance from any collection affected by Nazi persecution of Jewish people.
29 Reitlinger 1961–70, III, p.570. For a very long period, Christie's took bids in guineas (a guinea was 1 pound 1 shilling, i.e. £1.05) and paid vendors in pounds, thus taking a five per cent commission.
30 Reitlinger 1961–70, II, p.502. The roundel is V&A, 175-1885

Opposite: detail of no.**7**

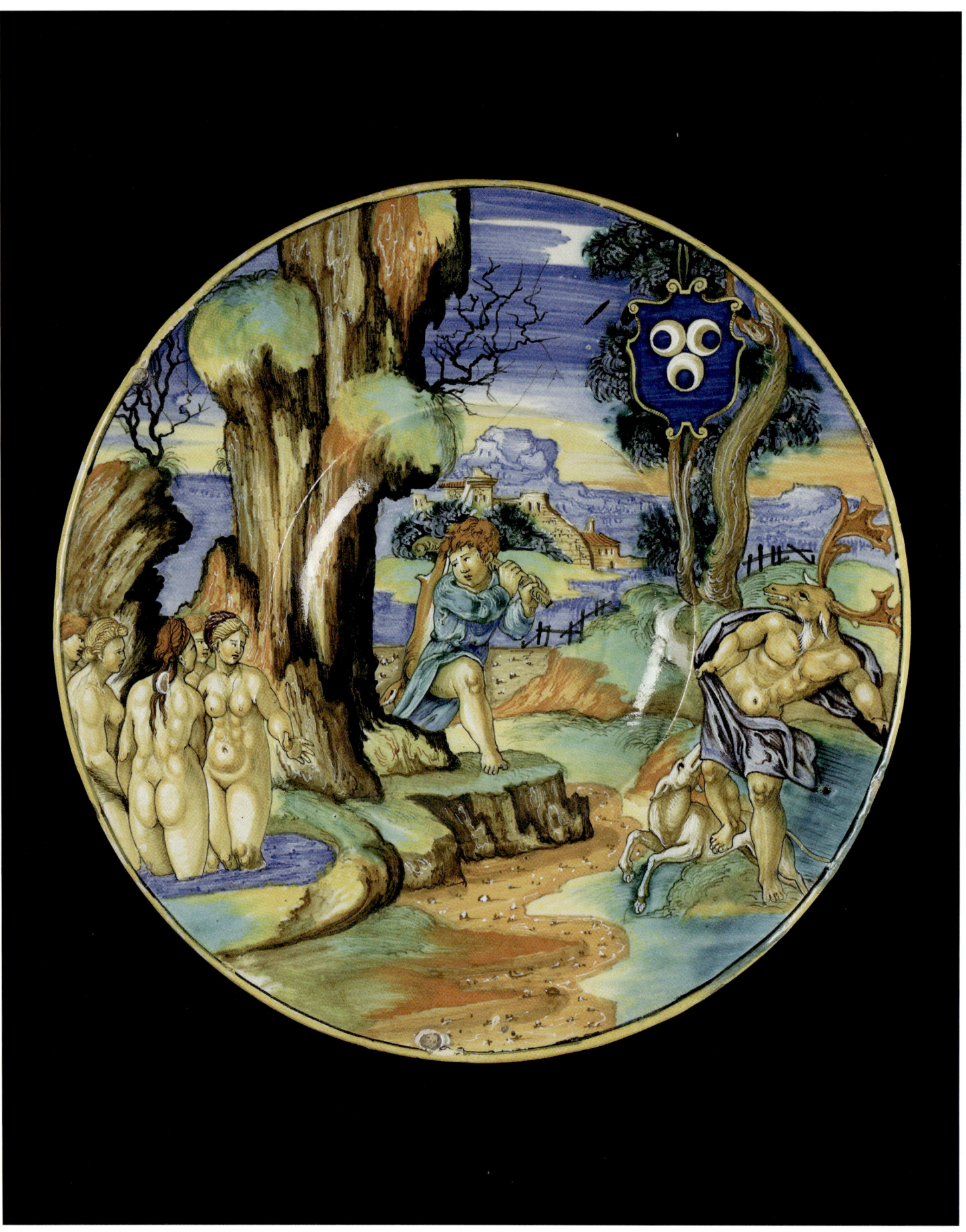

2

Plate, Diana and Actaeon

Urbino, Francesco Xanto Avelli, 1530
Accepted by H. M. Government in lieu of inheritance tax from the estate of
Samuel Airlie Holden-Hindley and allocated to the Ashmolean, WA2022.703.

Tin-glazed front and back. Inscribed on the reverse in blue, *Dov'alsuo amâte si Diana piacque. fabula* followed by a sign resembling a letter *y*. There is an edge-moulding in relief on the back. At the bottom on the front, between 6 and 7 o'clock, is a patch where the glaze has pooled away from the earthenware body; this 'crawling' can easily happen with tin-glaze pottery if dust or grease gets onto the vessel before it is dipped in the glaze.

Diameter: 29.1 cm

CONDITION: cleanly broken and repaired.

PROVENANCE: possibly Alexander Barker; Cook collection (by 1903); Humphrey W. Cook sale, Christie's, London, 7 July 1925, lot 49; bought by Tancred Borenius for 135 guineas; Walter Burns, North Mymms Park, Hertfordshire; his estate;

offered for sale, Sotheby's, London, 25 June 1931, lot 29; Mrs Walter Burns; her sale, Christie's, London, 28 June 1935, lot 30, bought for 50 guineas; an extract from this last sale is stuck to the reverse. Acquired by Mrs Arthur Hindley. This is a distinguished provenance. The maiolica in the Sir Francis Cook collection at Doughty House, Richmond, was a superb group of which the greater part was bought *en bloc* around 1870 from the celebrated connoisseur-dealer Alexander Barker of Piccadilly. Mrs Walter Burns was the sister of J. Pierpont Morgan.

Lent to the exhibition *Ceramic Art of the Italian Renaissance*, British Museum, 1987, but not included in the catalogue. On loan to the Ashmolean Museum since 1990.

BIBLIOGRAPHY: Rackham 1904, no.62; Rackham 1957, pp.99–111, pl.54; Rasmussen 1989, p.131; Poole 1995, pp.315–6; Triolo 1996, pp.263–4; Wilson 1996, p.188, no.2; Sani 2007, p.193, no.102; Wilson 2007, pp.258–61, fig.11; Kaucher 2024, p.316, no.v.

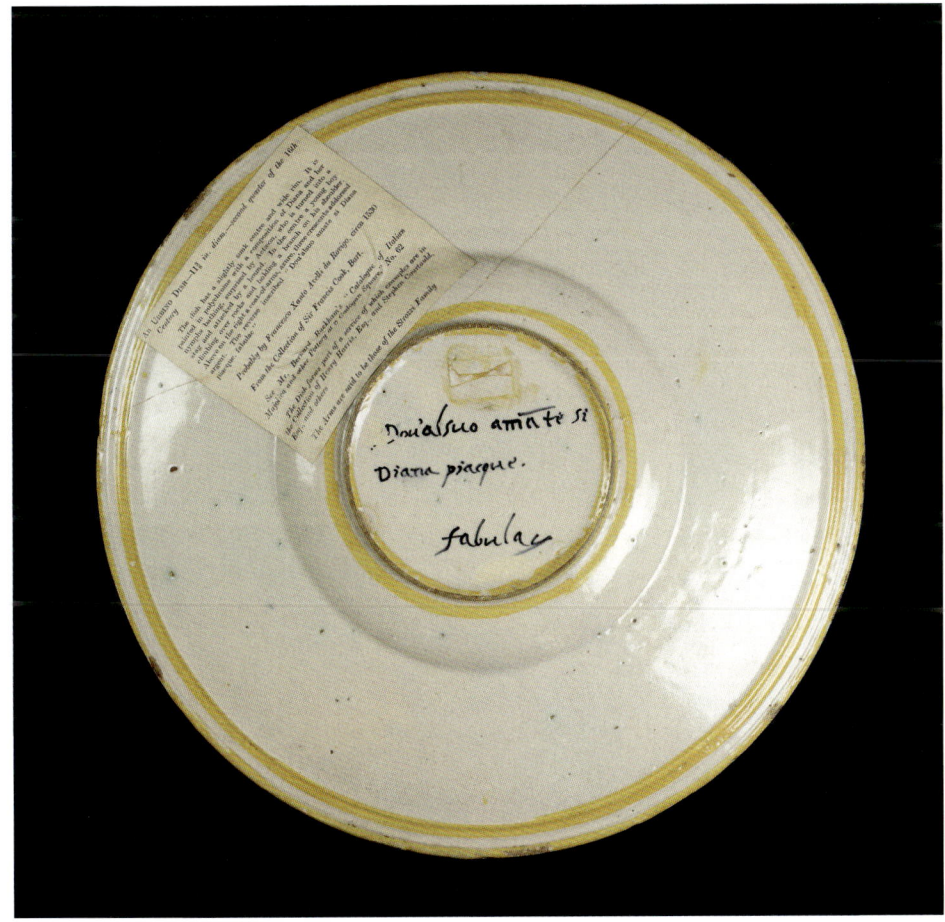

This plate is an early work by the most interesting character in the history of Renaissance maiolica: Francesco Xanto Avelli. Xanto came from Rovigo, near Padua, and had settled in Urbino by 1530 (perhaps several years earlier). There, between 1530 and 1542, he painted a stream of works, which he signed and dated more regularly than any other maiolica artist. He aspired to be a man of culture and a poet, and there is a manuscript of a sonnet sequence written by him in praise of Francesco Maria Della Rovere, Duke of Urbino (1490–1538), in the Vatican Library. He was a specialist maiolica painter, perhaps never an independent workshop or kiln owner like his contemporaries Nicola da Urbino and Guido Durantino, and his choice of subject matter for maiolica is eccentric and ambitious, including allegories of contemporary politics and subjects from Classical history and literature. He is one of the few ceramic artists to have been the subject of a major monographic exhibition: *Xanto: Pottery-painter, poet, man of the Italian Renaissance,* organised by John Mallet at the Wallace Collection in 2007.[31]

The inscription *Dov'alsuo amâte si Diana piacque. fabula* (where Diana so pleased her lover. A fable) is followed by two strokes of the brush resembling a *y*, which are often found on work by Xanto in this period and may possibly represent 'etc.'.[32] Like many of Xanto's inscriptions, the words on the back are an echo of

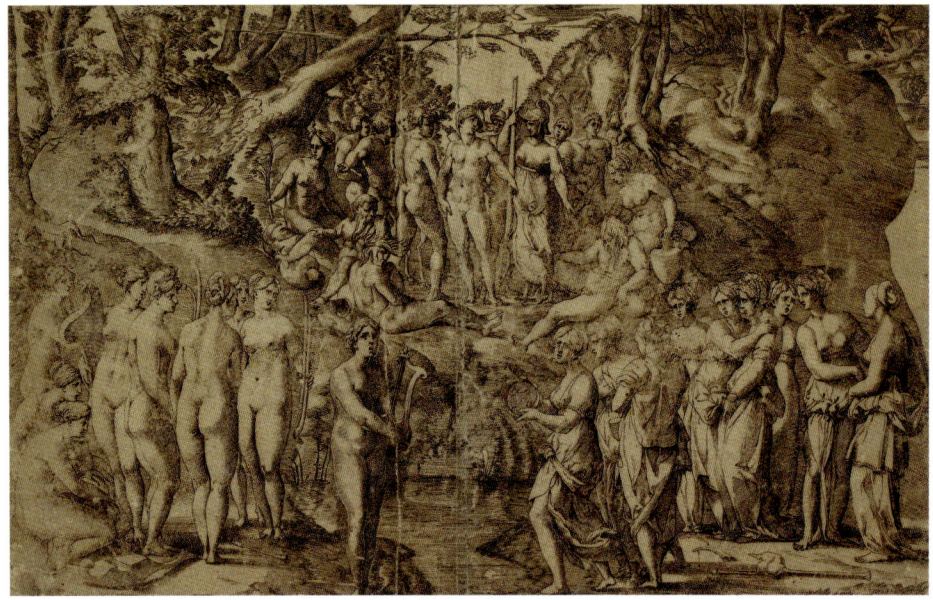

Fig.2 *The Muses and the Pierides*. Engraving by Gian Giacomo Ceraglio. Ashmolean Museum, WA1863.5068

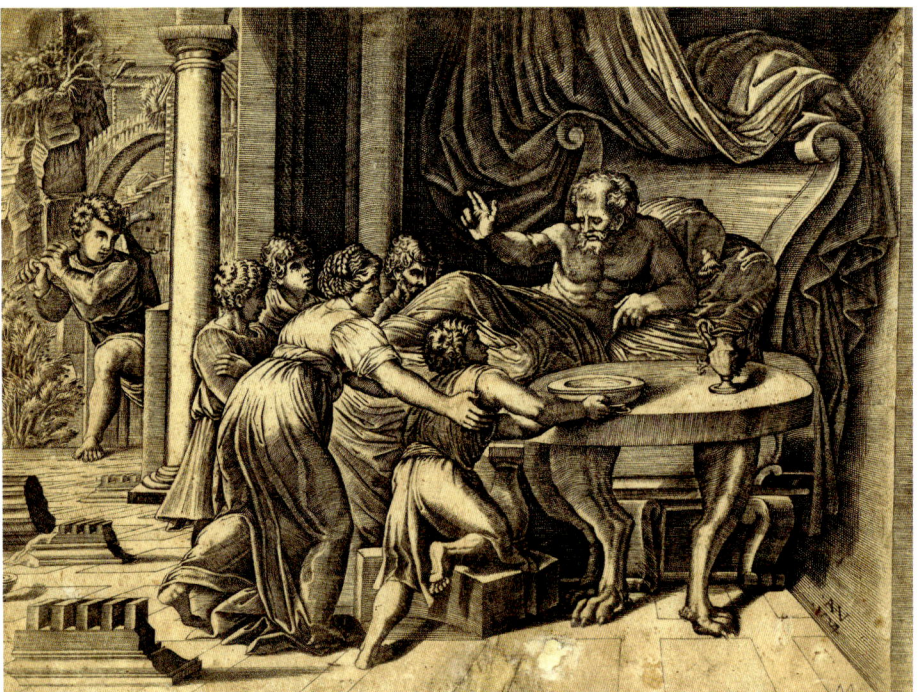

Fig.3 *Isaac blessing Jacob*. Engraving by Agostino Veneziano. Ashmolean Museum, WA1863.1769

tunic he wears is painted in greenish turquoise with white highlights, a favourite chromatic effect of Xanto's. In a manner typical of the artist, the design is a composite creation with figures taken from a number of diverse print sources. The group of Diana and her attendants is derived from figures on the left in an engraving of *The Muses and the Pierides* by Gian Giacomo Caraglio after Rosso Fiorentino (fig.2).[35] The figure in the centre comes from the figure on the left in an engraving by Agostino Veneziano, after Raphael, of *Isaac blessing Jacob* (fig.3).[36]

The plate is one of the best pieces from one of the most ambitious early Urbino *istoriato* sets to carry the arms of a patron. The arms may be those of the Ghini family of Cesena or, as has recently been argued in detail by Greta Kaucher, of a French nobleman, Jacques De Banes of the Dauphiné.[37] They may, alternatively, be of another family altogether. Twenty pieces from the set by Xanto are known.[38] One plate (in the Robert Lehman Collection at The Metropolitan Museum of Art, New York), is dated 1530.[39] Ten other plates and two salts have the crescents differently arranged and are by a different painter, known as the 'Milan Marsyas painter', indicating that work on the set was divided between two painters and perhaps two workshops.[40]

31 Mallet 2007, with comprehensive discussion of the biographical and attributional uncertainties. The most recent addition to the now extensive literature on Xanto is a volume of studies in *Faenza* 110/2 (2024).

32 On other pieces by Xanto in these years the final stroke more resembles a Greek letter phi; it is sometimes known in the specialist literature as the 'y/φ flourish'.

33 *Rime* 52; Holcroft 1988, pp.225–34.

34 Ovid, *Metamorphoses*, III.

35 Bartsch XV, p.89, no.53; British Museum, P&D, 1874,0808.279.

36 Bartsch XIV, p.7, no.6; British Museum, P&D, H,7.4.

37 Kaucher 2024, pp.67–8.

38 Kaucher 2024, pp.312–31.

39 Rasmussen 1989, no.76; Wilson 2018, pp.224–5.

40 Kaucher 2024.

Petrarch (1304–1374), a poet he evidently knew well.[33] It is quite typical of Xanto that the inscription is only tangentially descriptive of the scene.

The story of Actaeon, from Ovid's *Metamorphoses*, was the most popular of all Classical stories among Renaissance maiolica painters.[34] After a day spent hunting, Actaeon chanced upon Diana bathing with her attendants in a

sacred grove. The goddess saw him and transformed him into a stag so that he could not relate to anyone that he had seen the chaste Diana naked. Actaeon was subsequently killed by his own hounds. The figure of a boy with a stick in the centre is there more for compositional than narrative reasons, but may be intended to represent Actaeon at the moment he catches sight of Diana. The

3

Plate, Abraham and the angels

Urbino, probably workshop of Guido Durantino, c.1540–50
Accepted by H. M. Government in lieu of inheritance tax from the estate of
Samuel Airlie Holden-Hindley and allocated to the Ashmolean, WA2022.704.

Tin-glazed front and back. On the reverse, yellow rings and, in blue: *Tresviditet unû Adoravit* (he saw three and adored one) around a shield of arms of Lancierini. A nineteenth-century label on the reverse wrongly identifies the subject as Joseph of Arimathea.

Diameter: 24 cm

CONDITION: chips to edge.

PROVENANCE: unrecorded.

On loan to the Ashmolean Museum since 2005.

BIBLIOGRAPHY: Thornton and Wilson 2009, p.310; Wilson 2017, p.183, figs 68, 69.

The subject is Abraham welcoming three angels (Genesis 18); the text is from the Roman Catholic Latin liturgy and refers to the long-standing Christian interpretation of the three angels as an emblem of the Trinity.[41]

Nos **3** and **4** are from one of the most substantial Urbino *istoriato* armorial services, which has on the back the arms of the Lancierini family of Rome. The individual member of the family for whom the series were made has not yet been definitely identified, but could be Leone Lancierini, who died in 1555. It is unusual to find *istoriato* maiolica with arms on the back, rather than incorporated in the decoration on the front. Of the 30 pieces of the set so far recorded, 25 plates (including one bequeathed to the Ashmolean by C. D. E. Fortnum in 1899) and a salt have subjects from Ovid's *Metamorphoses* or ancient history; and four (including this plate) have Old Testament subjects.[42] The set is likely to have been made in the leading workshop in Urbino at the time, that run by Guido Durantino; Guido's son, Orazio Fontana (c.1520–1571), may have been involved in the painting of some.

41 Responsory for Quinquagesima.
42 For a listing, see Thornton and Wilson 2009, pp.310–11; to which should be added a *Rape of Proserpina* sold at Christie's, London, 19 May 2016, lot 129; also an *Orpheus Killed by the Bacchants* and a *Maenads Changed into Trees*, for which see the addenda and corrigenda to no.73 of Wilson 2017 on the website https://timothywilson.co.uk/publications

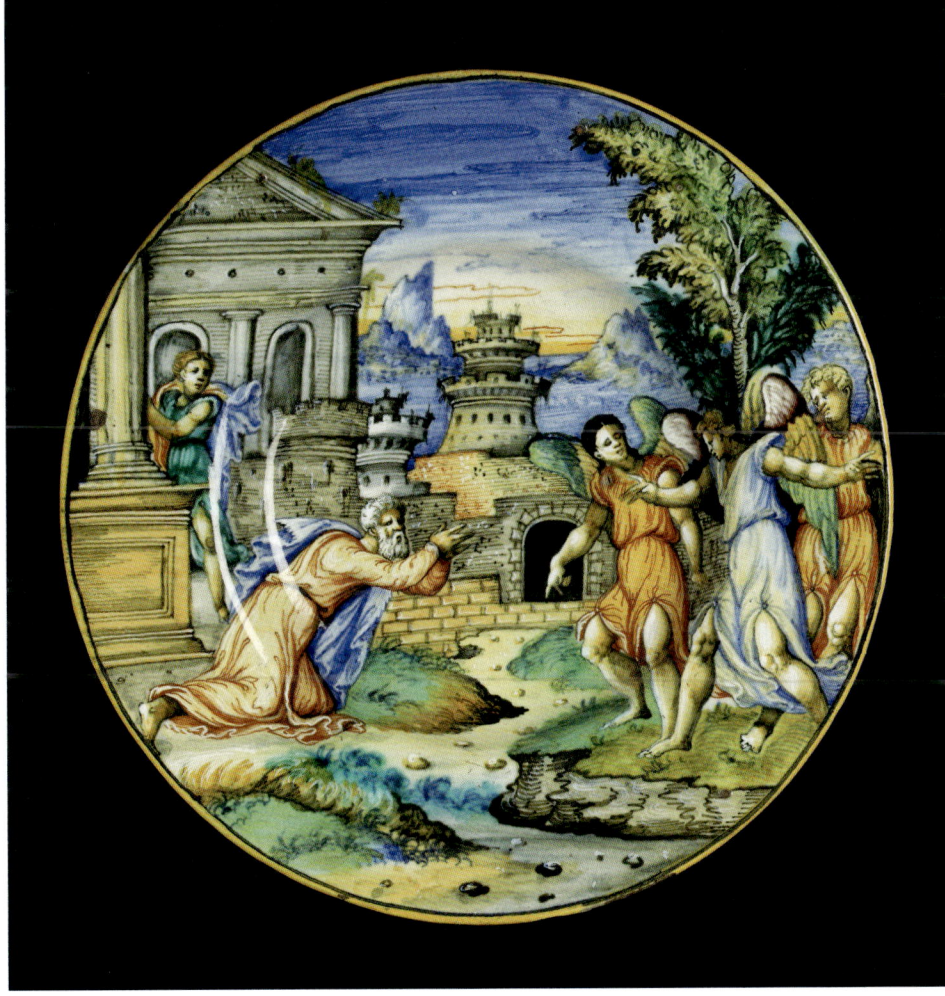

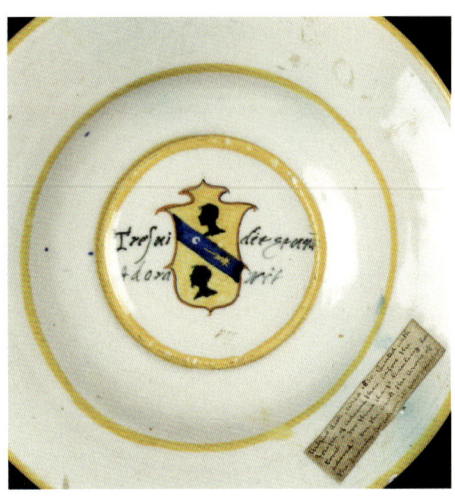

4

Plate, a legend of the infancy of Octavian

Urbino, probably workshop of Guido Durantino, *c.*1540–50
Accepted by H. M. Government in lieu of inheritance tax from the estate of
Samuel Airlie Holden-Hindley and allocated to the Ashmolean, WA2022.705.

Tin-glazed front and back. On the reverse, yellow rings and, in blue: *ottaviano inperatore* (the emperor Octavian) around a shield of arms of Lancierini.

Diameter: 27 cm

CONDITION: repaired and retouched breaks between 11 and 12 o'clock and between 8 and 9 o'clock.

PROVENANCE: unrecorded.

On loan to the Ashmolean Museum since 2005.

BIBLIOGRAPHY: Thornton and Wilson 2009, pp.312, 321; Wilson 2017, p.183, figs 70, 71.

From the same service as no.**3**. The painting on the front seems to be by the same artist, but the handwriting and painting of the shield of arms on the back appear not to be by the same hand.[43] At least three painters apparently worked on the set.

The subject is a legend told by Suetonius of how the infant Octavian (later the Emperor Augustus), left in his cradle overnight, could not be found in the morning. He was eventually found on a tower, facing the sun, a symbolic indication of his future eminence.[44] The subject was treated by Giulio Romano (*c.*1499–1546) in the Palazzo Ducale in Mantua, but that is not the source of the present plate.

43 The handwriting and the painting of the shield are by the same hand as on the *Bull of Perillus* from the same set already in the Ashmolean, 1899.CDEF.C445; Wilson 2017, no.73.

44 Suetonius, *Life of Augustus*, ch.94.

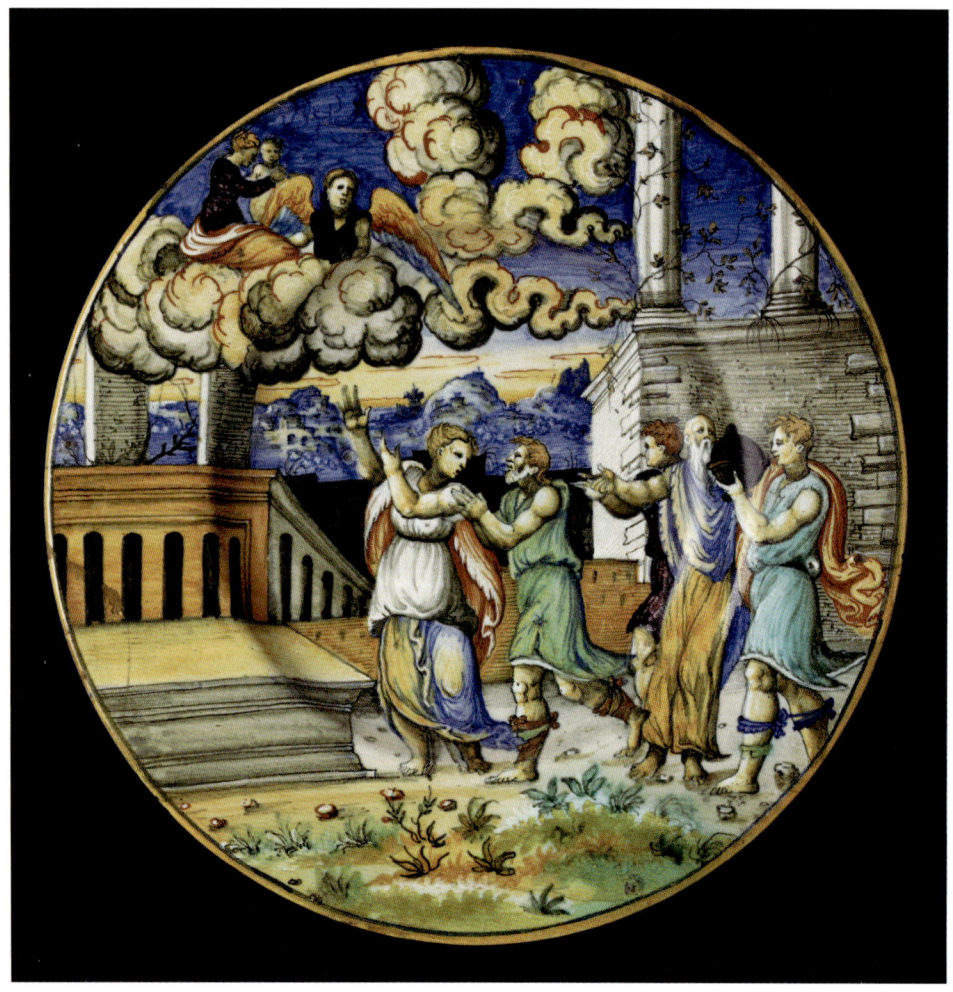

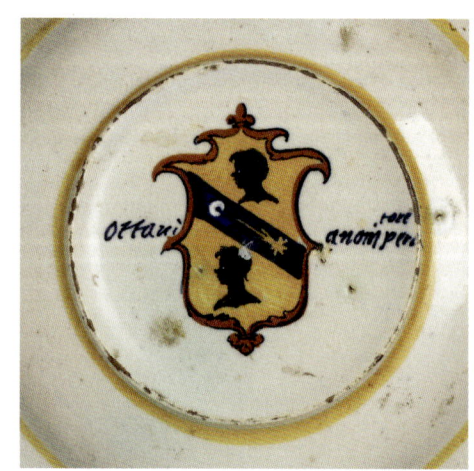

5

Bowl on low foot depicting the capture of Sinon

Urbino, by a painter signing "P", *c*.1540–45, perhaps made in the workshop of Guido di Merlino
Accepted by H. M. Government in lieu of inheritance tax from the estate of Samuel Airlie
Holden-Hindley and allocated to the Ashmolean, WA2022.706.

Tin-glazed front and back. Inscribed in brownish black with a garbled inscription, which refers to the Greek Sinon deceitfully allowing himself to be captured by Trojan shepherds and taken to King Priam: *Sinon ecco intento i pastor troianisieme conducano Al re Conalte grigda aninte un buon tre havea lonea lornandietre P.* Yellow rings around the edge.

Diameter: 27.8 cm

CONDITION: some chipping and scuffing.

PROVENANCE: W. M. de Zoete (1854 –1934); his sale (*Catalogue of the Valuable Collections of Bronzes, Sculpture, Ceramics, Textiles, etc. The Property of W. M. de Zoete, Esq. (deceased) of Layer Breton, Colchester, and Blenheim House, North Berwick,* Sotheby's, London, 1–3 April 1935), lot 248.[45] Bought by the dealers Cecil Leitch and Kerin of Bruton Place, London, for Mrs Arthur Hindley.

On loan to the Ashmolean Museum since 2005.

BIBLIOGRAPHY: Wilson 2017, p.175, figs 65, 66.

In a landscape with trees and rudimentary mountains, four men seize a fifth (Sinon), who has his hands forced behind his back. Upper right is a kneeling shepherd with his dogs, below are two sheepdogs.

The initial *P* at the end of the inscription, apparently but not certainly representing the initial of the painter, occurs on a few other pieces including examples at Erddig and in the Ashmolean, both of which are dated 1543. These were discussed in an article published in 2004, where the hypothesis is considered that they may have been painted by Paolo di Marino in the Urbino workshop of Guido di Merlino.[46] Guido had taken on Paolo di Marino as an apprentice in 1537 and renewed his contract as maiolica painter in 1540.[47] Guido di Merlino's workshop was second only, among Urbino workshops, to that of his brother-in-law, Guido Durantino in the production of *istoriato*.[48] However, the painting on the present bowl is by a different painter and the *P* may be unconnected with these pieces or with Paolo. The handwriting of the inscription resembles that of Francesco Durantino, who was also working for Guido in 1543.

The subject is from book 2 of Virgil's *Aeneid*, lines 57 to 62. Aeneas tells Dido

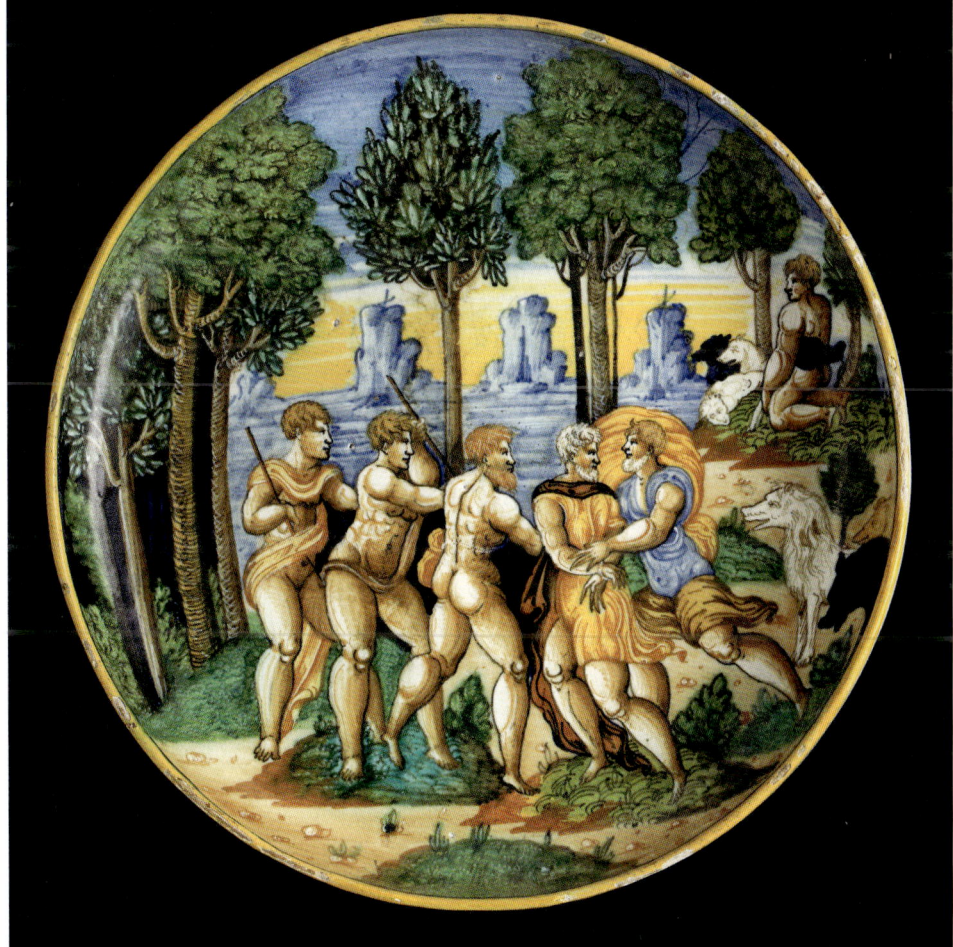

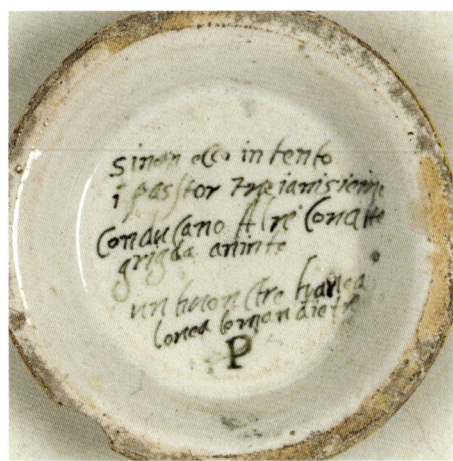

how, after ten years of unavailing assault on Troy, the Greek armies sailed offshore and pretended to have given up but left behind a huge wooden horse, which was in fact filled with armed men. As part of the deceit, a Greek called Sinon allowed himself to be captured by a group of Trojan shepherds and was taken with much shouting (*magno clamore* in the Latin) to King Priam. Falsely claiming to have escaped death at the hands of the Greeks, he helped to persuade the

Trojans to bring the horse inside the walls of Troy, thus ensuring the fall of the city. The inscription is not readily decipherable but describes Sinon taken by the shouting shepherds to the king.[49]

Episodes from Virgil are much rarer on Renaissance maiolica than subjects from Ovid.

45 Walter de Zoete, a member of an eminent family of London stockbrokers, was owner and restorer of Layer Marney Tower, Essex. His maiolica collection had been begun by 1887, when he

lent to the exhibition of Hispano-Moresque and Maiolica at the Burlington Fine Arts Club in London.
46 Wilson 2004, pp.136–9; see also Mallet 1978, pp.42–3; Wilson 2017, pp.174–7.
47 Gardelli 1999, pp.233–43.
48 For a recent summary of information on Guido di Merlino's workshop, see Wilson 2018, pp.298–300. An article by Giovanna Bandini and others including further discussion of *istoriati* from this group is awaited.
49 I thank Ela Tandello and Richard Cooper for sharing my attempts at decipherment.

6

Footed bowl and cover from a birth set (*tazza da impagliata*)

Probably Urbino, *c.*1540–60
Accepted by H. M. Government in lieu of inheritance tax from the estate of
Samuel Airlie Holden-Hindley and allocated to the Ashmolean, WA2022.707.

Tin-glazed overall.

Cup: height: 10.1 cm; diameter: 16.5 cm

Cover: diameter: 18.1 cm

CONDITION: some chipping, especially to the exposed edges of the cup.

PROVENANCE: W. M. de Zoete; his sale (*Catalogue of the Valuable Collections of Bronzes, Sculpture, Ceramics, Textiles, etc. The Property of W.M. de Zoete, Esq. (deceased) of Layer Breton, Colchester, and Blenheim House, North Berwick*, Sotheby's, London, 1–3 April 1935), lot 226. Bought by Cecil Leitch and Kerin for Mrs Arthur Hindley.

On loan to the Ashmolean Museum since 2005.

The cup (*scudella*) stands on a high, hollow foot. Inside is painted a scene of three women with a child amidst buildings, while around the outside is a landscape with water and buildings. The exterior of the upstand has a running foliate garland painted in orange on a yellow ground. On the top of the flanged cover (*tagliere*) is an angel with a sword and two women, unidentified but perhaps an Old Testament subject.

On the underside is an angel with a pair of dividers on a yellow ground within a ring of clouds. The iconography of these scenes is without known parallel and awaits elucidation.[50] On the outside of the flange is a leaf garland with flowers.

The painting is by a good Urbino-school painter of the 1540s or 1550s. It may, as first suggested by Justin Raccanello, be by Luca di Bartolomeo Baldi, who, in 1550–51, made a service for Cardinal Robert de Lenoncourt (d.1561). There are stylistic resemblances with pieces from the Lenoncourt set, but the specific stylistic comparisons seem not quite conclusive.[51]

These are pieces from one of the stacking sets described by Cipriano Piccolpasso in his manuscript *Li tre libri dell'arte del vasaio* (*c.*1557) as being made to contain broth and as presents for women who had just given birth. However, the iconography is less closely related to childbirth than is often the case.[52] Piccolpasso's drawing shows a

five-piece set, in which these forms are labelled as *SCHUDELLA* and *TAGLIERE*, but he notes that sets can be made up of as many as nine component parts.[53]

50 We thank Jacki Musacchio and Paul Taylor for observations on the problematic iconography.
51 For Luca Baldi, see Wilson 2018, no.116; Pesante 2018; also the addenda and corrigenda to no.116 of Wilson 2018 on https://timothywilson.co.uk/publications; most recently, with judicious lucidity, Triolo 2023, p.23, note 9.
52 This enchanting type of maiolica is discussed in detail by Musacchio 1999; see also Crainz 1986; Däubler 1994, pp.26–39; Bandini 1996.
53 Piccolpasso 2007, Book 1, fol.11; Wilson 2017, pp.222–4, fig.86.

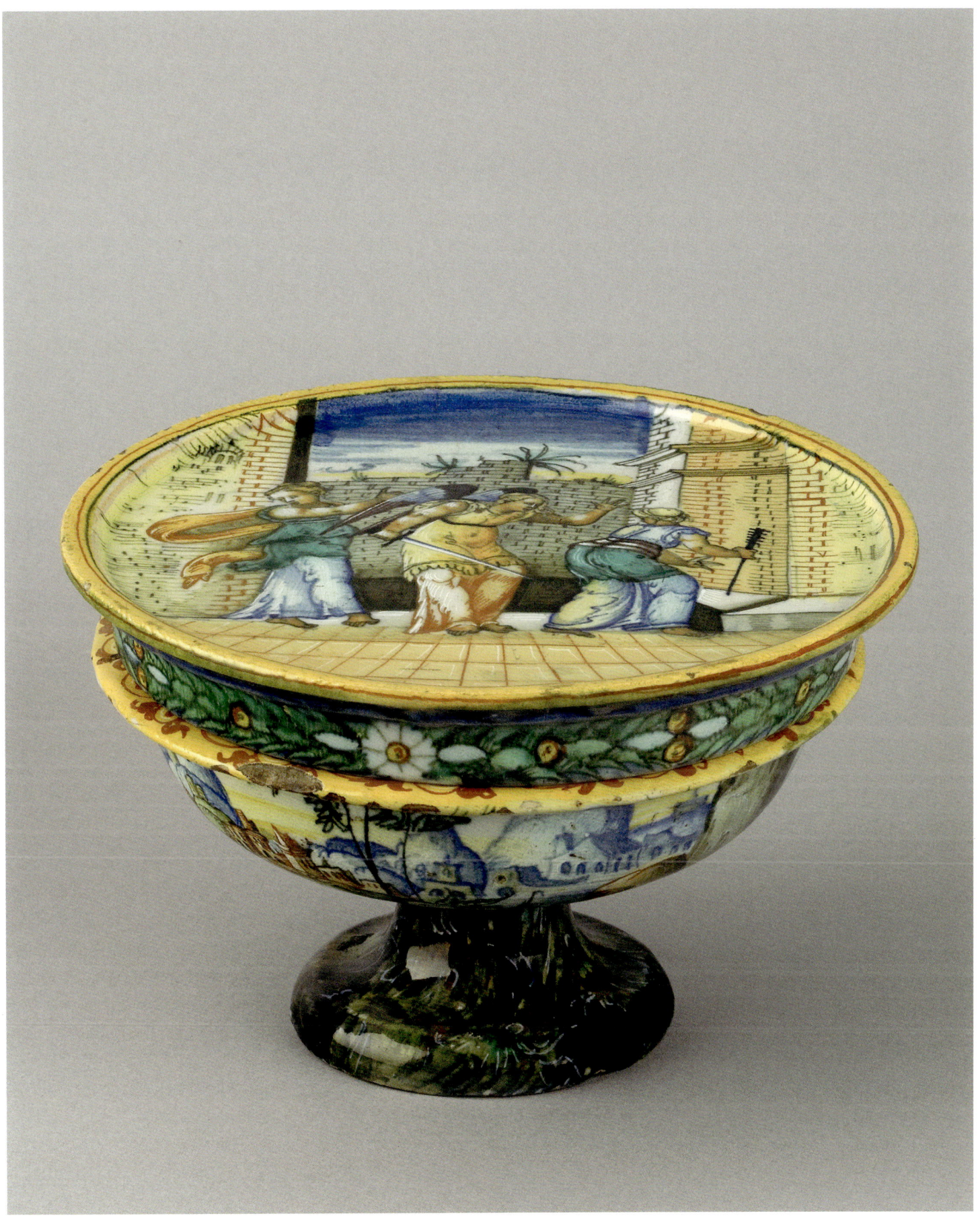

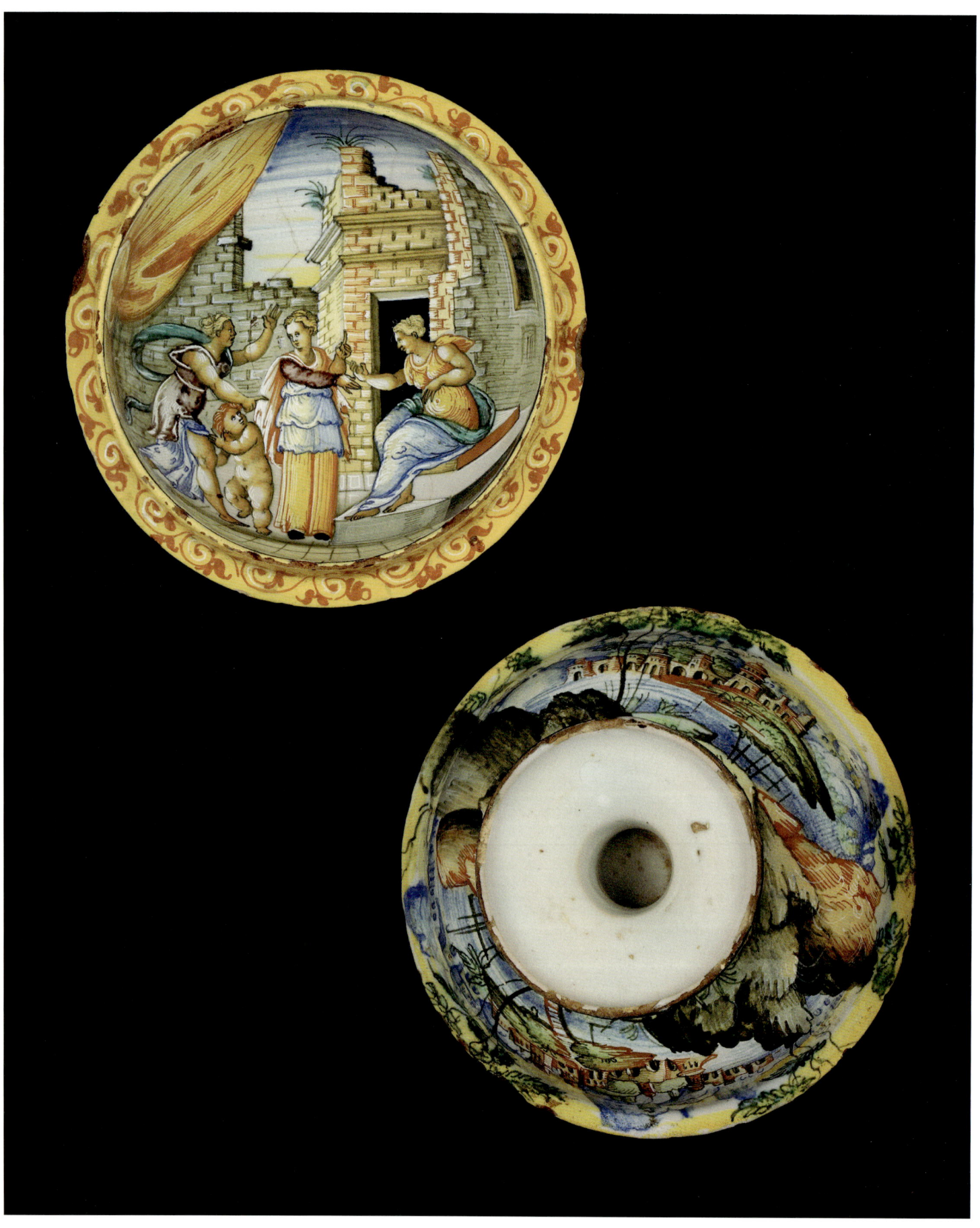

No.**6** (Cup)

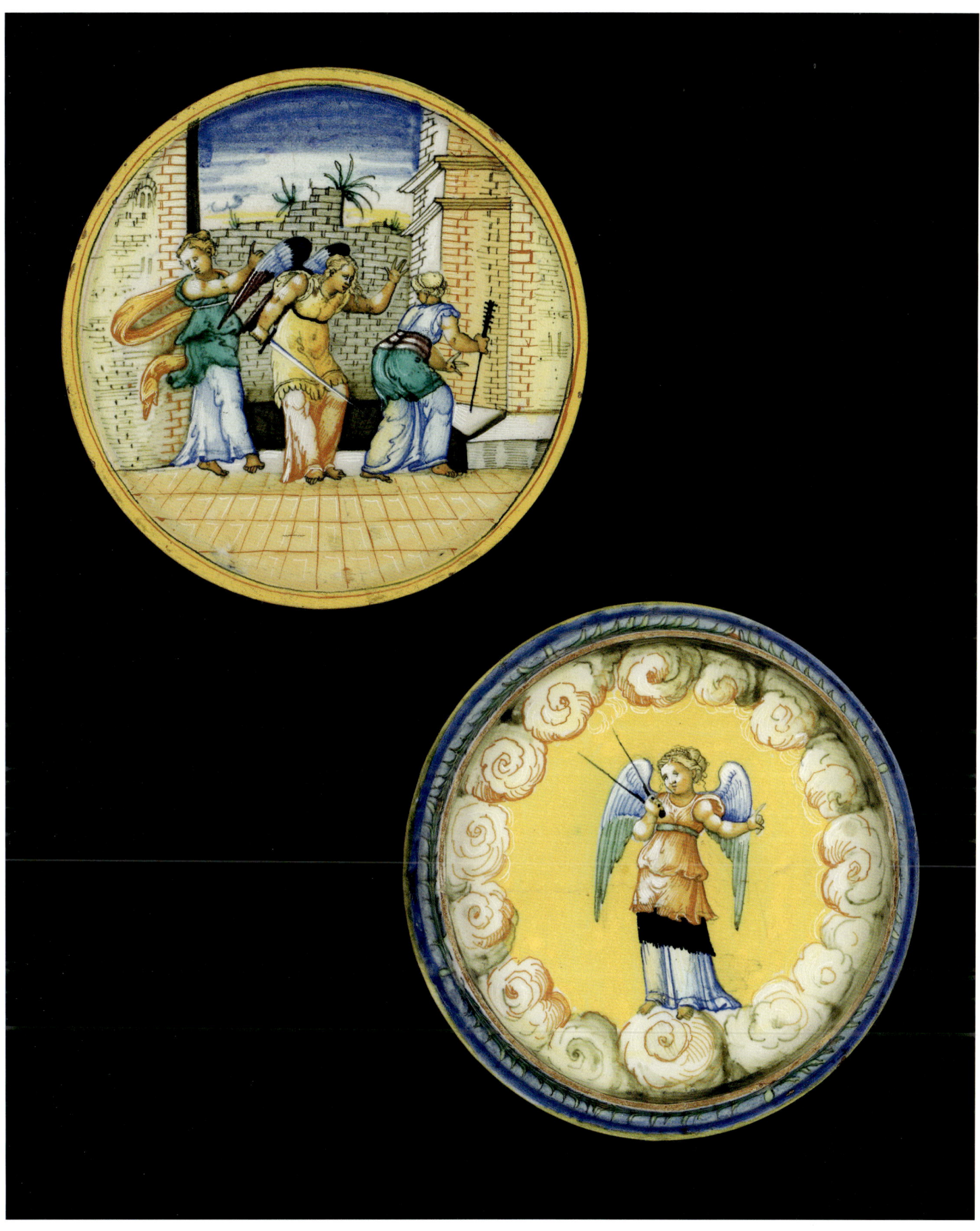

No.**6** (Cover)

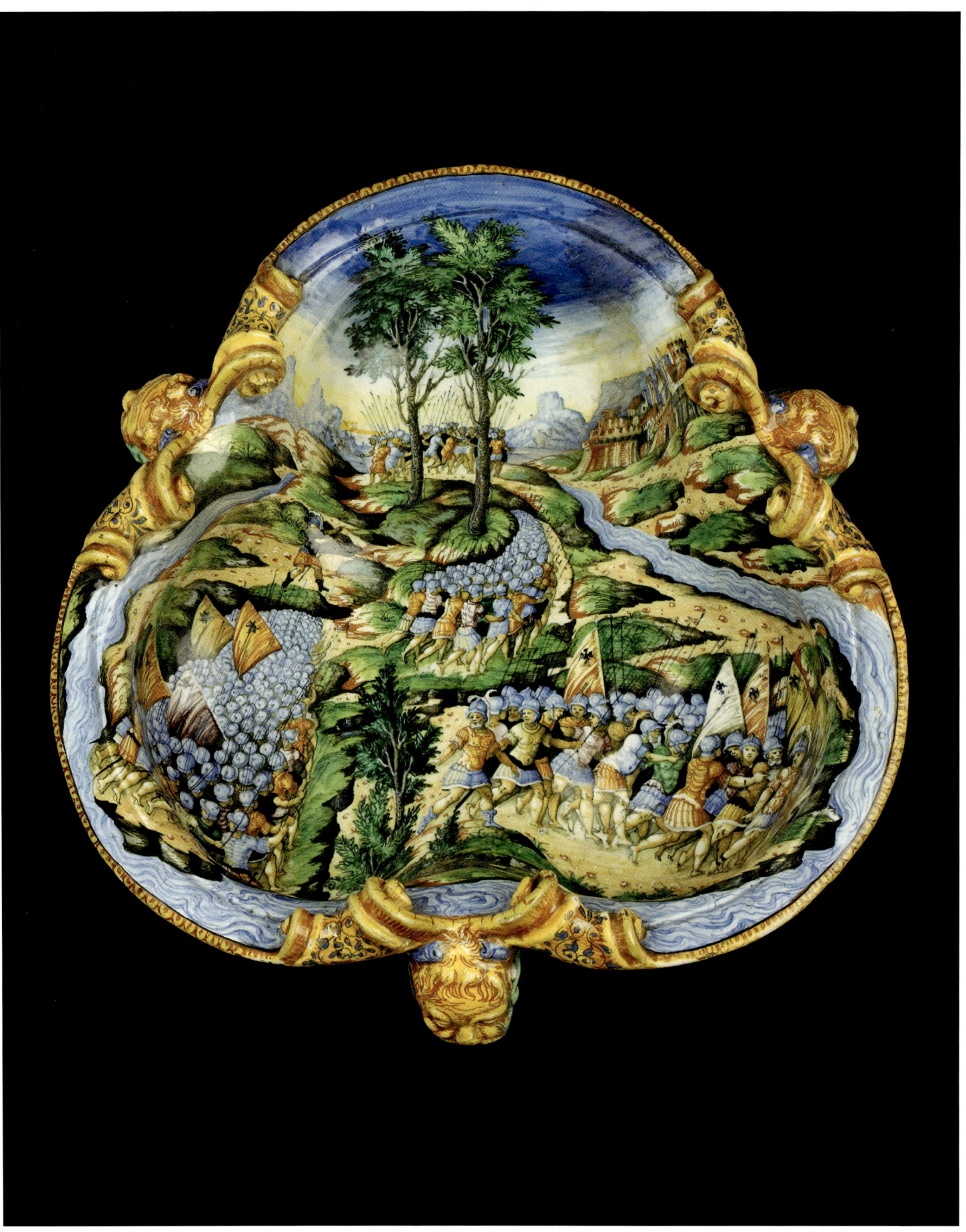

7

Large trilobed basin, the battle of the Allia

Urbino, workshop of the Fontana family, c.1550–60
Accepted by H. M. Government in lieu of inheritance tax from the estate of
Samuel Airlie Holden-Hindley and allocated to the Ashmolean, WA2022.708.

Tin-glazed overall.

Max width: 48 cm; max height: 22.5 cm

CONDITION: broken and repaired, with extensive
overpaint, between 9 and 12 o'clock; the foot has
been broken off and re-stuck. The side panel with
the inscription is not affected by any retouching or
overpaint.[54]

PROVENANCE: bought from Cecil Leitch
and Kerin, May 1936, for £225 (the most
expensive of Mrs Hindley's purchases). Stated
on the invoice to be from the Hermitage.
Painted within the foot is '47' in black, an
inventory number for an as yet unidentified old
collection, possibly one of the constituent

collections which now make up the collections
of the Hermitage Museum.[55]
On loan to the Ashmolean Museum since 2005.
BIBLIOGRAPHY: Wilson 1996, p.292, note 2.

This is *istoriato* maiolica at its most
grandiose. The monumental, deep
trilobed basin, which has three satyr-
mask handles and three lion-paw feet,
is of the form called in the Renaissance
and to the present day a *rinfrescatoio*, and
was used for mixing and cooling wine.
This form seems to have been introduced

into Urbino maiolica by around 1540
and became a focal object in large table
services. The best were made in the
workshop of the Fontana family.

Three columns of soldiers march
through a rocky landscape, with a river
and a city to the right; on raised ground
at the top is a fourth group of soldiers;
the river flows round most of the edge
of the basin. On a fictive sheet of paper
on the outside is the descriptive verse
inscription:

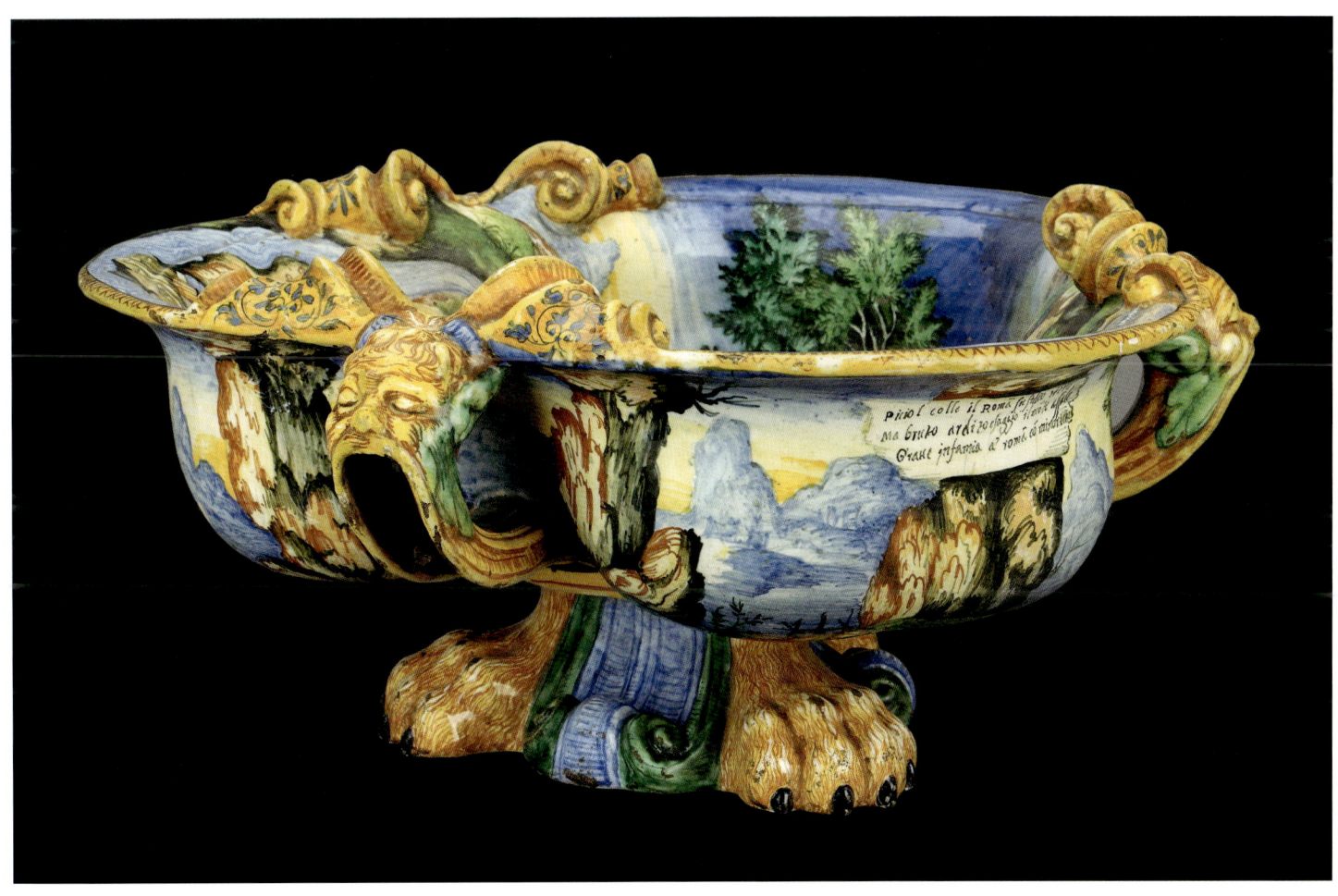

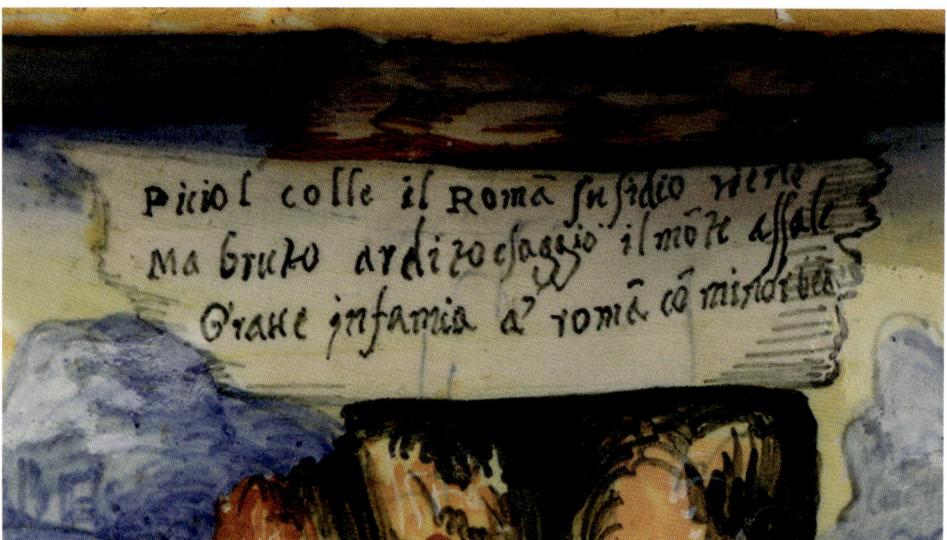
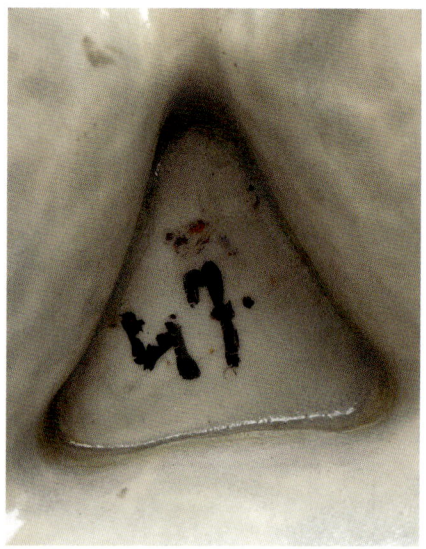

Piciol colle il Roma[no] susidio tiene
Ma bruto ardito esaggio il mo[n]te assale
Grave infamia a' roma[n] co[n] minor
   ben[e]

(A little hill holds the Roman reserves,
   but Brutus, brave and clever, attacks
   the mountain
a severe disgrace for the Roman[s] with
   little advantage)

The banners of the soldiers in the right
foreground have eagles, those of the
soldiers in the left foreground have what
appear to be turtles or frogs. On the
exterior are landscapes with trees and
rocks.

No corresponding episode that fits the
inscription has yet been identified in the
life either of the sixth-century Roman
Junius Brutus, regarded as founder of the
Roman Republic, or of the much later
Brutus, one of those who assassinated
Julius Caesar. The probability is that *bruto*
is a painter's error in copying a text he
has been given and that the name should
read *brenno*, Brennus. If this is the case,
the episode portrayed is the Battle of
Allia, at the confluence of the rivers Allia
and Tiber north of Rome, around 387 BC,
in which Roman troops, including
reserves set on top of a hill, were attacked
and routed by Brennus, leader of the
Gallic tribe the Senones. This battle was
followed by the sacking of Rome by the
Gauls.[56]

The manner of painting and the use
of verse explanations strongly recalls the
series made, probably in the Fontana
workshop, with subjects relating to
Hannibal from the Punic Wars.[57] The
painter who carried out most of the
Hannibal service may also have painted
this basin. Three similar basins from the
Punic War series are in the Bargello from
the Medici Grand-Ducal collections;
they may be among the six *rinfrescatoi a
triangolo* mentioned in a Medici inventory
of 1588.[58] The plates of the Hannibal series
have inscriptions in rhyming couplets,
not, as here, *terza rima*.

A basin almost identical to this one is
in the Speed Museum of Art, Louisville,
Kentucky.[59] The inscription on the Speed
Museum cooler was probably the same
as that on the present one, but is only
partly legible, having run in the kiln. It is
possible that the present basin replaced
the Speed Museum one because of the
kiln defect. No other pieces that seem
likely to be from the same set have been
noted, but there may once have been a
series illustrating early Roman history.

The stated provenance from the
Hermitage, Saint Petersburg, has not
been confirmed and the records of the
dealers Cecil Leitch and Kerin are not
known to survive. However, it is entirely
plausible, since the Russian government
did make numerous covert sales of works
of art to the West around 1928–32. The
fact that the Hermitage still holds a
comparable basin with a different subject,
suggests that this one might have been
sold as a sort of duplicate.[60] Full records
of these sales, however, have not yet, as
far as I know, been published by Russian
colleagues.[61]

54 We are indebted to Kelly Domoney for the
    results of examination under ultra-violet light.
55 No similar large-painted numbers, however,
    have been found on Hermitage pieces described
    in Ivanova 2019.
56 Livy, v, 38. We owe this explanation to Jane
    Wilson.
57 Drey 1991; update in Wilson 2018, pp.320–22.
    Addenda to the listings of the plates of
    the Hannibal set are listed under no.192 in
    the addenda to the 2009 British Museum
    catalogue on https://timothywilson.co.uk/
    italian-renaissance-ceramics-catalogue-british-
    museum-addenda-and-corrigenda/
58 Spallanzani 1994, p.82, tav.29; see now Marini
    2024, nos 249a–c.
59 Ladis 1989, no.24.
60 Kube 1976, no.84.
61 On sales from the Hermitage around 1930 to
    Calouste Gulbenkian, Andrew Mellon, and
    others see Walker 1974; Norman 1997, pp.179–
    201; Odom and Salmond 2009; Ekserdjian 2010.

8 and 9

Two pilgrim flasks

Probably Urbino, *c*.1553–70
Accepted by H. M. Government in lieu of inheritance tax from the estate of
Samuel Airlie Holden-Hindley and allocated to the Ashmolean, WA2022.709 and 710.

Tin-glazed earthenware. Both have lion masks from which rise scrolling handles resembling horns; slots are cut into the hollow foot of each.

8: height: 36 cm

9: height: 36.5 cm

CONDITION: wear and chipping to masks and handles. The invoice from Durlacher notes that both stoppers are replacements, but they are a good approximation to what the flasks would originally have had. The stoppers were originally fixed by screw fittings.

PROVENANCE: bought from Durlacher Bros, London, September 1933, for £100.[62]

8 (WA2022.709) is painted on one side with the scene of Pluto abducting Proserpina from Ovid's *Metamorphoses*, and on the other with four women throwing themselves into the sea, which is populated by half-human sea creatures. The falling women are probably the daughters of Achelous, who had been companions of Proserpina, transformed into Sirens.[63]

9 (WA2022.710) is painted on one side with the river god Achelous on the right, holding a banquet for Theseus at a table with legs set astride a stream.[64] On the other side is the goddess Minerva and the daughters of Mnemosyne (the Muses) at the spring of Helicon; the fountain is surmounted by a figure of Minerva.[65]

The four scenes are based, more or less closely, on woodcuts from a free verse version of the *Metamorphoses*, the *Trasformationi di M. Lodovico Dolce*, first published by Gabriele Giolito in Venice in 1553, of which one is illustrated here (fig.4).[66]

The form is derived from drinking vessels made out of gourds or of leather, as used by medieval pilgrims and other travellers. Such 'pilgrim flasks' became popular in maiolica services from the

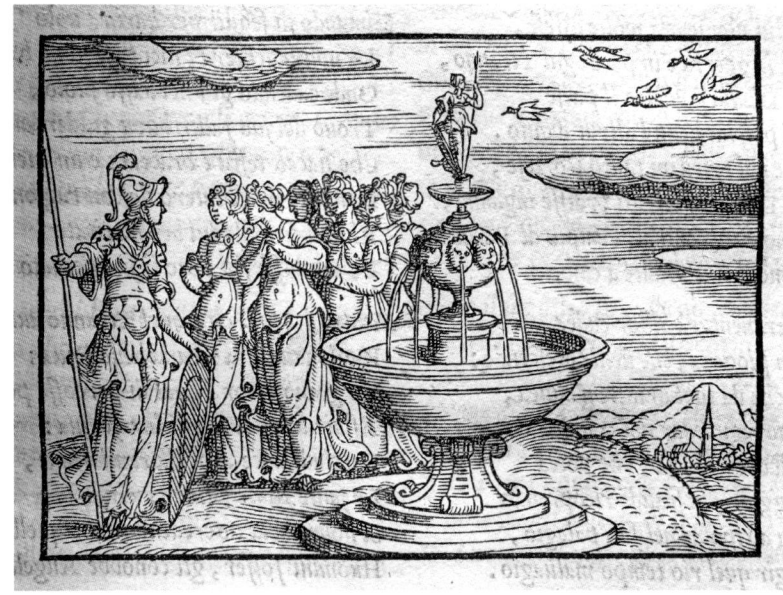

Fig.4 *Minerva and the Muses at the Spring of Helicon.* Woodcut from L. Dolce, *le Trasformationi …* (Venice, 1553). Bodleian Library, Oxford

1530s in Urbino and elsewhere, not so much as functional bottles but as part of the *credenza* for display. They were a regular part of Urbino *credenze* from the 1530s for the rest of the sixteenth century. The Ashmolean collection did not hitherto contain any maiolica example.

The original caps were attached by screw fittings, fitting a threaded upstand on the flasks. This was a virtuoso pottery technique, described by Cipriano Piccolpasso, who noted that some maiolica bottles were made 'with a screw mouth, in the manner of silver flasks. I would not wish to pass lightly over this secret, because it is a thing too beautiful and ingenious and very difficult'.[67]

The two pilgrim flasks were acquired together and are very likely to have been part of the same set. They are probably by the same painter, but this is not beyond debate. No.**8**, especially the group

of falling women, is close in style to Francesco Durantino, who by the likely date of these flasks had left Urbino.[68] It is possible that the painter may have been trained in Urbino alongside Francesco.

62 Copies of correspondence kindly supplied by Mark Holden-Hindley. The records of Durlacher Brothers for this period preserved in the Getty Research Center cover only the New York side of the business.

63 Ovid, *Metamorphoses*, V, 552–63.

64 Ovid, *Metamorphoses*, VIII, 571–3.

65 Ovid, *Metamorphoses*, VI, 254–67.

66 *Le Trasformationi di M. Lodovico Dolce* (Venice, 1553), p.111, illustrating *Minerva and the Muses at the spring of Helicon*; the *Abduction of Proserpina* is on p.115; the *Banquet of Achelous* on p.181. The *Daughters of Achelous* is not illustrated in the Dolce version, but the maiolica painter has made use of figures from a woodcut of a different subject, *Tereus, Procne, and Philomela*, on p.142.

67 Piccolpasso 2007, Book 1, p.51.

68 Wilson 2017, p.167.

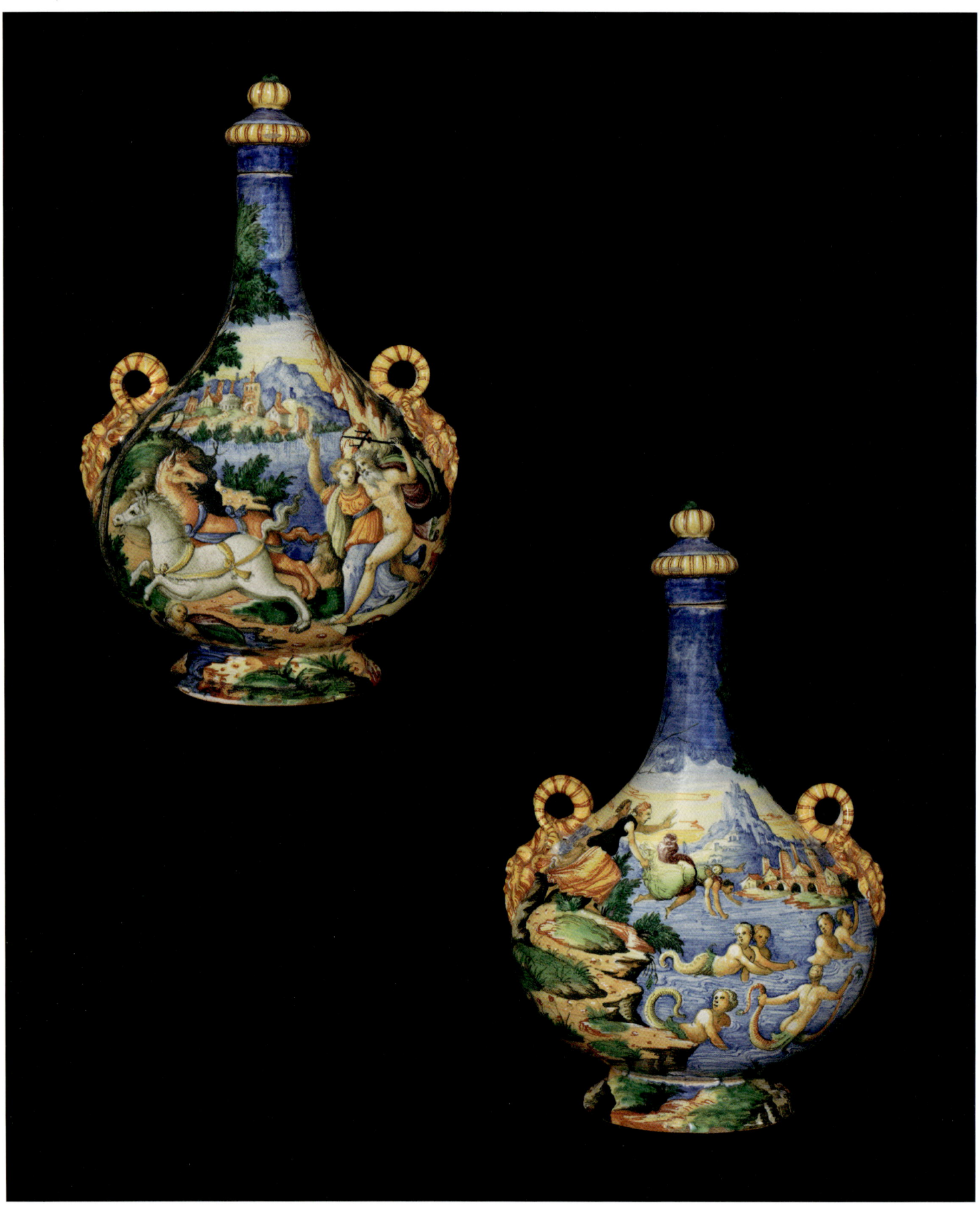

No.**8**

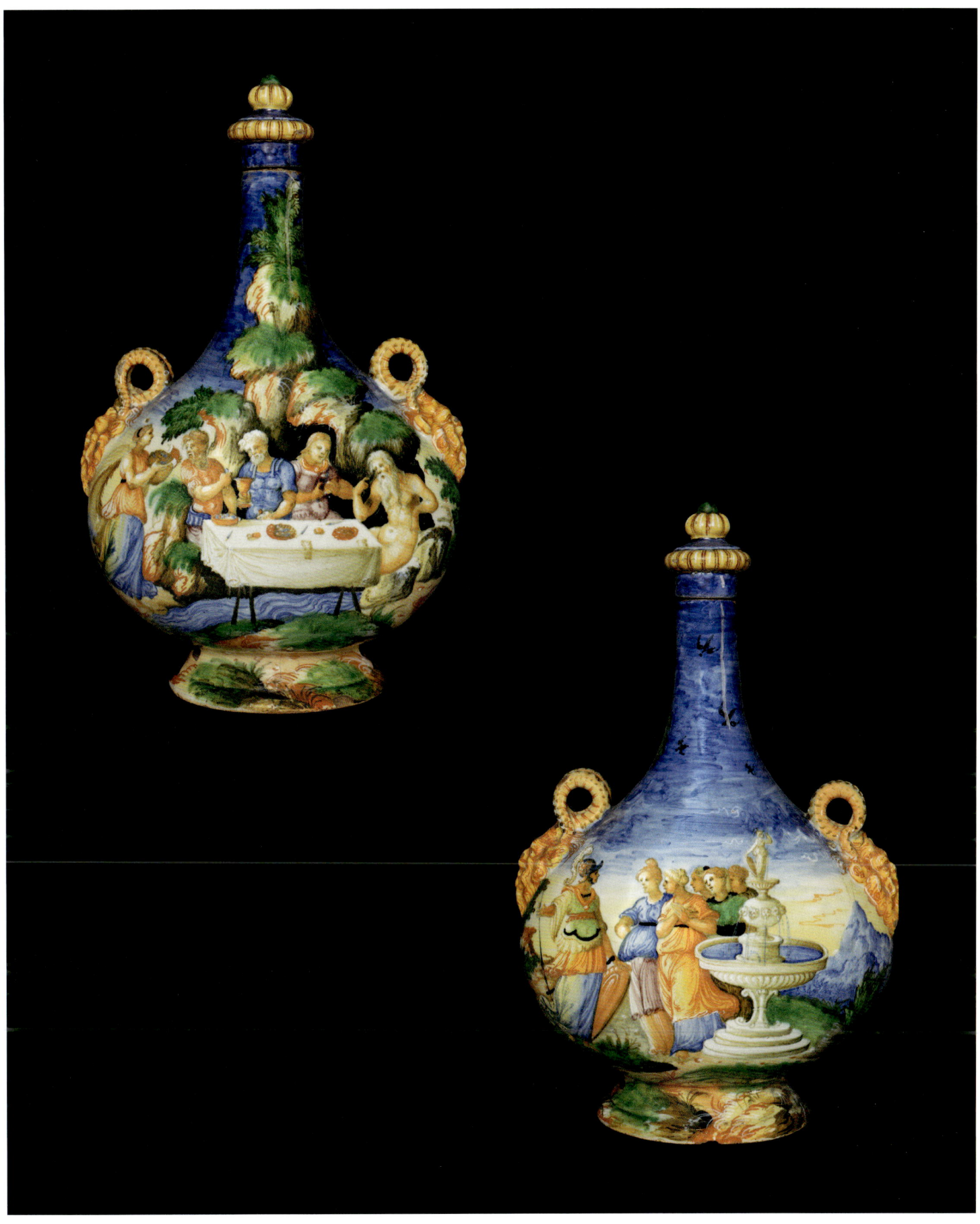

No.**9**

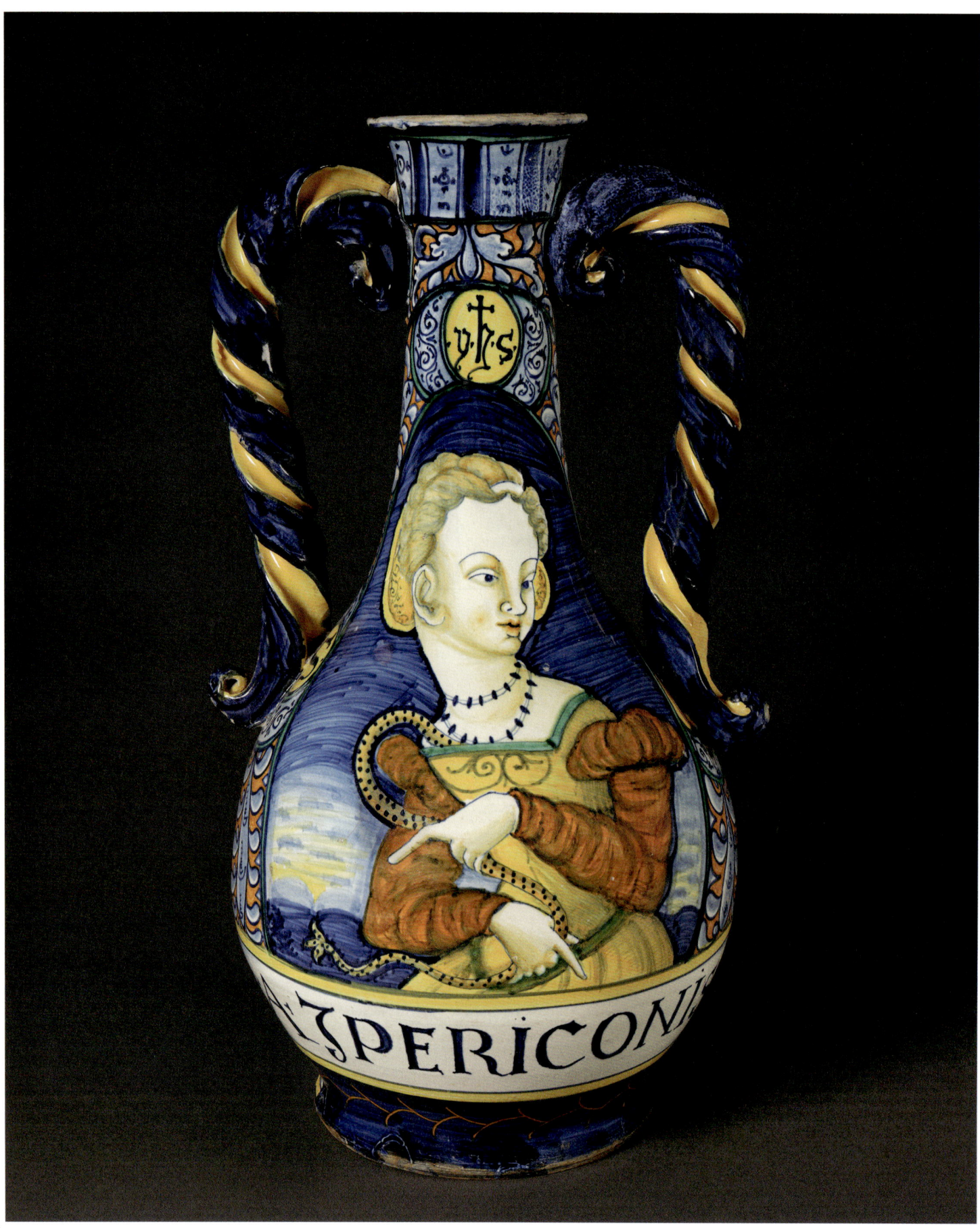

10

Pharmacy bottle, Cleopatra and the asp

Castelli, workshop of Orazio Pompei, c.1550–60
Accepted by H. M. Government in lieu of inheritance tax from the estate of
Samuel Airlie Holden-Hindley and allocated to the Ashmolean, WA2022.711.

Tall bottle with flaring rim, tin-glazed inside and out; two twisted handles.

Height: 33.5 cm

CONDITION: retouching around the rim and on the front; restored by Loretta Hogan, 1991. Very often bottles of this form have lost their handles or had them replaced, but this does not seem to be the case with this jar.[69]

PROVENANCE: W. M. de Zoete; his sale, *Catalogue of the Valuable Collections of Bronzes, Sculpture, Ceramics, Textiles, etc. The Property of W. M. de Zoete, Esq. (deceased) of Layer Breton, Colchester, and Blenheim House, North Berwick,* Sotheby's, London, 1–3 April 1935, lot 252. Bought by Cecil Leitch and Kerin for Mrs Arthur Hindley. Unidentified pencil (ownership?) marking under the base *SP*

BIBLIOGRAPHY: Pescara 1989, no.506.

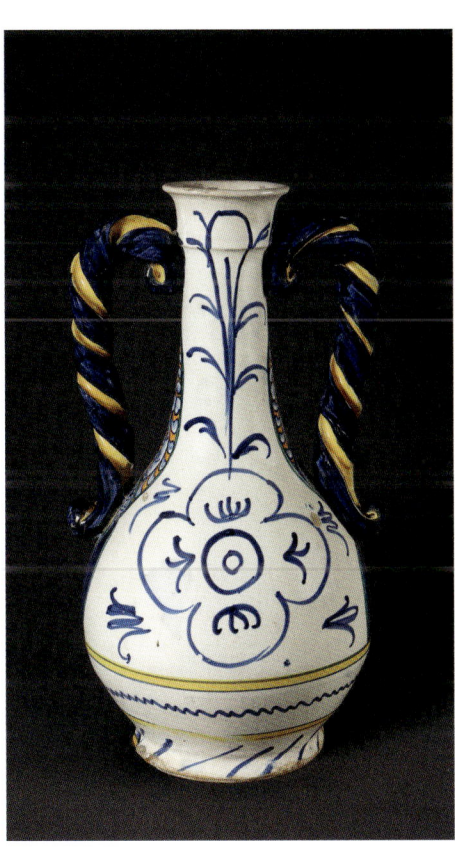

On the front, Cleopatra commits suicide by putting the asp to her breast, which (unusually in representations of the subject) remains concealed within her dress. The contents inscription is *A.YPERICONIS*. At the springing of the left handle is the letter *S* in a roundel. At the top are the letters of the sacred trigram (the first three letters of the name of Jesus in Greek), *.y.h.s.*, with a bar crossing the upright of the *h*. On the back is a fern-scroll rising from a lobed quatrefoil.

The contents indicated by the inscription were a medicinal water made from Hypericum (*hipericon* in Italian Renaissance pharmaceutical manuals), Saint John's wort.

Archaeological work in the 1980s showed that jars of this type (named Orsini-Colonna jars after an example in the British Museum with a bear for the Orsini hugging a column for the Colonna) were made in Castelli, in the Abruzzo mountains from around 1540 for several decades.[70] Most were made in the workshop of Orazio Pompei, the town's most successful pottery owner. Numerous painters were involved, including Orazio himself.

The subject, which occurs on other Orsini-Colonna jars, is characteristic of the slightly kinky subject matter sometimes favoured in the Pompei workshop, for instance 'Roman Charity', or Lucretia or Judith represented naked.[71]

The *S* in a roundel is difficult to parallel on jars of this type. One possibility is that this is the initial of the painter, but no member of Orazio Pompei's family with this initial is recorded at the time.

A jar of Orsini-Colonna type has long been a desideratum for the Ashmolean

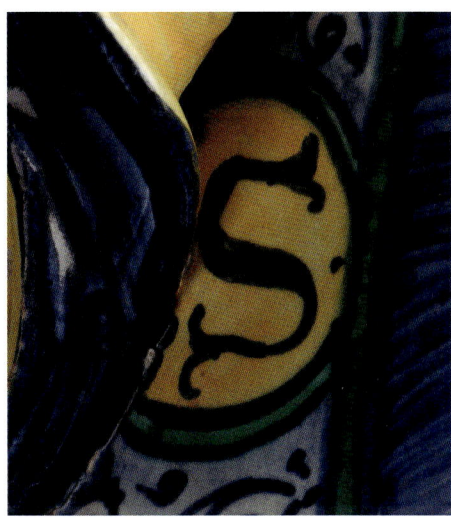

collection, and this is an excellent and characteristic example.

69 We thank Kelly Domoney for examining the bottle under ultra-violet light.
70 Thornton and Wilson 2009, no.338, with discussion and references.
71 For parallels to the form, subject, and style, see Pescara 1989, especially nos 503–5; no.432 is another Cleopatra, this time represented naked. See also Marini 2024, no.324b, with analogies. A particularly fine example with Cleopatra naked is in the National Gallery of Art, Washington, DC, 2014.136.313, from the Corcoran collection (Watson 1986, no. 16).

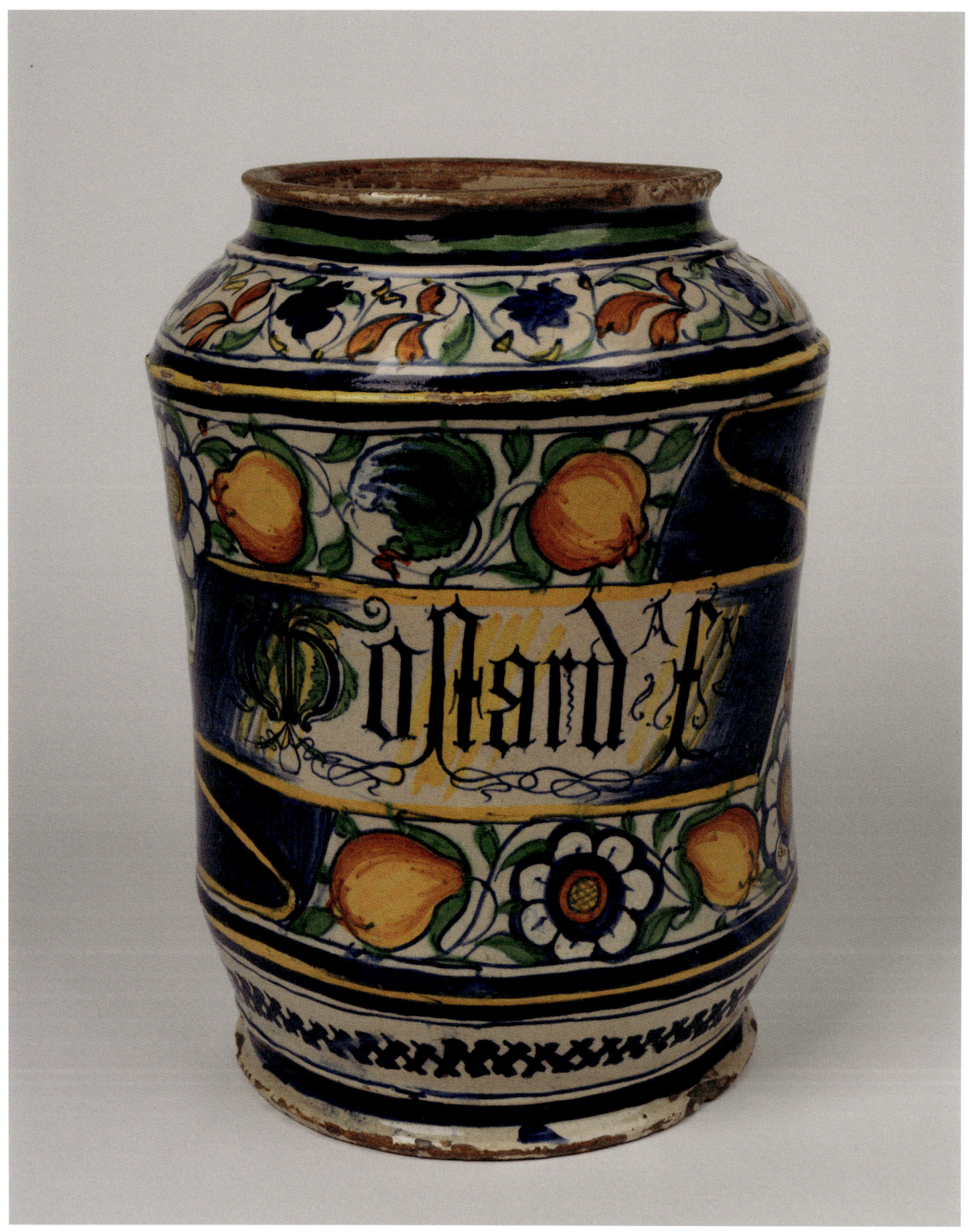

11

Storage jar for *mostarda*

Venice, *c.*1530–70
Purchased from Justin Raccanello, London, with the aid of the late Martin Foley,
the ACE/V&A Purchase Grant Fund, and the Oxford Ceramics Group, WA2024.53.

Albarello, straight-sided, with two pairs of small protruding ridges where the body narrows top and bottom; throwing ridges visible inside; flanged at the rim. Earthenware, covered outside and inside with a whitish tin-glaze.

Height: 36 cm

CONDITION: some wear and chipping, especially at rim and base. A hole has been drilled in the base to allow the jar to be used as a plant pot or lamp.

PROVENANCE: Cambi, Milan, 25 October 2016, lot 11; private collection; Wannenes, Genoa, 30 November 2023, lot 153; bought by Justin Raccanello.

BIBLIOGRAPHY: Wilson 2018, no.197.

On a ribbon cartouche on the front of this handsome *albarello* is the contents inscription *MostardA fNA*. The rest of the main area of the body is painted with leaf scrolls, fruit and flowers. Near the neck is a band of leaf scrolls, while near the base is a band of *X*s.

The designated contents, *mostarda fina*, was not mustard but a fine *mostarda*, the sweet fruit pickle which was, and still is, a speciality of the north-east of Italy. In *Dizionario del dialetto Veneziano*, Giuseppe Boerio notes that 'Our *mostarda* is a foodstuff, or rather a most precious condiment, sold by confectioners and made essentially of quinces flavoured with mustard and honey or sugar'.[72] The predominant fruit in the decoration here are quinces, reflecting the intended contents.

Several large handsome Venetian *albarelli* so inscribed and with this ornament survive.[73] Some, including this one, may have been made in the workshop of Jacomo da Pesaro, the leading Venetian workshop for much of the first half of the sixteenth century, but this is unproven. The ornament evidently has reference to the contents, though

the same decoration is found on *albarelli* and globular jars inscribed as to contain other products, such as rose syrup.[74] *Mostarda* jars were probably mainly used in retail outlets, *spezierie*, though they might sometimes have been used for

domestic storage in large households. Equally capacious *mostarda* jars exist with different ornament, probably later and all or most made in the workshop of Domenego da Venezia.[75]

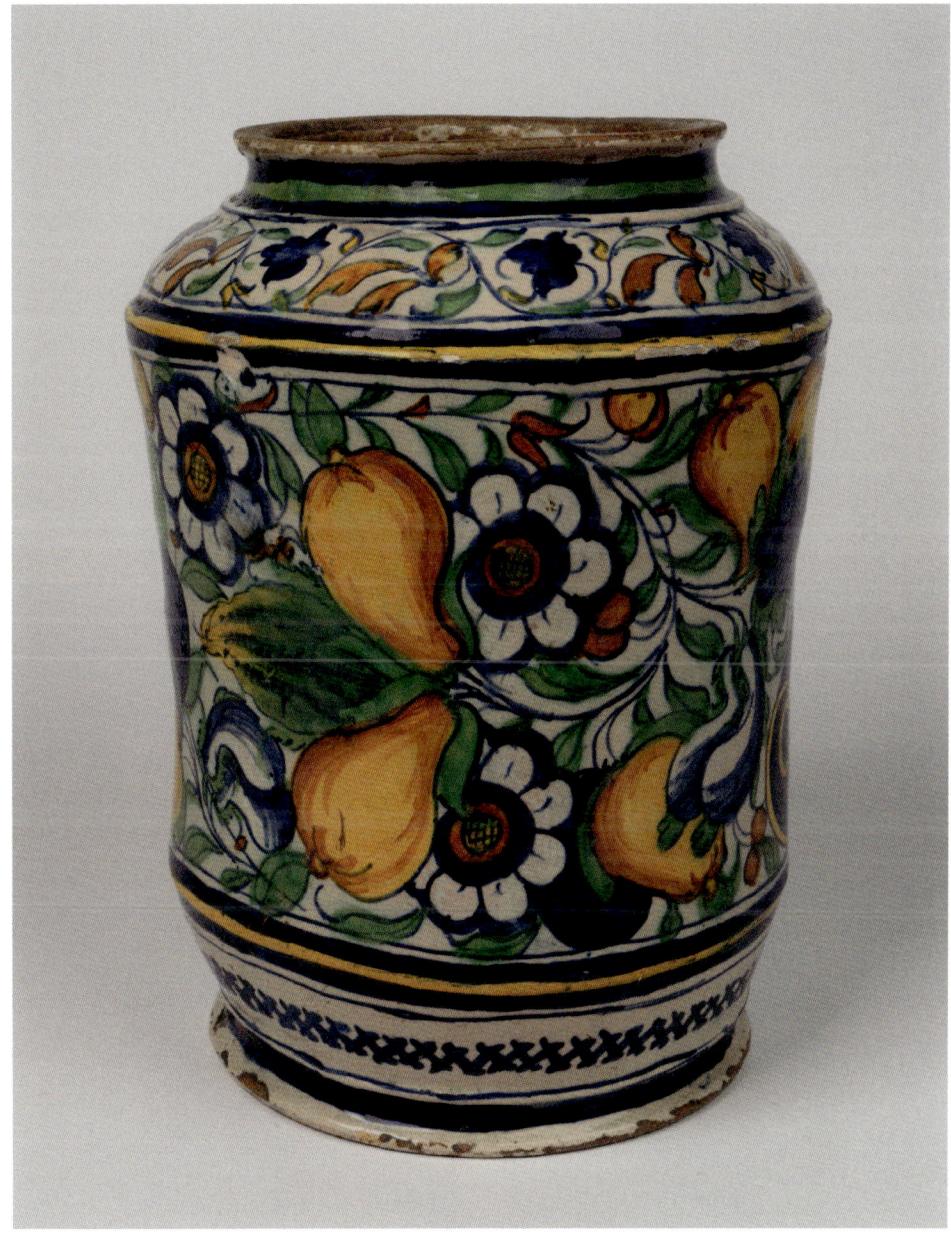

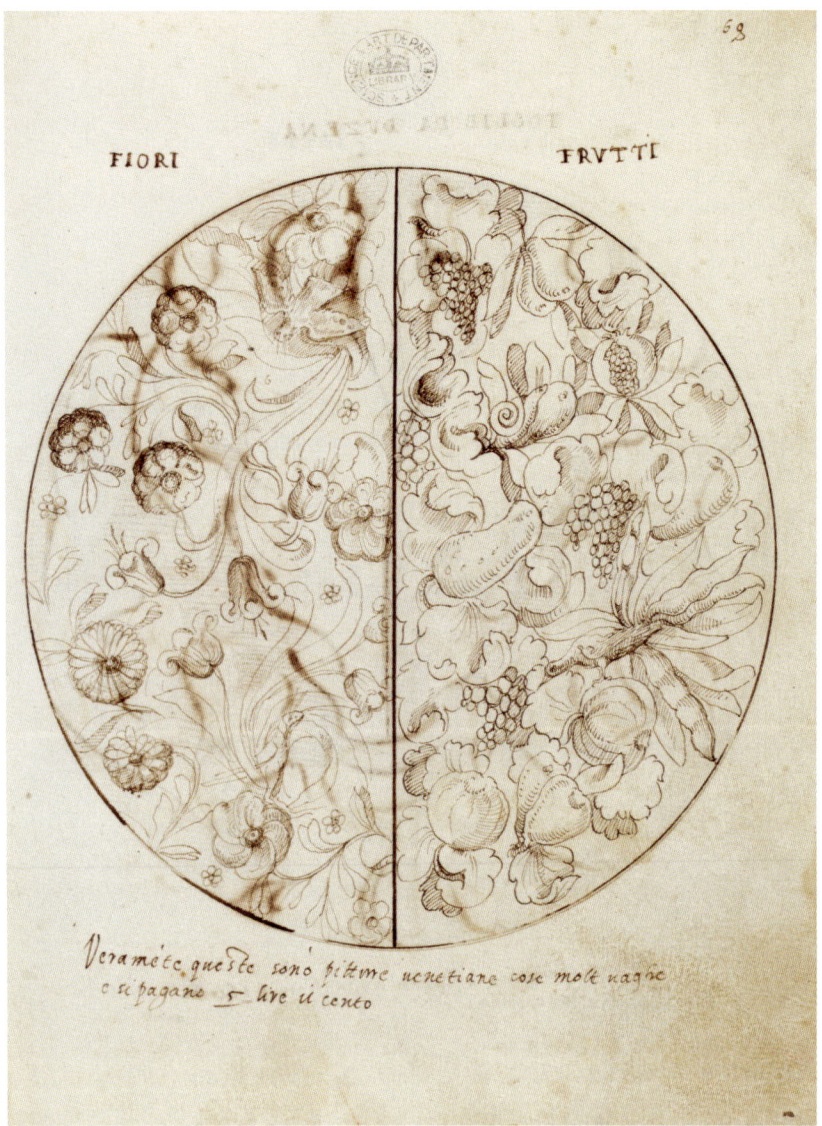

This type of characteristically Venetian ornament was illustrated as *frutti* and *fiori* about 1557 by Cipriano Piccolpasso in his *Three Books of the Potter's Art* (fig.5). He comments on both flower and fruit decoration: 'Truly these are a Venetian type of painting and very charming'.

Jars with this type of ornament raise interesting issues about the diffusion of Italian maiolica ornament to what are now Belgium and the Netherlands, since examples have been attributed to Italian potters working in Antwerp.[76] Whether or not any of the globular jars or *albarelli* with this ornament were actually made in northern Europe, there is no reason to suppose this example is anything other than Venetian.

72 Boerio 1867, p.429: *La nostra Mostarda è un una vivanda, o sia un sapore preziosissimo venduta da' Confettieri e fatto essenzialmente di mele cotogne condite di senapa e miele, ovvero di zucchero.*

73 Examples are cited by Wilson 2018, p.434.

74 For example, Wilson and Sani 2006–7, I, no.73, a globular jar inscribed as for *so.roxati.simp*; and other examples there cited.

75 Examples are listed in Wilson 2018, p.434, to which may be added four at Pandolfini, Florence, 2 October 2024, lots 18, 19, 25, 27, and generally comparable jars illustrated by Perale 2021.

76 Poole 1995, no.443, discusses an older attribution to Antwerp of a jar in the Fitzwilliam. See also Alverà Bortolotto and Dumortier 1990, pp.55–74, noting (distantly) comparable ornament on tiles from the Antwerp workshop of Guido Andries (Guido di Savino). A plate in the British Museum, BEP, 1885,0508.40, with a fruit and flower border is dated 1583 and marked with a monogram of *C* and *L*. It was attributed by Wilson 1987, no.259, to Cornelis Lubbertz, Haarlem, but by Dumortier 2002, p.211, to Lambrecht Collegie, Antwerp. I am unaware of any direct archaeological evidence from Antwerp for the production there of large jars resembling this and consider the frequently made attributions of jars of this type are unproven.

No.**11** (detail)

12

Plate with the arms of Dethick and grotesques

Pisa, workshop of Niccolò Sisti, c.1593–1602
Purchased 2021 from Justin Raccanello (Bazaart), with the assistance of the Madan Bequest Fund, Art
Fund, the ACE/V&A Purchase Grant Fund, the late Dinah Reynolds in memory of Margaret Macfarlane,
the late Martin Foley, and the Oxford Ceramics Group, WA2021.91.

Plate with narrow rim, high foot-ring; tin-glazed front and back, with one kiln-support mark at 6 o'clock. On the reverse are yellow-ochre rings; there are numerous pinholes in the glaze on the back.

Diameter: 46.5 cm

CONDITION: some cracking and wear to glaze. UV examination by Dr Kelly Domoney indicated that there is no restoration or overpaint but noted a crack through the body upper right.

PROVENANCE: private collection, Arezzo; G. Asioli Martini, Imola; from whom bought at the Florence Biennale, 2019, by Bazaart, London.

BIBLIOGRAPHY: Asioli Martini 2019, no.16; T. Wilson in *Oxford Ceramics Group Newsletter* 53 (June 2022), pp.3–4.

The large maiolica plate is painted with flamboyant all-over grotesques on a white ground, including Diana of the Ephesians, a pavilion, two winged putti holding torches, fantastical half-human, half-bird, and half-animal creatures, sphinxes, insects, a rather comical owl, and snails.[77] At the bottom are two cameo-style medallions with facing portraits of a man in a contemporary ruff and a woman. The composition is divided at the four compass points by rods.[78] In the centre is a shield of arms with sideways helm and closed visor, mantling, and a crest of a nag's head charged with a crescent; the crescent in English heraldry is the mark for difference of a second son.

The plate has been convincingly attributed to the workshop in Pisa of Niccolò Sisti, under the patronage of the Medici Grand Dukes of Tuscany. Niccolò di Maestro Sisto was from Norcia in Umbria and was a specialist in kiln technology of various types. He is first recorded as recipient of a regular salary from the Tuscan Grand Ducal treasury

in 1571.[79] He recurs in Medici service in 1577, described as *stillatore* (master of distilling techniques), and apparently in connection with the recently successful project to make Medici porcelain.[80] In 1580, he is recorded in connection with making *cristallo* in Florence and as running a *fonderia* (foundry). In 1592–3, he was operating a glass kiln in Pisa and apparently also making porcelain there. In or around 1593, he started running an operation to make maiolica in Pisa, having received an advance of 500 ducats from the treasury by an order from Grand Duke Ferdinando I in 1592. He was then described as *fonditore* (foundry-master), and it was noted that he had been charged with introducing into Florence and the Grand Duchy maiolica in the Faenza style (*introdurre in Firenze e nello Stato l'esercitio delle maioliche alla faentina*); the reference is presumably to a version of *bianco di Faenza*.

As a young man Niccolò Sisti came to work alongside his father in the Medici laboratories in the Palazzo Vecchio. It has been suggested that the central standing figure in the painting of *The Alchemists* in the Studiolo of Grand-Duke Francesco I de' Medici (fig.6) represents Niccolò Sisti.

In 1619, Sisti successfully petitioned Grand Duke Cosimo II, who had succeeded his father in 1609, to be relieved from paying back the outstanding part of the advance made to him in 1592.[81] He noted that he had never been paid for numerous pieces of maiolica. These included the large sum of 440 *scudi* worth of *bellissima robba a grottesche*, which had been stored in one of the Medici palaces and which had been sent by Francesco Paulsanti, a court official, into England.

Sisti stated that he believed this was by order of Ferdinando, so the delivery to England must have predated 1609.

Despite this large consignment, maiolica painted with grotesques was rare in England and not generally traded from Italy to England: only two fragments have been noted from excavations in England.[82] However, a remarkable group of comparable plates excavated at Enkhuizen in the Netherlands, a port that had trading links with Tuscany, includes several plates that look as if they may come from Sisti's workshop (note the snail at 2 o'clock); one of these has a possibly Tuscan coat of arms (fig.7).[83] This plate too needs research – both on the arms and on the Italian merchants active in this Netherlandish port – but corroborates the existing evidence that Sisti's products reached international markets.

The documents suggest that Sisti's skill was as a kiln-master and that he employed several painters, rather than being one himself.

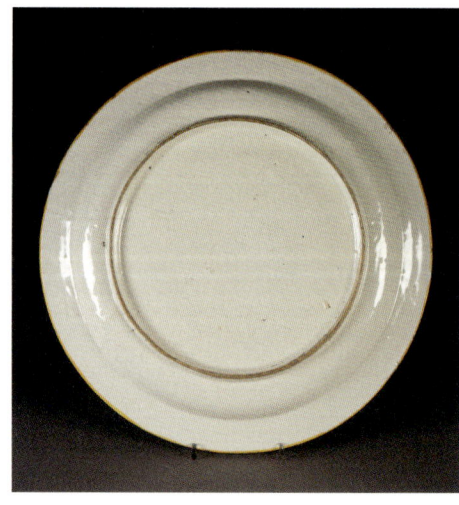

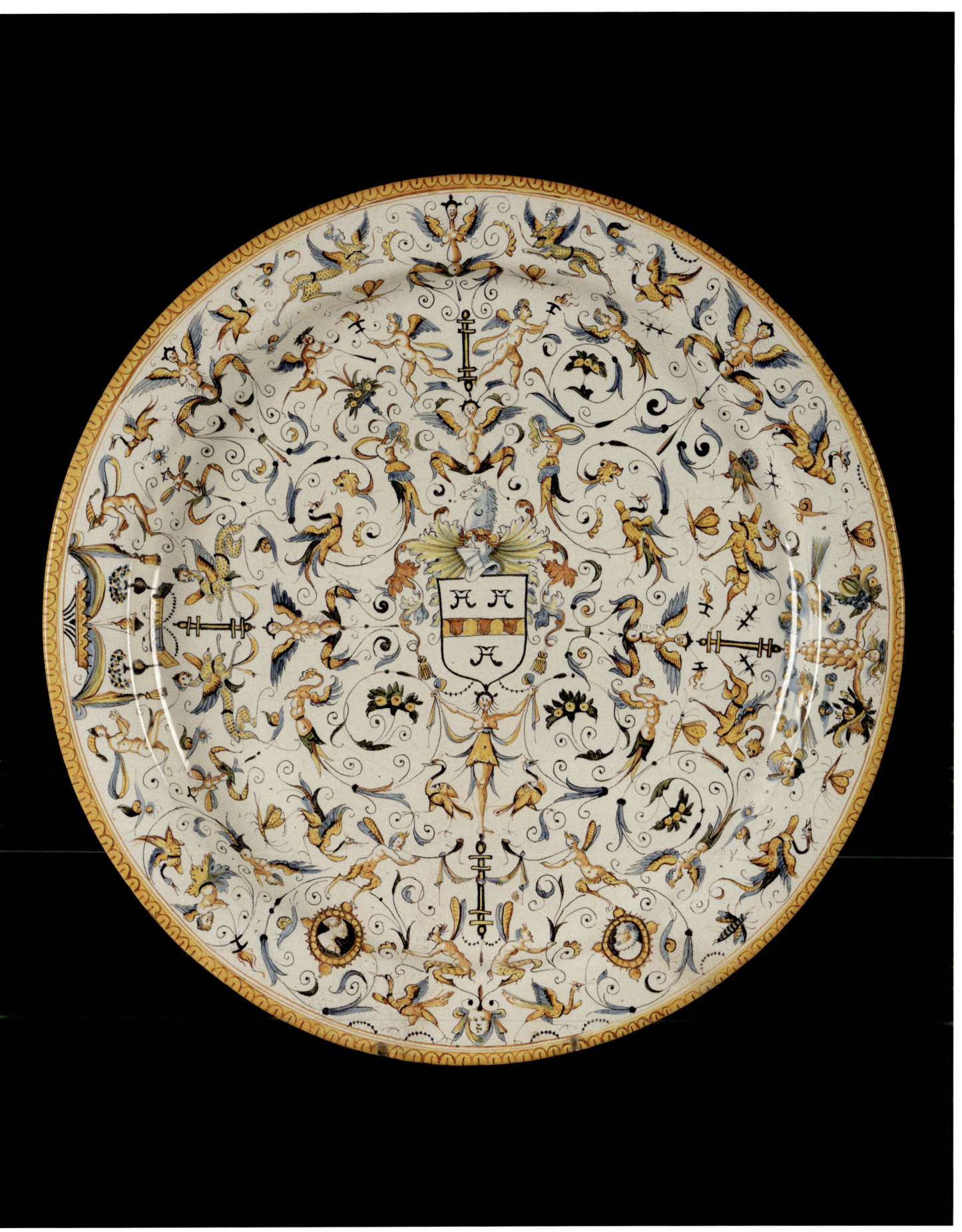

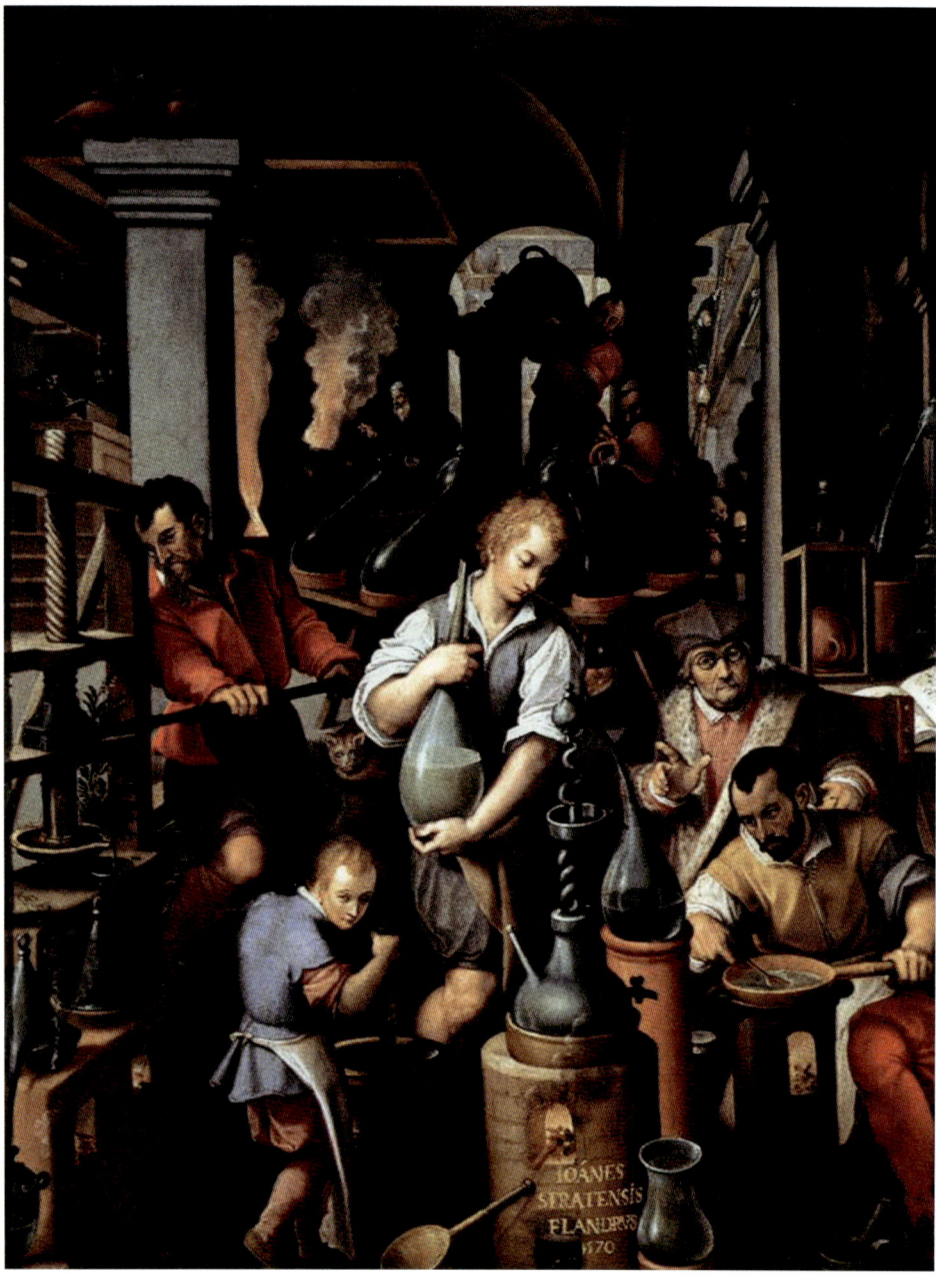

Fig.6 Jan van der Straet, called Stradanus, *The Alchemists*, oil on slate, 1570; from the Studiolo of Grand-Duke Francesco I de' Medici in the Palazzo Vecchio, Florence. The central standing figure in the painting may be Niccolò Sisti. Lower right is Grand-Duke Francesco; over his shoulder perhaps Sisti's father, Sisto da Norcia.

In the absence of any kiln waste from Pisa itself, all attributions to Sisti's workshop have to start from a grandiose vase in the Museo Internazionale delle Ceramiche, Faenza, marked *PISA* on a cartouche.[84] The vase is painted with grotesques, broadly speaking in the Urbino style, corresponding, no doubt, to some cups sent from Pisa to the Medici villa at Artimino in 1601, described in the archive document as *terra di Urbino, cioè fatte in Pisa a modo di terra di Urbino*.[85]

Several pieces with similar grotesques have been more or less convincingly attributed to Sisti's workshop, including a fluted bowl dated 1596 in the Faenza museum.[86] They often include spirited representations of creatures, notably snails, which seem almost to have been a distinguishing motif of the workshop.[87] Among the pieces that seem convincingly attributed to the same workshop as the marked vase is a large plate with a depiction of *Susanna and the Elders* and

grotesques (including snails), seemingly by the same hand as the marked vase.[88] The grotesques on the Dethick plate may not be by the same painter, but the form and facture of the two plates are so strikingly similar as to make the attribution of the Dethick plate to Sisti's workshop convincing.[89]

The arms on the shield on the maiolica plate correspond to the arms of Dethick of Derbyshire, drawn (for maiolica) with some precision: *argent a fess vairy or and gules between three bougets sable*.[90] On the crest, a nag's head, is a crescent, the mark of a second son.

When the plate was acquired by the Ashmolean it was thought that the arms were those of Sir Willam Dethick (1543–1612), who was appointed Garter King of Arms, head of the English College of Arms, in 1586. He was a noted antiquary, who visited Italy as a young man.[91] He was his father's second son, so used the crescent for difference in his arms. The hypothesis was that the plate might have been a gift from the Grand Duke of Tuscany, perhaps while on diplomatic business in Italy. However, while this remains an outside possibility, no evidence has been found that Sir William Dethick visited the court at Florence (no Italian was made a Knight of the Order of the Garter in Queen Elizabeth's reign), or Italy at all during his tenure of office.[92]

Sir William Dethick was a passionate and sometimes violent man, who on one occasion scandalously poured the contents of a chamber pot over the head of the wife of a fellow herald. However, subsequent research in the British State Papers has led to the emergence of an even more startlingly colourful individual as a more likely candidate.[93] This is a man from another branch of the extensive and complicated Dethick family of Derbyshire: Humphrey Dethick.[94] He was born in Derbyshire in 1567, the third son, but perhaps the second to survive into adulthood, of William Dethick and his wife Ellen (*née* Alsop).[95] He started to attend Cambridge University, but withdrew early due to ill health and later went to sea. Subsequently, he worked for a London merchant, Richard May, and by 1595 was based in Florence, where he was agent for the wealthy London textile merchant Baptist Hicks (later Viscount Campden). He was evidently a man of some education and professional competence. In 1601–2, he travelled to France and on to Scotland. There, in Dunfermline, he stabbed and killed a man and was suspected of having been part of an international plot, together with a mysterious Italian accomplice, to assassinate James VI of Scotland.[96] The dramatic events caused a widespread stir and are documented in almost tabloid excitement in contemporary correspondence. He was taken into custody and examined. The Scottish records contain his revealing deposition, reprinted here. The examiners were suspicious of a valuable 'stomacher', perhaps a jewelled breast piece, that he was wearing. He stated that he had

received it from Lorenzo Usimbardi, who was secretary to Grand Duke Ferdinando I. Dethick stated that he had got to know Usimbardi through 'ane huir' [whore], presumably a Florentine courtesan whose services both men used.

In England, Sir Robert Cecil, Queen Elizabeth's hyperactive Secretary of State, took an interest in the well-being of James VI, the heir apparent to the throne of England, and received informative reports from correspondents in Scotland about the case, quoted below.[97] Dethick was considered by the Scottish authorities to have gone mad in prison, but it was noted that James regarded his case with sympathy. The contemporary Scottish church historian David Calderwood (1575–1650) reported that Dethick had:

> cryed lyke a mad man 'The houre! the houre! the king! the king!' &c. Being examined he confessed

that he and an Italian sould have slaine the king, as is reported. He was transported to the Castell of Edinburgh and keeped in the yrons, but within a quarter of a yeere was set at libertie. It was reported that the king thought not muche of the mater but tooke the man to be somewhat distracted in his witts.[98]

The subsequent course of events in Humphrey's life has been reconstructed by Janet Kinrade Dethick. At some time after 1602, he was released from prison, apparently through the intervention of the king, and went to Ireland, doubtless as one of the Protestant English settlers who established themselves for a time in an ultimately unsuccessful colonial venture into Munster. On 31 March 1611, he was made one of the burgesses of Tralee in County Kerry, and in 1618 he was one of two representatives of the borough.[99]

The reasons to think that the maiolica plate was made for Humphrey Dethick are circumstantial but compelling. He was in Florence in the years between 1595 and 1601 and spent some time in Pisa, where Sisti's workshop was situated, before coming to Scotland. Most cogent is the evidence that he was a friend of 'Laurenso Lucenbardis'.[100] Lorenzo Usimbardi was in charge of the Medici craft workshops (*intendente delle fabbricche*) for Grand Duke Francesco I de' Medici and had played a key administrative role, after Ferdinando de' Medici succeeded his brother as Grand Duke in 1587, in setting up the Pisan workshop of Niccolò Sisti, where the plate was almost certainly made.[101] It seems a more than plausible speculation that the plate was commissioned by Usimbardi and intended as a present to Dethick; or that it was ordered by Dethick himself through the agency of Usimbardi. It is noteworthy, in view of the precision with which the shield of arms on the plate is represented, that Dethick had an interest in heraldry. Among his luggage in 1602 were found, according to George Nicolson (letter of 4 May 1602) 'other books and papers of arms and genealogies'.[102] It is unlikely that

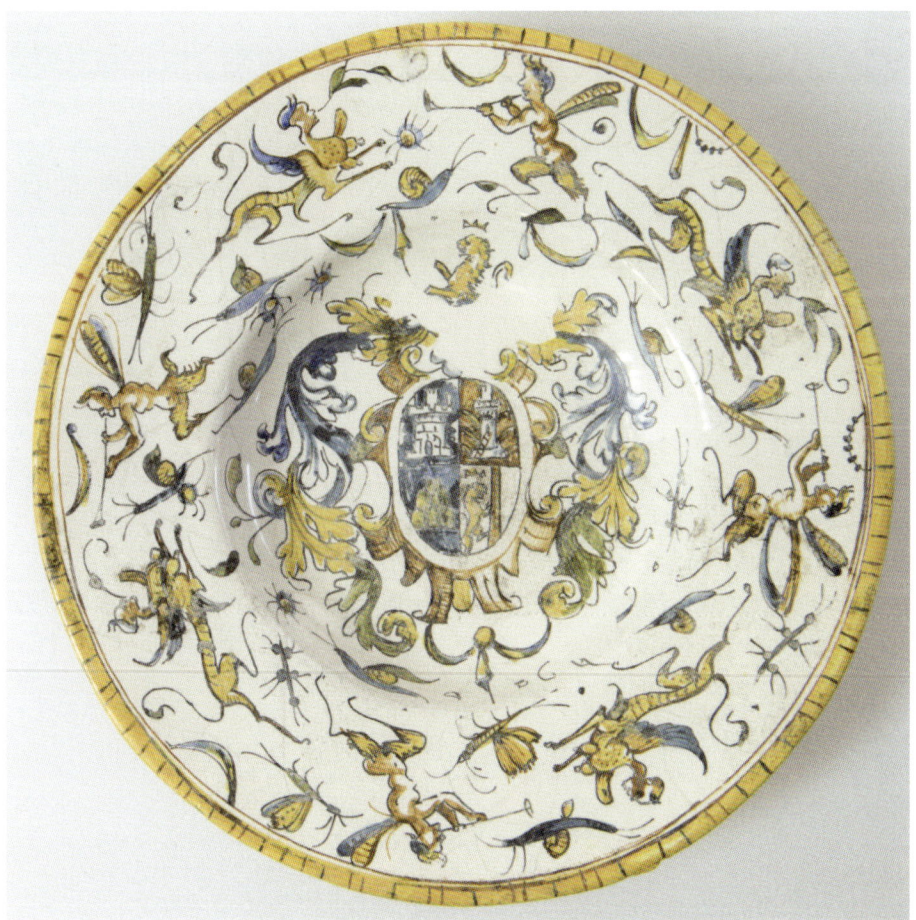

Fig.7 Armorial plate (restored) probably made in the Pisan workshop of Niccolò Sisti, excavated at Enkhuizen, Netherlands

of the wealthy merchants of Augsburg and Nuremberg; while Italian potteries, especially in Tuscany and Liguria, had extensive export markets to northern Europe in relatively routine wares.[104] Yet, until the identification of the arms on this plate, no definite example had ever been found with the arms of an identifiable English or English-based individual earlier than a Deruta salt from 1625, which bears the arms of Henrietta Maria, Queen of England, and is now in Plymouth City Museum, published recently by Elisa Paola Sani.[105] The Dethick plate, which was very likely made for a man who was at the centre of a dramatic supposed attempt to assassinate James VI of Scotland, less than a year before the heir-apparent acceded to the throne of England, is therefore of unique historical interest.

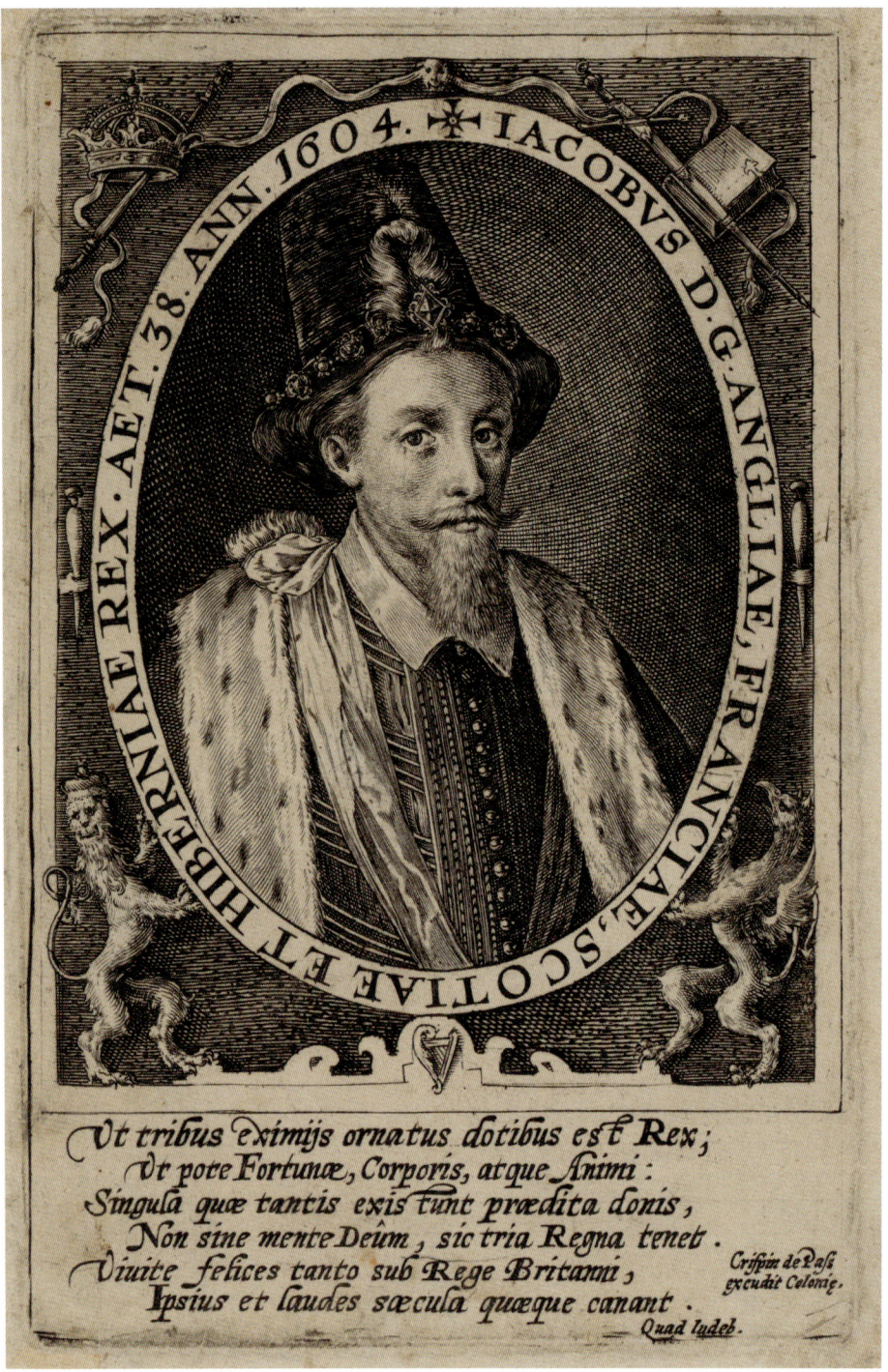

Fig.8 *King James VI and I*. Etching by Crispijn de Passe the elder, 1604. Ashmolean Museum, WA HP11250

Dethick brought the plate back to Britain in 1601–2, and, indeed, he may never have received it. It may not be coincidence that the earliest modern provenance for the plate is a collection in Arezzo, which is not far from the Usimbardi family home in Colle Val d'Elsa.

This plate is a rare convincingly identifiable product of the work of the workshop of Niccolò Sisti in Pisa, but its importance and interest are mainly historical.[103] At its most ambitious, Italian Renaissance maiolica was a successful luxury product with international reach. Clients of or recipients of gifts in the sixteenth century included the King of Spain, the Grand Master and the Chancellor of France, and several

77 The grotesques may be compared with those described as '*compendiario* grotesque' by Mallet 2004.

78 Similar rods appear on a smaller plate in Braunschweig: Lessmann 1979, no.88.

79 Spallanzani 1994, pp.65, 160, doc.27.

80 Cora and Fanfani 1986, p.27.

81 Guasti 1902, p.371. On Sisti, see most recently, with a bibliographical update, Spallanzani 2024.

82 Williams and Wilson 1989, pp.207–8; see also Brown and Curnow 2015, p.193, in the context of grotesque-painted maiolica recovered from a Spanish shipwreck off the coast at Kinlochbervie, Scotland.

83 'Excavations Enkhuizen', Provincie Noord-Holland, 2013, https://collectie.huisvanhilde.nl/?query=Records/relatedid=%5bSite 1426%5d&label=Zoekopdracht&showt ype=record#3035ec03-3bd7-4d26-aaf7-55e549013906. The dexter impalement might be for Tanini of Florence, see https://www.archiviodistato.firenze.it/ceramellipapiani/index.php?page=Famiglia&id=7270. We thank Marco Spallanzani and Niccolò Orsini De Marzo for comments on the arms and Justin Raccanello for further comments, and for information relating to Sisti more widely.

84 Cora 1964, pp.25–30; Bojani et al. 1985, no.666.

85 Cora 1964, p.26.

86 Cora 1964, tav.IIIa; Bojani et al. 1985, no.667; Ravanelli Guidotti 1997–8, no.107. For other attributions of maiolica of this sort to Pisa, see G. de Simone in Baldassari 2018, pp.155–60, including a fluted bowl dated 1593.

87 However, a note of caution about attributions of such '*compendiario* grotesques' to Pisa is implied by Marini 2024, no.420, where a plate

on high foot with similar grotesques, including snails, formerly attributed to Sisti's workshop, is instead attributed to 'Duchy of Urbino (or Castel Durante)'. Snails also occur on two pieces that are undoubtedly from the Duchy of Urbino, the plates at Waddesdon Manor marked as made by Giovan Paolo Savini in the Castel Durante workshop of Cesare Compagno in 1609, studied by Mallet 2004.

88   Currently with Justin Raccanello, London.

89   Grotesques of similar sort were made around the same date elsewhere in Tuscany (at Siena and Montelupo), but these have no close similarities either to the marked Pisa vase or to the Dethick plate.

90   See Maxwell Craven, 'A Derbyshire Armorial', *Derbyshire Record Society* 17 (1991), pp.53–4. The original identification of the arms as Dethick was due to Justin Raccanello.

91   A. Adolph, 'Sir William Dethick', *Oxford Dictionary of National Biography*

92   Marco Spallanzani's gleanings in the 'England' files for the *Principato* in the Archivio di Stato di Firenze produced no record of a likely occasion for such a commission by or gift to Sir William. No likely reference to him (or to Humphrey) occurs in the papers recorded by the Medici Archive Project. James Lloyd tells us he has found no papers that look likely to shed light on the question in the Archives of the College of Arms. We thank Professor Spallanzani and Dr Lloyd, and also Nigel Ramsay, for their kind assistance.

93   The initial suggestion of Humphrey as a more likely candidate than William was made following an online search by Matthew Winterbottom.

94   For the family, see W. C. Metcalfe, *Derbyshire Visitation Pedigrees, 1569 and 1611* (London, 1895), pp.30–32, and the family tree in Dethick 2008, p.vii, where the complications caused by the multiple Humphreys in the Dethick family are sorted out. She speculates that an elder brother, Ralph, may have died in infancy; Humphrey, if then the second surviving son of his parents, might have used the crescent for difference in his arms.

95   The Wikipedia entry gives his birth date as 1577, but in his deposition in Dunfermline in 1602 he gives his age as 35.

96   There were good relations between the Medici Grand Dukes and the English crown during the reign of Elizabeth I, and a plot hatched in court circles in Florence to assassinate her designated successor seems improbable.

97   Others, less closely concerned with the events, reported on them. Both John Chamberlain (letter to Dudley Carleton, 17 June 1602, in S. Williams, *The Letters of John Chamberlain* (London, 1861), p.139) and Philip Gawdy (letter to Lady Dorothy Gawdy, 27 June 1602, in I. H. Jeayes, *Letters of Philip Gawdy of West Harling, Norfolk, and of London, to various members of his family, 1579–1616* (Roxburghe Club, London, 1906), pp.123–4) believed that the events in Dunfermline were a real assassination attempt. The Wikipedia entry on Humphrey gives online links to these letters.

98   Calderwood 1845, VI, p.151.

99   Dethick 2008, p.26.

100 Sir Robert Cecil in the letter of 8 June 1602 quoted here notes that Dethick had received letters from 'a secretary of the Duke of Florence'. It seems likely, if not certain, that this was Usimbardi.

101 Cora and Fanfani 1986, pp.29–34, transcribe correspondence between Sisti and Usimbardi between 1592 and 1596. On the prominent role of various members of the Usimbardi family in general in the administration of the Grand Duchy, see Fantoni 1994, pp.139–68.

102 Letter 4 May 1602, below.

103 In the last 30 years, the Ashmolean has assembled a wide-ranging group of white-ground grotesque-painted maiolica in the style first developed in Urbino about 1560, which now includes most of the known production centres, but hitherto nothing from Pisa. The only example of Pisa maiolica identified in any UK museum is a bowl in the Bowes Museum, Barnard Castle (no.x.2162), with the arms of the Pio da Carpi family, which was I think correctly attributed to Sisti by Brown and Curnow 2015, p.193; other examples from the set, as noted by Brown and Curnow, are in the Louvre, two at Écouen, one at Faenza, and one recorded as sold in Paris, Fraysse et associés, Drouot, 5 June 2003, lot 143.

104 Hurst 1991, pp.212–31; Gaimster 1999.

105 Sani 2019. The impaled arms could refer jointly to Charles I and Henrietta Maria, but seem more likely to have specific reference to her.

Documents relating to Humphrey Dethick

**Henry Wotton to a noble acquaintance
(the Earl of Essex?), *c.*1595:**

There is farther in Florence one Dethick, an English factor, and withal a very good scholar, who no doubt to your lordship will be a most sufficient instrument in this kind.[106]

George Nicolson (English Resident in Scotland) to Sir Robert Cecil (English Secretary of State), from Edinburgh, 4 May 1602:

An unhappy Englishman come by sea out of France some 10 days or more ago, spending his time some days here at Leith and other places without desire of acquaintance of any of his countrymen, went to Dunfermline on Tuesday 'sennett', spending his time with Robert Douglas, a very good young gentleman that serves the French King and with whom this man met in the ship in France and came hither, and seeking access to the King as having matter of moment to impart to him, as he seemed to some, but to others and openly only to see the King as he pretended, on Friday morn about break of day began to rage and cry The King, the King, God keep the King, he was to see him but could not being hindered by his countrymen; and so continued raging a long time as for want of the King's sight, till Mr. Aston came to him and gave him all the comfort he could to relieve his rage, though for his pains this man calling himself now Humphry Dethick rose in his shirt and suddenly thought to have done Mr. Aston a displeasure but that wisely he prevented him … After, Christopher Hammon came to him to comfort him, who soon after grew very quiet and was brought to the King, fell down as grovelling and kissed the King's foot, who was very wary on him, and after being asked if he had got his contentment in seeking the King and kissing his hand, he said he had but he was to speak the King privately but so returned to his lodging not without that hope. Yet after he was retired some gentlemen drinking and being 'barbing' in the next room espied him laid on his bed with his rapier and dagger drawn by him, at which hearing of his former rage they began to wonder and had resolved to have stolen in upon him and taken away his weapons that he should not have in any new rage done any hurt, but that Chambers, the man he slew, dissuaded it, wishing them to let him alone with these reasons, that

he had been with the King, was well or might awake well, and that such discourtesy might offend the King and put him in new rage; persuading the quiet shutting of the door between him and them. Which was done, yet not so fast but in a small time after he rose on a sudden and suddenly broke open the door and with his rapier before they could draw any weapons struck Chambers through the body and killed him behind, hurt the barber and persevered raging and striking till he could no more, but cast away his weapons and yielded to be taken, which was a wonder they should do and not kill him. Hereon, he was presently put in the Tolbooth in irons. The King, President and Council advising what to do, resolved they could not execute him because he was mad, but that he should be removed to Edinburgh, let blood and quieted and well used to be brought to his wit if it may be and then to be further examined again to see what can be found with him. His coffers are taken and both gold and jewels found in them with letters of merchandise to and from him, all agreeing with his own declaration and confession. There was a written book of the particular handling of and speeches passed in the matter of the late Earl of Essex [Robert Devereux, 2nd Earl of Essex, executed 1601], with other books and papers of arms and genealogies, for his dealings wherein, as I hear, he said he had been a dealer in England and Paris to come to England. He has a free licence in his favour of Cardinal Cagitons [Enrico Caetani, cardinal Protector of England from 1594, died 1599], the King says, as also that he was to buy hides here. The King pities and favours him. Browne the messenger for France that is now here with these Dutchmen saw him in Paris, he says, and that he was great with the Bishop of Glasgow and her Majesty's agent there and had dealing and sent letters between Sir Thomas Shirley and his son. The King desires that he may have knowledge out of England what he is and that his brother or some friends may be advertised of this matter and he or some friends come hither to intermeddle with his money, jewels and letters and satisfy the poor widow and fatherless children of the man's. I see the King very careful to handle this matter as a thing that either Englishmen's eyes will be upon or as in some extraordinary favour and pity to the man. For this day one that had been with him yesternight came and told that he had confessed that he was to have slain the King for the good of England; and an Italian was to have met him to that effect. Whereon the King, though not believing it, yet caused him be examined by the Council, who finding no constancy but still follies in him, denying it sometimes and sometimes speaking but sparingly to it, has so showed the King who holds his determination anent him and prays that some of his friends may be sent hither as aforesaid and will proceed noway but very honourably and discreetly herein. [*In margin*: I was plain with the King and prayed him he would not spare or favour him because he was an Englishman, but try him to the uttermost and satisfy himself in any thing towards his estate or person, and in this matter of his fact also as he thought best. The Englishman does now say that he knows his fault and desires his goods may be given to the poor and party and that he may have time to repent and die.] It may therefore please your Honour cause to advertise his brother in London or his sometimes master [Richard May] in Watling Street, a woollen draper, and to direct them as shall be thought meet for the King's contentment. The rest to his first confession here enclosed.

The enclosure to the preceding letter:
Humphrey Dethick's examination at
Dunfermline, 1 May 1602:
Humphrey Dethick, Englishman, of the age of 35 years, examined, depones as follows. To wit, that he is son lawful to William Dethick, procreated betwixt him and Helen Dethick, and that he was born in Smithstoun[107] in Derbyshire and that he was first put to the school in Ashbourne in Derbyshire and removing therefrom to Cambridge, after 20 days remaining there he fell sick and was brought away. After that he passed to the sea with Captain Glegmond where they got sundry prizes of Spaniards and one of Frenchmen and brought the same to England, and that he remained with the said captain the space of six months and then he addressed himself to London and entered in service with Richard May, merchant, and remained with him five or six years. During the which space he [was?] accustomed to write Mr. Smith's preachings. Being demanded of what occupation his father was, depones that he was a gentleman and had three sons. The youngest of his sons named Edward is in London and keeps a silk shop there, and his eldest brother named William was slain at the hawking, and that his eldest brother was never married, and that his father sold his heritage to a Londoner named Storie. Being demanded how long it is since he came out of Italy, depones that in August or September last he came from Italy and that he came first to Marseilles and from that to Paris where he remained a month. Depones also that in March last he was in Paris and came therefrom

to Rouen where he stayed three weeks and then came to Dieppe where he was stayed by contrarious winds 15 days and then he embarked in James Douglas>s fern> boat and landed in Leith. Being demanded what religion he exercised when he was in Italy and France, depones that the time of his being in Italy he passed to the mass and coming to Paris to see the King he passed once to the mass there. But he ever kept his own religion in his heart. Depones that when he was in France he was minded to have passed to Turkey, but being disappointed of his ship he took purpose to come in Scotland and wrote to Sir Thomas Shirley [Chirlie] for this effect and that the cause of his here coming was to have gained his Majesty's licence to have transported some hides to Ireland and that he brought with him to Scotland in gold and rings worth 120*l.* sterling. Depones also that he has been thrice in Italy. Being demanded anent the slaughter committed by him, depones that he knows not whether the devil or he slew him. Being demanded for what cause he drew his sword and dagger and laid the same on his bed, depones that there being a number of persons in the house where he lodged and he hearing a great din among them, he drew his sword but knows not to what end he drew it. Depones also that he got the 'stomaker' which was upon his breast from the Duke of Florence's secretary named Laurenso Lucenbardis and that his acquaintance with the said secretary was by the mean of 'ane huir'.[108]

James Hudson (Scottish Resident in London)
to Sir Robert Cecil, May 1602:
The enclosed packet … is from Mr. Baptist Hicks, touching the man now in trouble in Scotland named Dethick, who was Hicks's factor in Italy, and has not yet cleared his accounts with Hicks. Dethik is a very honest man.[109]

Sir Robert Cecil to George Nicolson, 19 May 1602:
I have considered of all the particulars contained in your letter of 4 May, wherein amongst other things you have made relation of the strange proceedings of one Dethick. I will send for the friends of the party and make them see how compassionately he is dealt withal by the King. If he be distracted (and in that fury only have committed those tragical acts) his blood being saved, is a work of mercy. But when I consider by your relation, which is all I have, that he seems to confess that, he came thither with a purpose to perform an abominable act before God and man, and that an Italian should be of the complot …

Since the writing of this letter I have received answer that the brother of this Dethick will within some few days repair towards Scotland. He is the man that he writes for, and now can I call to remembrance that he was a factor to a merchant in Watling Street and resided in Florence, by which occasion he had access unto me upon a complaint from the Duke of Florence of the taking of a ship going out of Lisbon towards Leghorn, the Duke's port, of which ship and goods some of his subjects pretended to be interested, to see if he could have recovered them, but within a little while it was proved but 'coloration'. It were not amiss to remember him of this circumstance, whereby it may appear in what state his mind is.[110]

Sir Robert Cecil to George Nicolson, 8 June 1602:
Mr. Nicolson. Although I have so lately written unto you of her Majesty's care, since she was advertised of this savage part of Dethick that the bottom of his villainy might be searched, yet there is another accident of late which in her Majesty's conceit ministers great cause of suspicion. For if it be true that you advertised me in your former letter that in the 'middest' of his unquietness he gave out some speeches as though he expected some Italian to follow him, her Majesty thinks that these letters which she sends you enclosed handle some circumstance belonging to that design, for who can think that it concerns merchandise if you will observe the manner of that style. Always it suffices that when the King knows all he can best judge of all, for which respect you shall receive herewith both the originals which were directed to him. They were enclosed in a letter from an Englishman in Florence who consigned them over to one Norden here, a plain honest merchant, whom he required to send the same unto him if he could tell where he was. He writes that they are written from one of the Grand Duke's secretaries. This is as much as her Majesty knows of the matter. The rest must be beaten out by wise and curious examination …

If you look well in the letters out of Italy you shall see some mention made of one sent back from Marseilles. I think it therefore not amiss to send you these four lines which are written from one Murres to this Dethick, between whom and him though it seems there is intercourse for debits, yet because the packs of practice and treason are bound up in cases of merchandise under which words they are carried, her Majesty was pleased that the copy of that letter should likewise be sent, which may peradventure help those whom the King appoints to examine to draw forth matter from him when he sees that many letters are intercepted, wherein he may think matters are more clearly discovered than they are, although her Majesty is contented that the King be advertised of all the particulars she knows. Therefore I acquaint you that it is said in a letter from thence that the Italian letters come to Dethick from a secretary of

the Duke of Florence. Yet it may well be that he abuses his name, for it is far from her Majesty's meaning or any of her ministers' to move the King to suspect the Grand Duke who is a prince of honour and virtue and one between whom and her Majesty there is great and good correspondency.[111]

Sir John Carey to Sir Robert Cecil, from Berwick-upon-Tweed, 11 June 1602:
[extract] As for Dethicke, of whom you ar deseyerus to hear of, he is styll in the castell of Edenborowghe, sensered bey menes disposityons, good or bad: but his facte and him selfe favered bey the Kinge – for that he feyndes that in trewthe his fact proseded ether out of a drunken frensey, or out of a certayen fear of some hurt to be dun to himself: for that the compeney wiche came into his chamber wear in a consultatyon to a taken awaye his wepones from him, seinge him ley slepinge uppon his bed, and his wepones drawen bey him – for that presentley uppon ther speches he waked and lept of his bed, being as it semes ether drunk or desperatley in fear, and ded that blodey ded, wherbey maney men doe talk according to ther fanseyes. No man cane knoe the sertentey of his confession, but the Counsell that examined him: but it is unlikeley he hathe confest any harme to himself; for that the Kinge favers himself and his cause, so muche as well he cane for the clamor of his pepell whose willes and consayetes ar to them a lawe.[112]

George Nicolson to Sir Robert Cecil, from Edinburgh, 23 June 1602:
[extract] Dethick had written a petition to the King and enclosed it to my Lord Treasurer to present to you before this last distraction, which I send to you here enclosed, beseeching you to return them to me by your next. For my Lord Treasurer has sent them to me by the King's direction and when Dethick shall be well, as he is growing thereto, I would not have them out of place.[113]

Copy of Humphrey Dethick's petition to King James VI of Scotland, May or June 1602:
[extract] Declares his innocency of Popery and 'athiesme'. He came hither because, while abroad, others have deprived him of his inheritance and of the name of his house, which has continued since 200 years before the Conquest. Speaks of an enterprise which he undertook, with a nobleman of England, to surprise a place of the enemy's where were great riches: but the design was overthrown for this year. He came to Scotland intending either a renewal of that attempt, or else to undertake a

merchant's voyage. Since his arrival he has fallen into this misfortune, whereby he has wrecked his life. Prays the King to remember his present misery, either relieving him by free grace, or remitting him to a final trial. If the King wills that he dies in these irons, he will patiently endure it.[114]

George Nicolson to Sir Robert Cecil, from Edinburgh, 20 June 1602:

On the 11 hereof I received your Honour's letter of the 3 directing me to show the King in her Majesty's name … and also her great contentment for his escape from the peril of Dethick; as likewise of the dislike of Henry Lee and his secret and suspicious creepings to Loudon. All which I did at good length deliver unto the King from her Majesty according to the exceeding well written directions set down to me in your said letter and found the King so glad to understand her Majesty's good liking of his course anent the pledges and her great care for his preservation … And for her Majesty's care of him anent the matter of Dethick he protested he took it as a sure token of her true care and love for him and would requite it to the utmost of his power in revealing to her whatsoever he should hear of King or subject that might import her or her estate and swore it with better words than I can write and wherein he has written with his own hands to her Majesty …

And receiving at Falkland on the 15 hereof your Honour's of the 8 with the Italian letters written to Dethick, etc., by which you likewise signify unto me that it is her Majesty's pleasure I should from her show the King both her still care to discover the bottom of Dethick's villainy and her interception and sending to him of Italian letters, etc. 'mistically', written to Dethick that he might try him the better by them, which I did according to the good directions in your letter to the King from her Majesty, and in her name, both show and deliver unto him with still notice to him as you have directed me that her Majesty would not have him spare Dethick because he is an Englishman and her subject, but to try him the more severely, adding that I was sure she would not spare her greatest subject if she knew him guilty of any evil thought to his Majesty but punish him herself, which he said he believed. I then said to him that he might now see by these her Majesty's cares of him that now when he was in these good courses her Majesty heaped her love(?) daily upon him more and more both in her goodness to him and plainness with him in showing him all that she knows; that it is said in a letter that the Italian letters come from a secretary to the Duke of Florence in which it is far from her Majesty to have that noble Duke, her worthy friend, any way suspected

by him, I said. For she conceives this secretary's name may be abused, and yet in love to the King and trust that he would 'respectively' use her therein had not stuck for his better trial of the truth to assure him all she knew … This much for these. Now for Dethick. He is grown mad again worse than ever, having 'riven' his clothes from his back and not spared to hare himself desperately and unmannerly, as no examination can he yet made for him till he be well again, which he is now beginning to be. The King had given order for examining him and to this end bade me give the Italian letters to he englished to Mr. David Foulis, which I did. If my Lord Treasurer and the Council can draw nothing from Dethick, he will examine him himself and try what he can of him either anent his own life, which I still see he distrusts him not for [or] on her Majesty's state, and will faithfully advertise her Majesty what he finds …

Thus I give your Honour but trouble to read these reports, the truths or untruths whereof you. I hope, know. Always they be the matters here in most marvel. If Dethick had taken this new distraction upon the news, as I told and prayed my Lord Treasurer to try certainly, it had been an argument very suspicious against him but my Lord sent me word he took it on Sunday before (this day 'sennet') which cleared my then doubts of it.[115]

Thomas Wilson from Venice to Sir Robert Cecil, 27 August/6 September 1602:[116]

Mr. Browne is the reporter to me from the mouth of Sir James Linsey … That there were 2,000 English gentlemen vowed to stand for King of Scots, though there were many that they knew did nothing but plot and work against him; whereof he said, of any that lives abroad, he knew me to be one of the chiefest and dangerousest: nay, more than that, that I was one of the chiefest plotters of the death of King of Scots in the last matter of Dethick! A heinous accusation, and I know Sherley is the author hereof, for he hath a mint for such inventions. Haply, he hath devised it upon this presumption, because Dethick and I were lodged both in a house at Pisa when he parted thence for England; and this matter they all conclude was wrought by England against King of Scots – matters too intolerable to be put up with silence.[117]

John Lingard in his *History of England* gives a variant account of the events:

It appears from letters in my possession that Dethick had been employed by Cecil as a spy in Florence, where James had much dealing with the grand duke, that he returned to London, and went thence to Edinburgh where he had an audience of the king but was afterwards refused access to the court. One morning, coming down from his chamber into the shop of the house in which he lodged, he drew his sword and killed one Jeamie and, on examination, answered that he had made a mistake and killed the wrong Jeamie. Cecil knew what suspicions this might arouse in the mind of James. He sent for the former host of Dethick from Florence, and induced the queen to require that the murderer should be hanged in Scotland, or put into her hands. But James saved the man's life under the conviction that he was insane, and confined him within the castle of Edinburgh.[118]

106 *Calendar of the Manuscripts of the Most Hon. The Marquis of Salisbury [Hatfield House]* (London, 1915), XIII, p.555.

107 Despite kind assistance on this and related matters from Benjamin Longden of the Derbyshire Record Office, no place of this name in Derbyshire has been found; Dethick 2008, p.24, suggests the Scottish court clerk might have mis-heard 'Snitterton', a hamlet in Derbyshire.

108 J. D. Mackie, *Calendar of the State Papers relating to Scotland and Mary, Queen of Scots* (Edinburgh, 1969), II, pp.978–81.

109 *Calendar of the Manuscripts of the Most Hon. The Marquis of Salisbury [Hatfield House]*, part XII (London, 1910) p.176.

110 Mackie, *Calendar of the State Papers relating to Scotland and Mary, Queen of Scots*, XIII, (1969), part 2, pp. 984–6.

111 Ibid., pp.1000–1.

112 Joseph Bain, *The Border Papers: Calendar of Letters and Papers relating to the Affairs of the Borders of England and Scotland* (Edinburgh, 1894–6), II, pp.788–9.

113 Mackie, *Calendar of the State Papers relating to Scotland and Mary, Queen of Scots*, XIII, (1969), part 2, p. 1009.

114 *Calendar of the Manuscripts of the Most Hon. The Marquis of Salisbury [Hatfield House]*, part XII (1910), p. 180.

115 J.D. Mackie, *Calendar of the State Papers relating to Scotland and Mary, Queen of Scots*, XIII, (1969), part 2, pp. 1004–7.

116 Thomas Wilson, *c.*1565–1629, correspondent of and secretary to Sir Robert Cecil.

117 *Calendar of the Manuscripts of the Most Hon. The Marquis of Salisbury [Hatfield House]*, part XII (1910), p. 324.

118 Lingard 1837–9, VIII, p.387, cited by Dethick 2008, p.25.

13

Plate on high foot

Probably Duchy of Urbino, *c.*1620–80
Bequeathed by Sidney R. Knafel, received 2023, WA2023.154

Flat plate with a raised ridge at the edge; set on a high, hollow, spreading foot; tin-glazed overall.

Diameter: 29.6 cm; height: 6.8 cm

CONDITION: repairs at 2 and 4 o'clock; overall wear and scuffing.

PROVENANCE: unrecorded

The plate is painted in the centre, with buildings surrounding a domed church. Around this is a band of rudimentary fictive gadroons between bands of rope pattern. The grotesques on the border include fantastic birds and winged figures. The underside is undecorated.

This is a late example of the tradition of white-ground grotesque decoration initiated in the Fontana family workshops in Urbino about 1570. It was probably made in the Duchy of Urbino, perhaps at Pesaro or Urbania, in the mid- to late seventeenth century.[119] It usefully extends the Ashmolean's representation of the variants of grotesque painting on maiolica.

119 For grotesques comparable in type and coarseness, compare a bowl and a jug in the Museo del Vino, Torgiano, which Fiocco and Gherardi judge may be as late as the eighteenth century: Fiocco and Gherardi 1991, nos 169, 173; also the pieces cited by Poole 1995, under no. 361; which Poole also judges to be eighteenth-century.

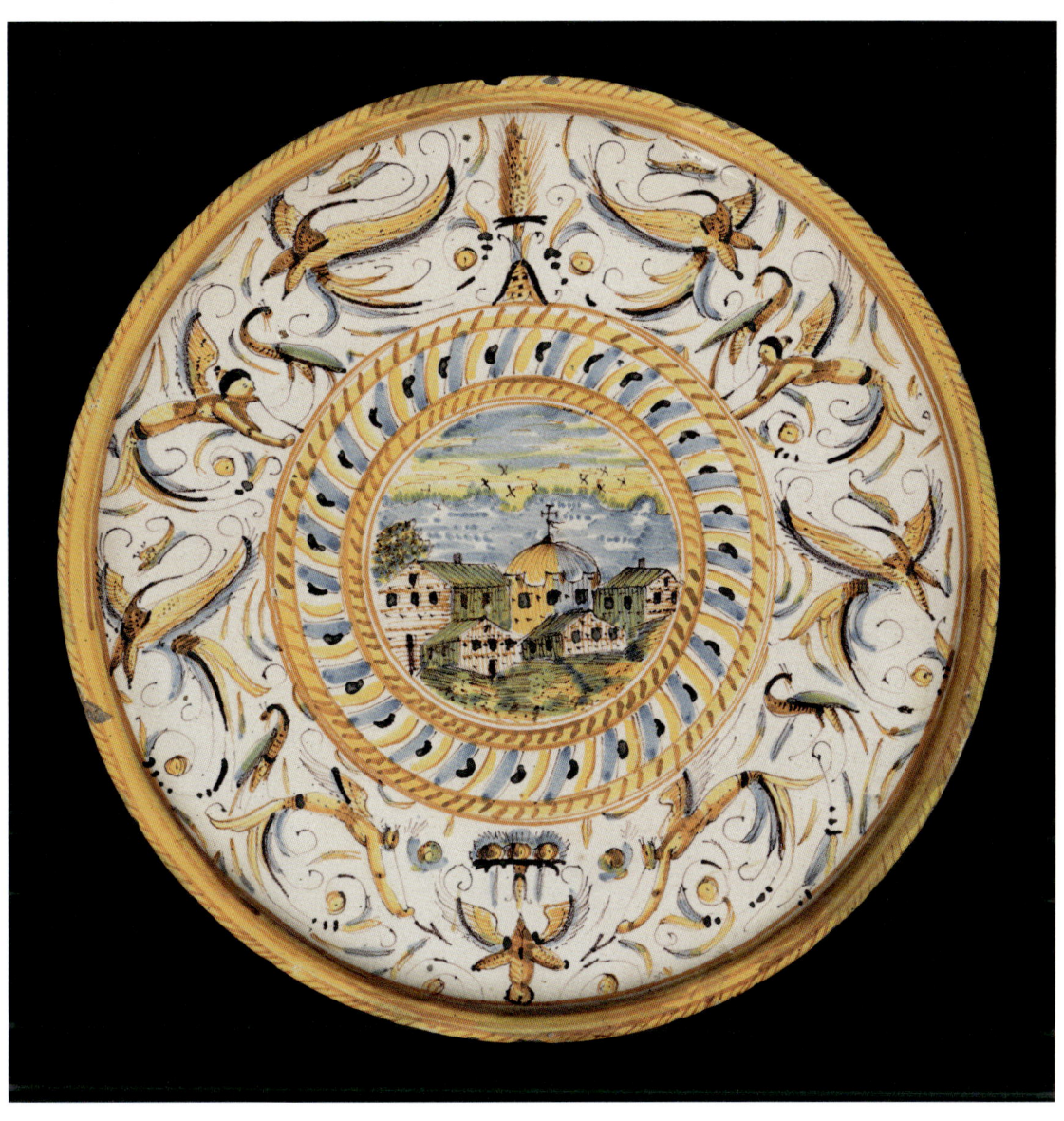

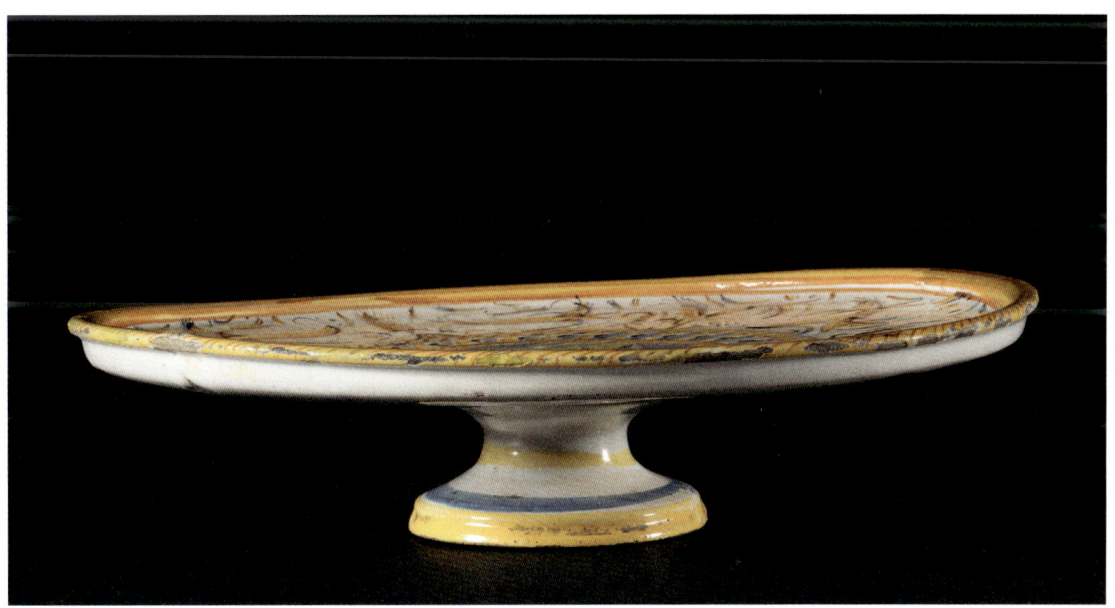

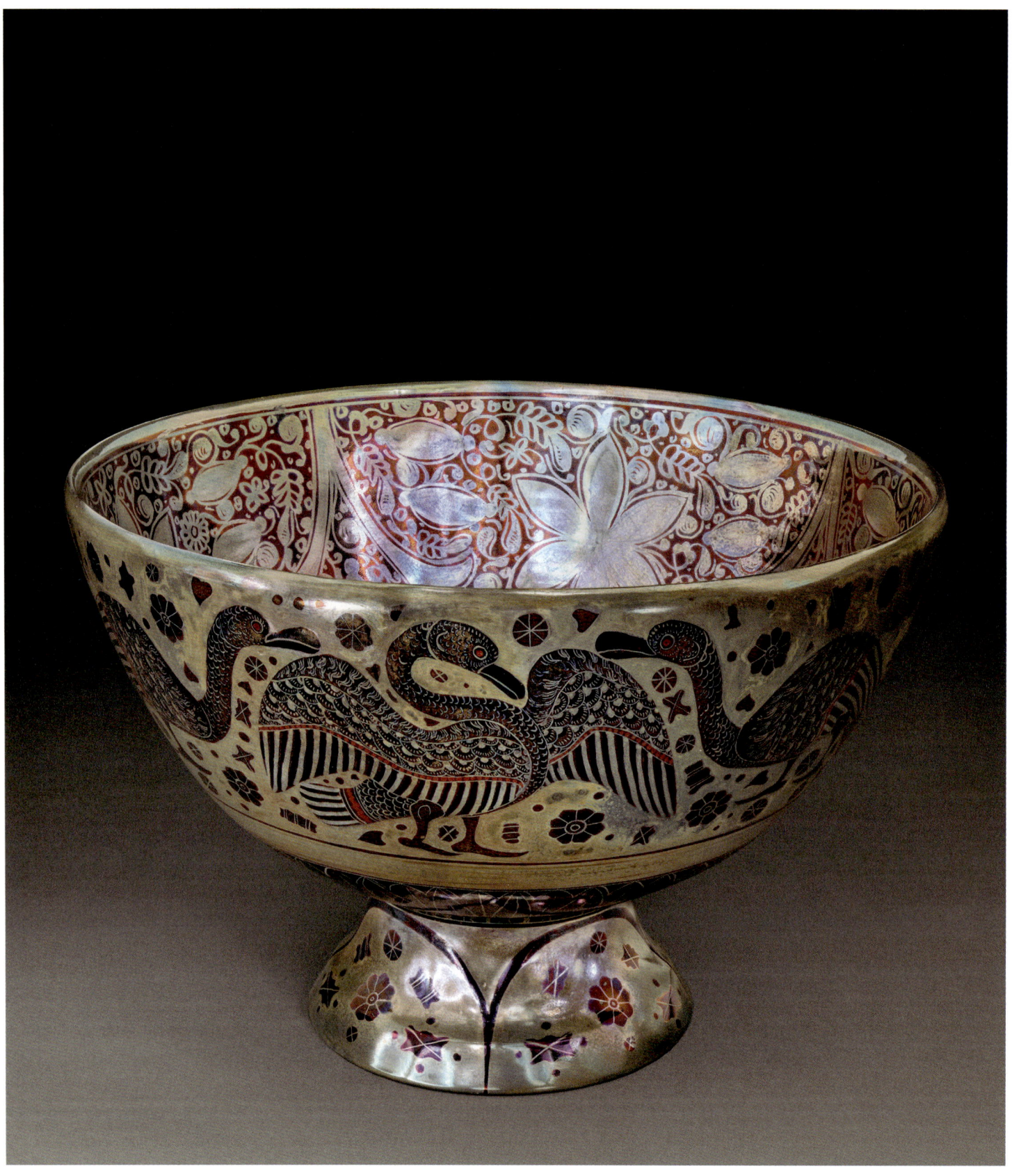

14

Large footed bowl

Florence, Manifattura di Maioliche Artistiche, Figli di Giuseppe Cantagalli, *c*.1901–10
Purchased 2019 from Justin Raccanello (Bazaart), with the aid of the late Martin Foley, WA2019.18.

Tin-glazed and painted with iridescent lustre and red lustre highlights. Marked with the cockerel mark of Cantagalli and the painter's mark *10*.

Depth: 28.3 cm; diameter: 41 cm

CONDITION: some wear to lustre.

PROVENANCE: bought by Justin Raccanello at a sale at Gorringe's, Lewes, 21 March 2017, lot 151.

BIBLIOGRAPHY: Raccanello 2018, no.16; Winterbottom 2019.

Made by the celebrated Florentine Manifattura di Maioliche Artistiche, Figli di Giuseppe Cantagalli, this bowl is decorated with geese or swans that are derived from an ancient skyphos-shaped vase in the Museo Archeologico Regionale di Syracuse.[120] However, it is the beautiful *lustri iridescenti*, the iridescent lustre that shines with metallic rainbow hues when the bowl's surface plays against the light that makes this bowl so exceptional. Cantagalli led the Italian revival of lustred pottery in the late nineteenth century and made many pieces with the more usual golden and red lustres. Only a handful of *lustri iridescenti* pieces are known to survive due to the major technical difficulties in achieving this beautiful, experimental effect. The technique of true lustre was introduced into thirteenth-century Spain by the Moors and subsequently into Italy by the early sixteenth century. Lustreware of high artistic quality ceased to be produced in Italy after the middle of the sixteenth century, and by the nineteenth century the technique had been completely forgotten. In Britain, William De Morgan (1839–1917) rediscovered the technique after extensive experimentation in the

1870s and 1880s. Many of his beautifully lustred ceramics can now be seen in the Ashmolean. Six are described below, nos **47–52**.

De Morgan spent his winters in Florence and was a friend and advisor to Ulisse Cantagalli (1839–1901). It is thought the two men collaborated in perfecting their lustre techniques. Cantagalli had transformed his family pottery after taking over in 1878. He specialised in making high-quality imitations of Italian maiolica, Hispano-Moresque, and Iznik wares. De Morgan described Cantagalli's gold and ruby lustres as 'the best I have seen'.[121] Before his death in 1901, Ulisse had been experimenting to create a new iridescent lustre to decorate ceramics in contemporary Art Nouveau taste. Production continued after his death,

led by his widow Margaret and daughter Flavia, but only a handful of pieces are known, including this bowl. It is probably the same bowl that appears in a photograph of the Cantagalli display at the 1911 Esposizione di Torino, when the factory won the Gran Premio. The firing is almost perfect and the play of light across the bowl's surface shows the complete colour spectrum, displaying the full iridescent effect that the decorator was striving for.

120 On Cantagalli in general and in the Ashmolean in particular, see Frescobaldi Malenchini and Rucellai 2011; Wilson 2017, pp.346–53 and literature there cited. A drawing of the vase with details of the bird decoration survives in the Fondo Cantagalli, MIC, Faenza, I.4274.

121 Hamilton 1997, p.201.

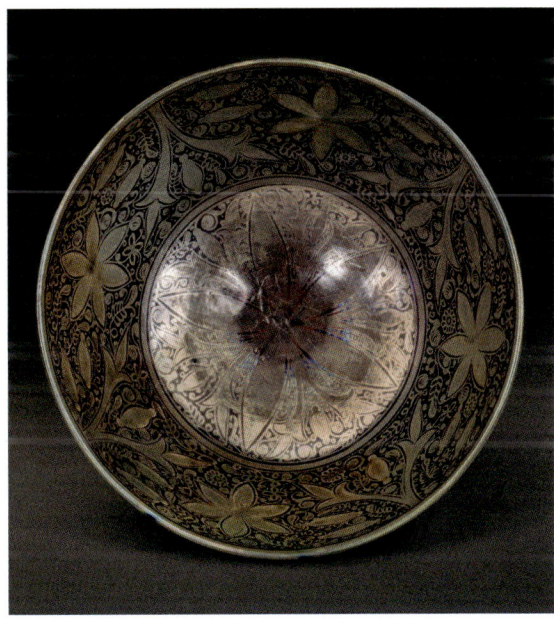

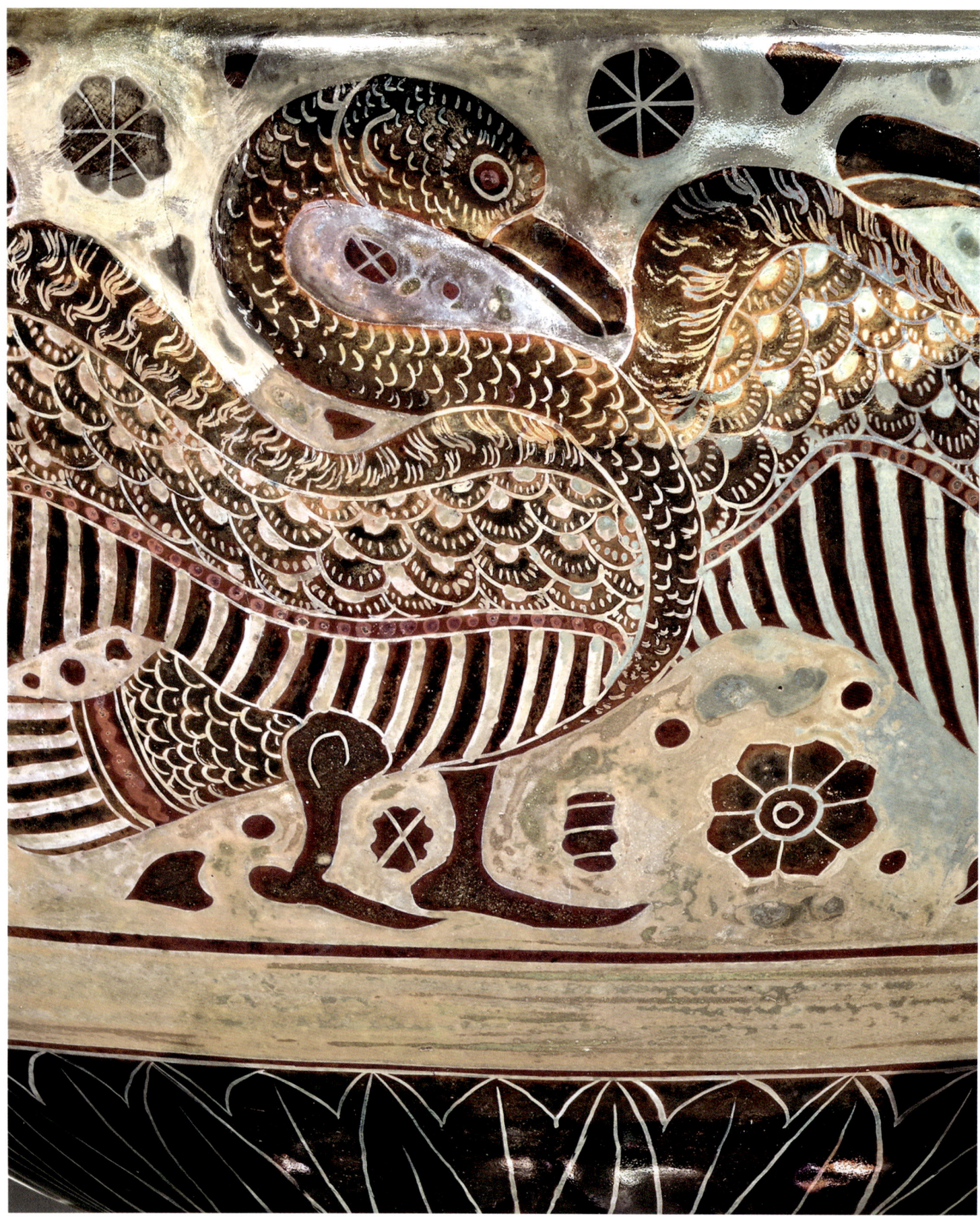

No.**14** (detail)

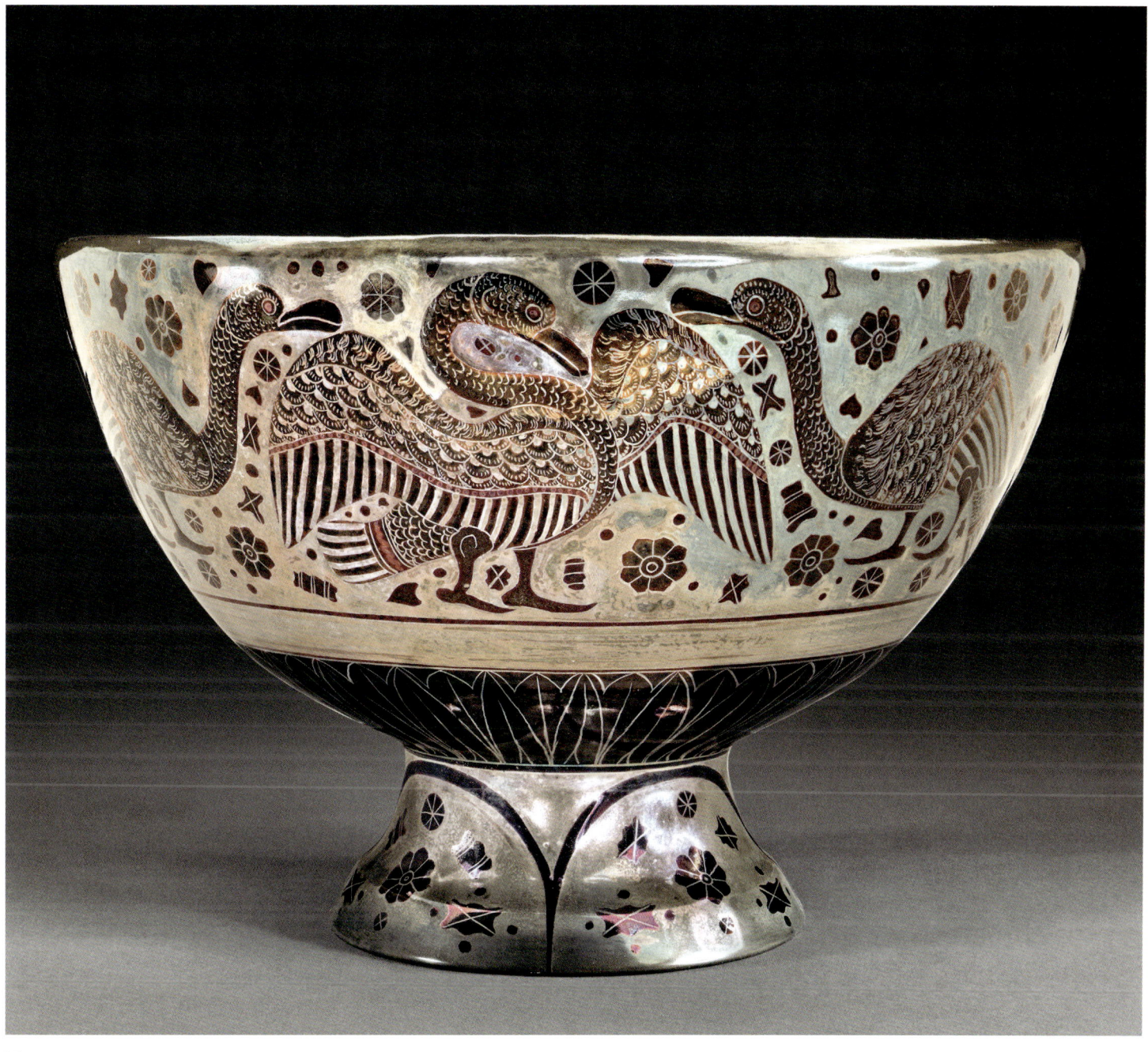

No.**14**

15

Cup and saucer, Attilio

Gualdo Tadino, Rubboli workshop, under the management of Daria Rubboli, *c.*1905
Presented by Timothy Wilson, 2023, WA2024.7.

The cup and saucer are painted on a white tin-glaze in blue and green, with red and golden-brown lustre. Unmarked.

Saucer: diameter: 14 cm

Cup: diameter: 10.6 cm; depth: 5.2 cm

CONDITION: minor wear

PROVENANCE: Given to Timothy Wilson, *c.*2010, by Maurizio Tittarelli Rubboli, together with a companion cup and saucer, *ELVIRA* (subsequently given to Elisa Paola Sani).

In the interior of the cup is a profile of *ATTILIO* in *all'antica* armour and a crested helmet. The exterior of the cup and the outer part of the saucer are painted with plant scrolls with flowers, winged masks, and bird or griffin heads.

The painting is in the manner of maiolica made in the workshop of Maestro Giorgio Andreoli (*c.*1470–1555) in Gubbio, in about 1515–30. The red and gold lustre have come out well.

One of the towns in Italy that, after the mid-nineteenth century, achieved the red and golden lustre for which the workshop of Maestro Giorgio had become famous in the Renaissance was Gualdo Tadino, in Umbria south-east of Gubbio. The industry in Gualdo Tadino was largely created by Paolo Rubboli (1838–1890), whose workshop was carried on after his death by his dynamic widow Daria (1852–1929). A service of cups and saucers in the Rubboli family collection at Gualdo Tadino, which looks identical in style, has been attributed to the painter Umberto Marinari and he may well have been the painter of the present cup and saucer.[122]

122 Caputo 2012, pl.LII and p.100. The Rubboli Collection set contains an *ELVIRA* very like the one that previously accompanied the present *ATTILIO*.

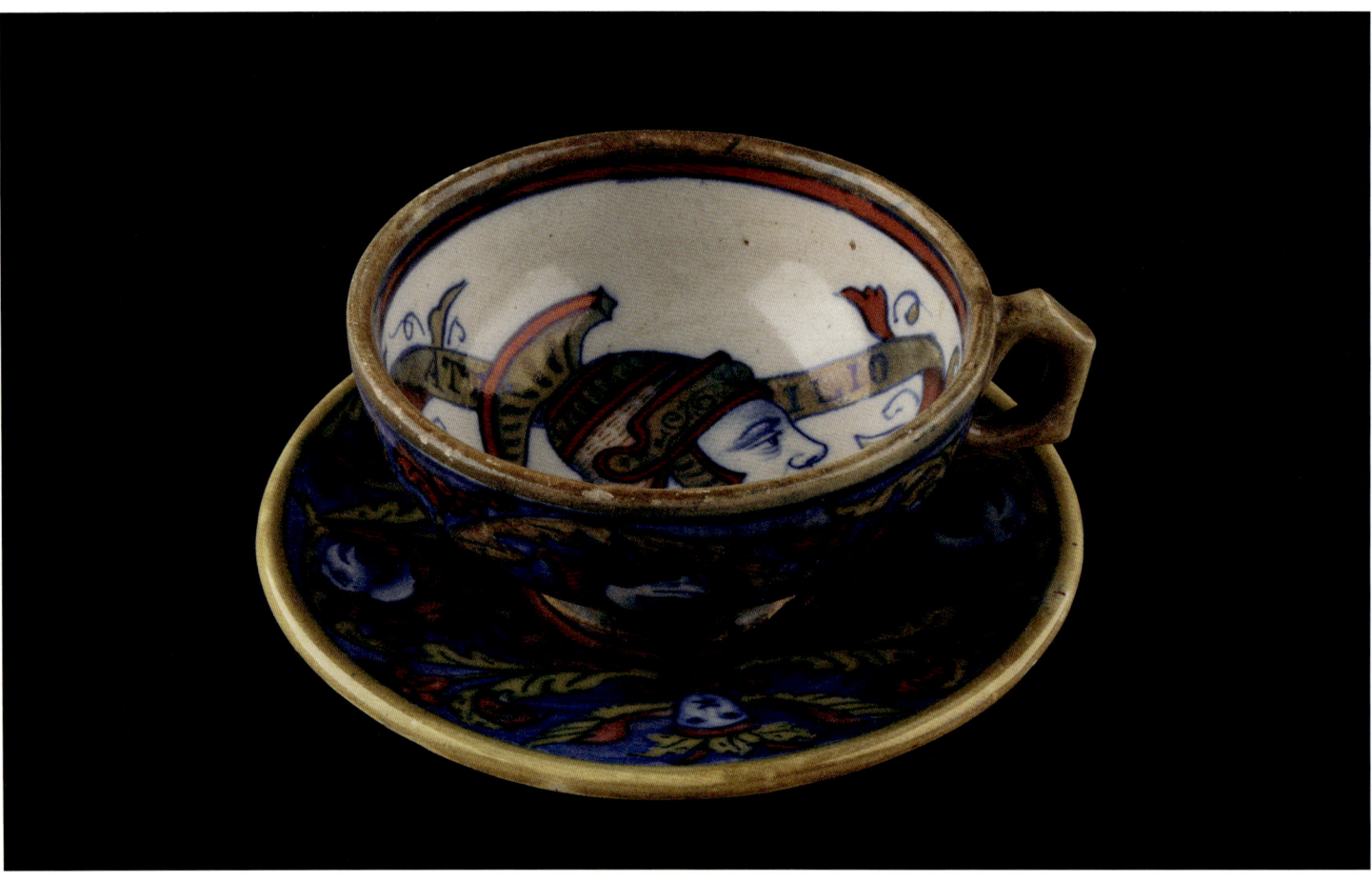

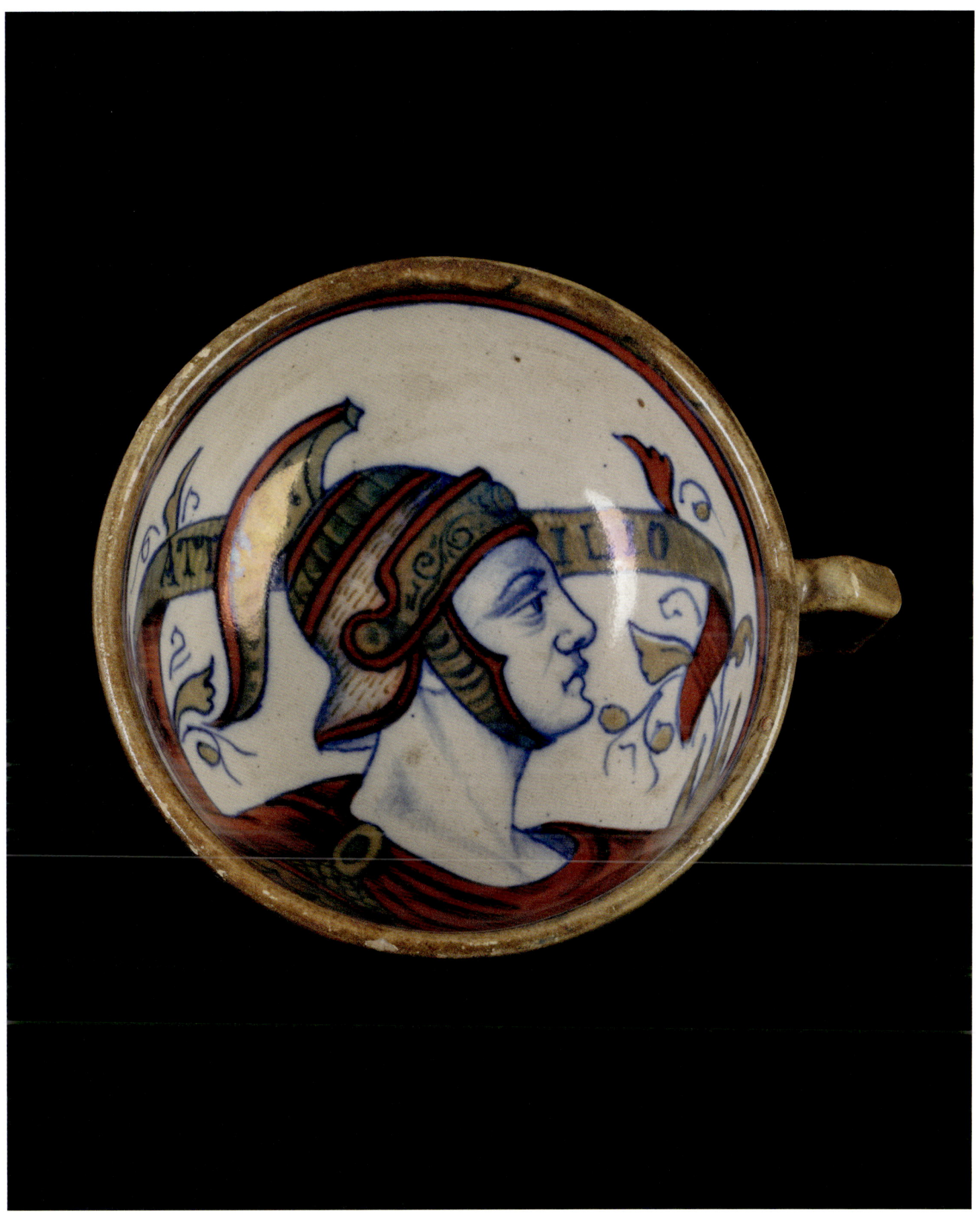

16

Roundel with an angel

Deruta, Patrizio Chiucchiù, 2006
Presented by Timothy Wilson in honour of Dinah Reynolds, 2023, WA2024.8.

Tin-glazed overall. The roundel has a small foot-ring but the upper surface is flat.

Diameter: 21.1 cm

CONDITION: good.

PROVENANCE: given by the artist to Timothy Wilson, 2006.

BIBLIOGRAPHY: *Oxford Ceramics Group Newsletter* 60 (October 2024), p.23, fig.2.

The painting is in blue with brilliant red and gold lustre, representing a half-length angel in an attitude of prayer before an open book, all set on a chequered tile floor. On the back are scale patterns and dots in red and gold lustre. Within the foot-ring, in blue, is written: *Chiucchiù Patrizio Deruta Es. unico 28 Sett. 2006*, and, in lustre, *Chiucchiù Patrizio* along with five stars. *Es. unico* indicates the piece is a unique example, not part of a series or edition.

The angel is of a type frequently painted on Deruta dishes of the first half of the sixteenth century, with the inclusion here of a book suggestive of the Virgin Annunciate.[123] The model is based on a type of angel recurrent in the work both of Perugino and of Pintoricchio.[124]

Patrizio Chiucchiù, born in Deruta in 1957, opened his own workshop in Deruta in 1978; he is a supreme virtuoso master of the traditional lustre technique.[125] The glaze is of a traditional tin-lead type, and the lustre firing was done in a wood-fired reduction kiln.

123 For examples see Thornton and Wilson 2009, no.280.
124 For example, in the Collegio del Cambio, Perugia and in the church of Sant'Andrea, Spello.
125 Sannipoli 2008, pp.35, 70–71.

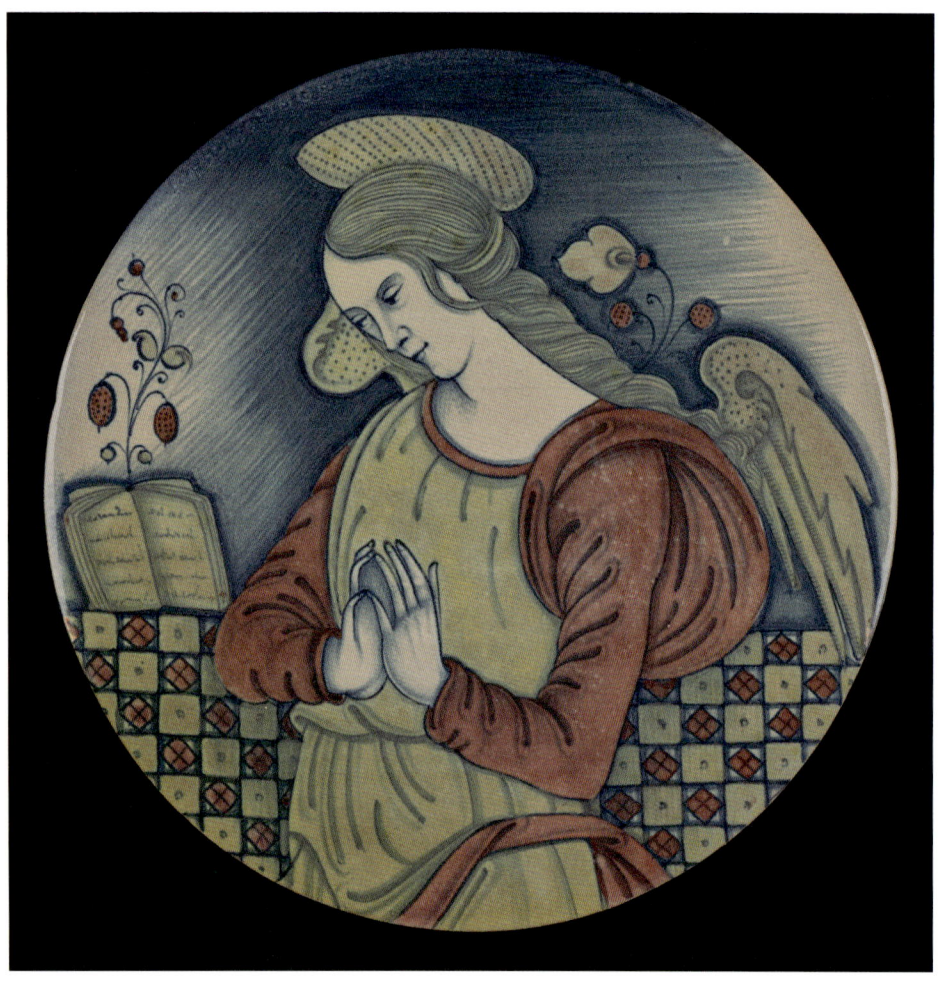

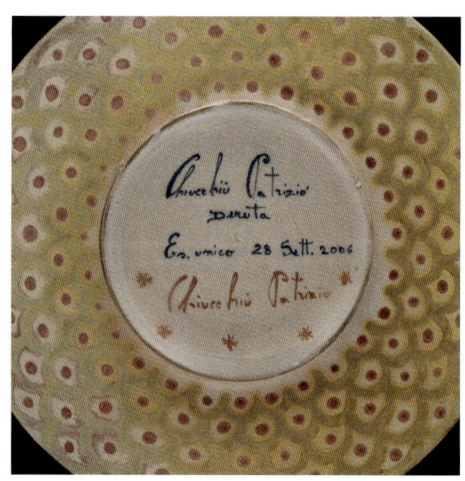

17

Lustred jug

Deruta, Giulio Busti, 2000
Presented by Timothy Wilson, 2024, WA2025.28.

Jug with sharply pinched lip, curling handle, splayed pedestal foot. Tin-glazed outside and in and beneath the foot. Painted in black, blue, green, and yellow, with red and golden lustre. Signed beneath the foot *BUSTI 2000*.

Height: 17 cm

CONDITION: good.

PROVENANCE: given by the artist to Timothy Wilson in the early 2000s.

BIBLIOGRAPHY: none.

Giulio Busti, born in Deruta in 1945, has contributed more to the revival and appreciation of the great sixteenth-century lustre tradition of the town than anyone else. He was trained as a potter and sculptor at the Istituto Statale per la Ceramica, Deruta, and the sculpture school of the Accademia di Belle Arti, Perugia, also serving an apprenticeship with the Perugia ceramic artist Edgardo Abbozzo (1937–2004). Around 1970, he set about renewing the technique of lustred maiolica in Deruta, which had been the glory of the town's potteries in the Renaissance, but had been virtually abandoned in the 1950s. He taught ceramics for many years at the Istituto Statale in Deruta and the Accademia 'Pietro Vannucci' in Perugia. He has also served a long and successful term as curator of the Museo Regionale della Ceramica in Deruta. As a ceramic historian, he, together with co-writer Franco Cocchi, has written a series of fundamental works on Deruta ceramics.

He states that 'from an artistic point of view, the jug and similar works I have exhibited are intended to be a model of combining tradition and innovation in a way that could be useful also to practising potters'.[126]

The lustre-firing of this jug was done in an electric kiln, using broom, the traditional material for lustre firings, to generate smoke.

126 Email to T. Wilson, 7 November 2024. On Busti's work, see the monographic exhibition catalogue, Bojani 1991, and the examples of contemporary Umbrian lustre pottery in Sannipoli 2008.

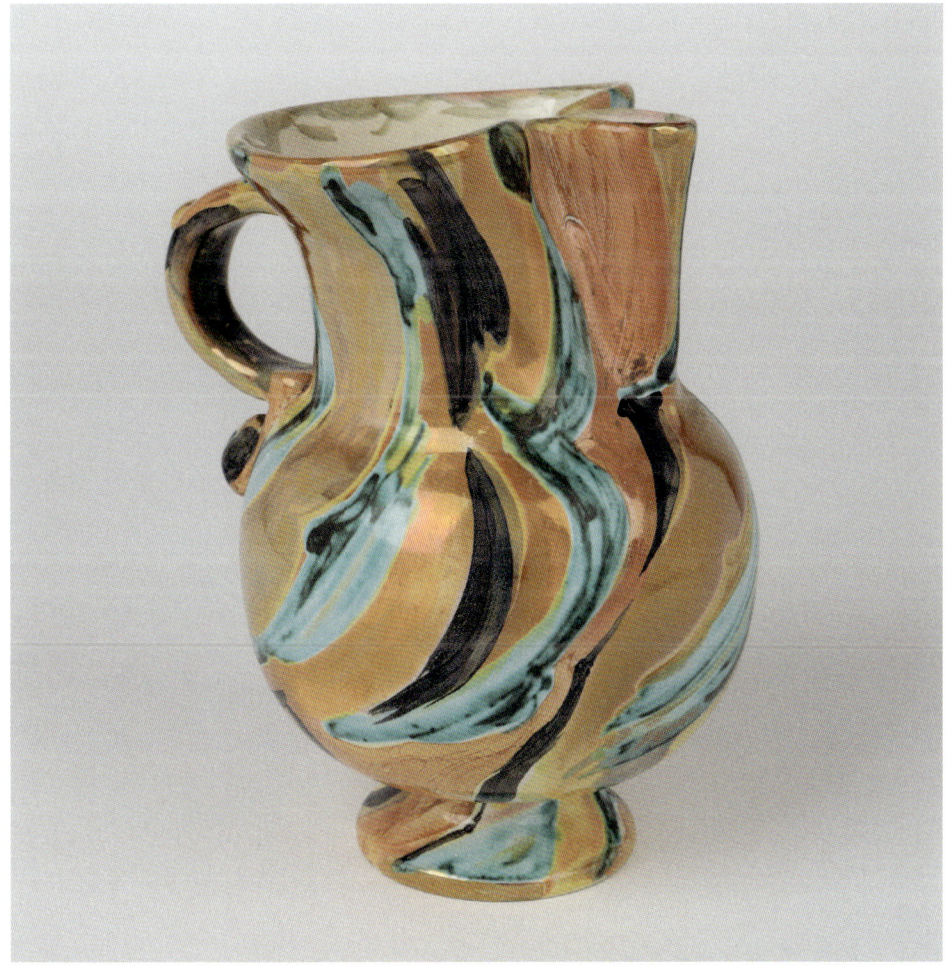

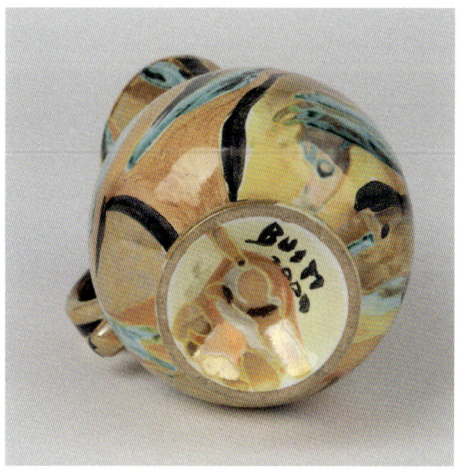

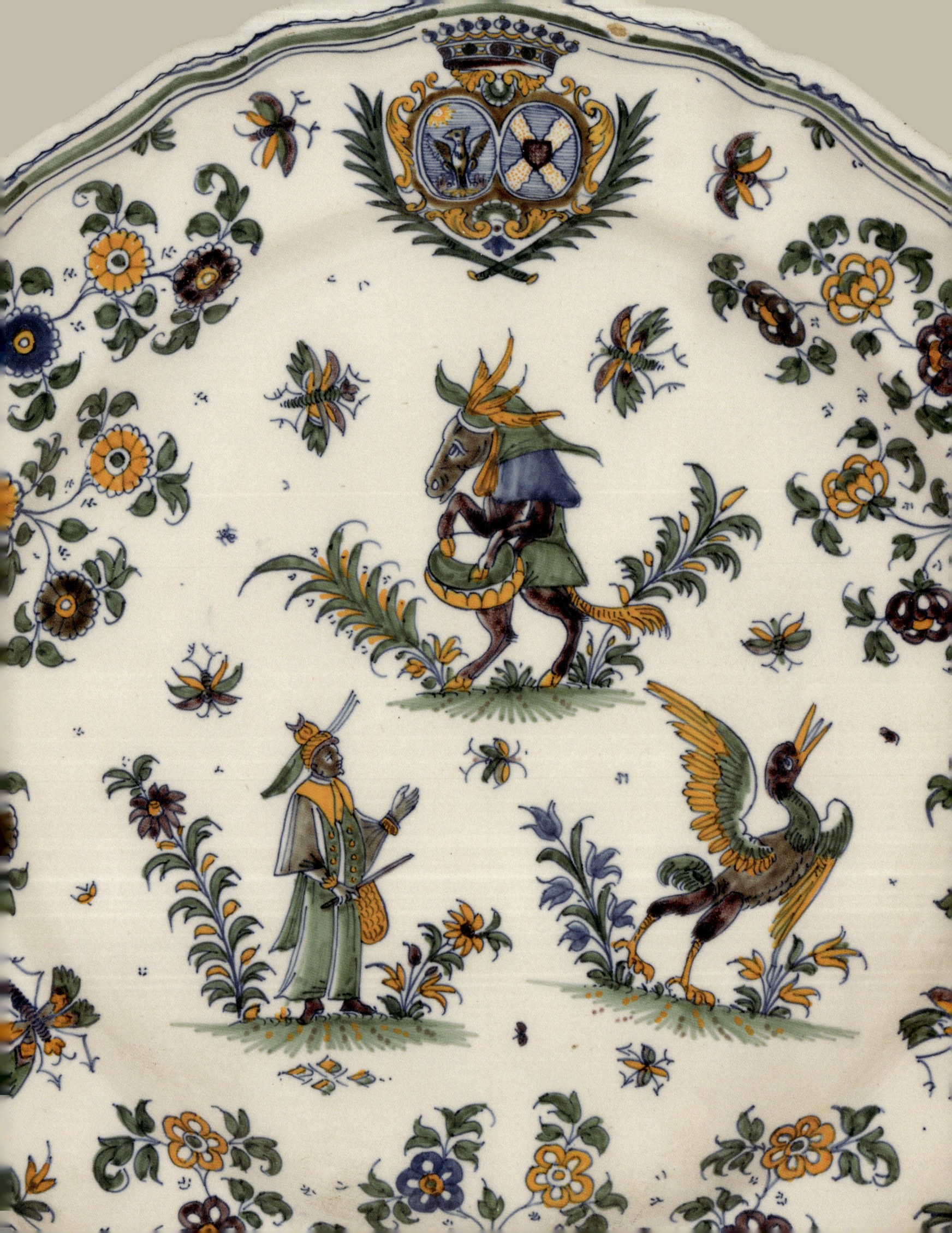

FRANCE

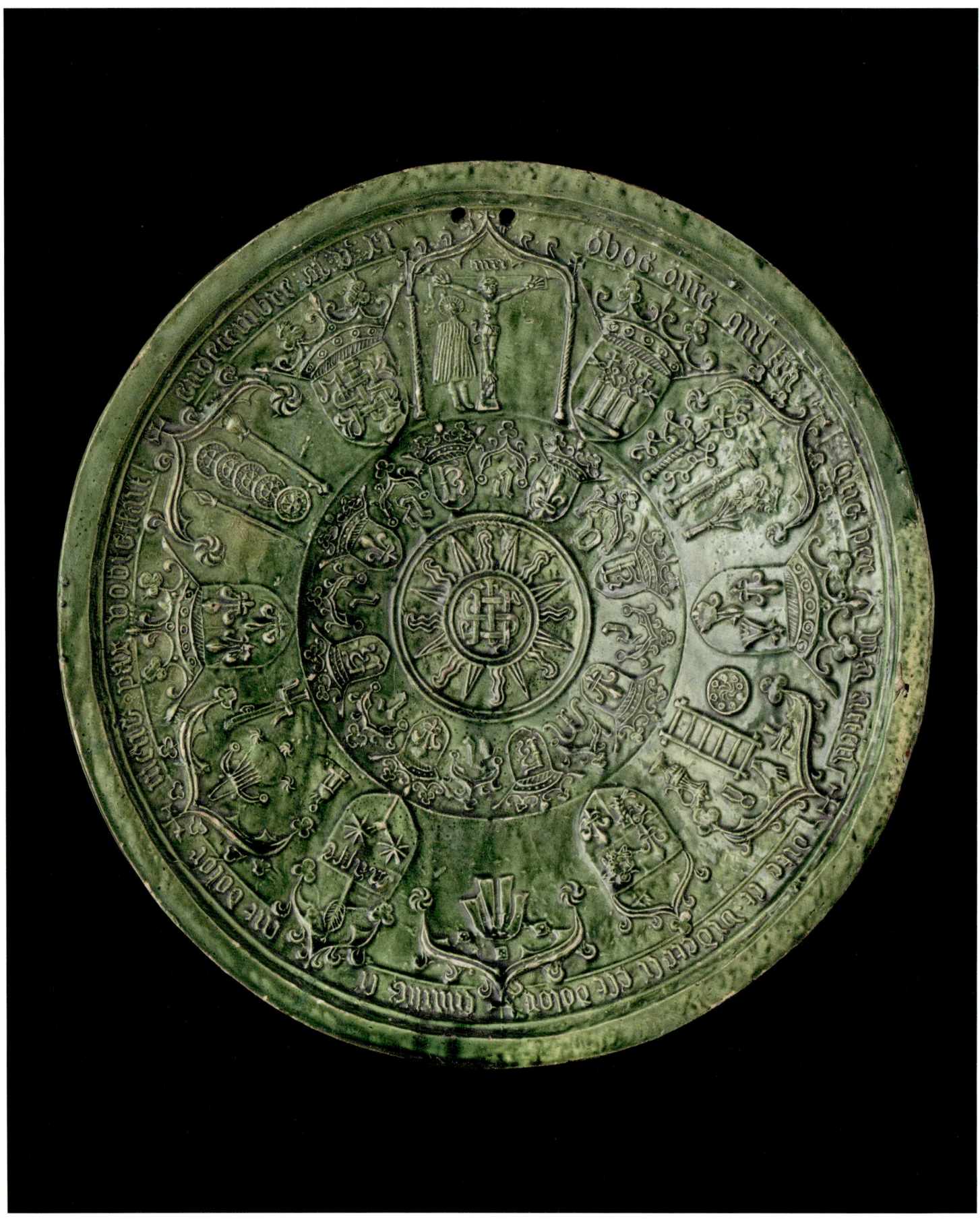

18

'Plat de la passion'

Beauvais or district, early sixteenth century
Purchased in honour of Timothy Wilson from E. & H. Manners Ceramics and Works of Art (Madan Bequest Fund) with the aid of the ACE/V&A Purchase Grant Fund, the late Brian Wilson, and the late Martin Foley, WA2017.1.

Green lead-glazed and moulded earthenware; reverse unglazed, with nineteenth-century paper label fragment. Beneath the base, apparently made in the wet clay, are scratched marks; the significance of these, if any, is uncertain.

Diameter: 37 cm

CONDITION: broken into five large sections that have been rebonded and the breaks overpainted.

PROVENANCE: Emile Chami (1910–1992); sold Paris (Beaussant Lefevre, Drouot-Richelieu), 9 December 2015, lot 108; purchased by E. & H. Manners Ceramics and Works of Art.

BIBLIOGRAPHY: Vergnet-Ruiz 1956; Chami 1963; Vergnet-Ruiz 1964; another similar dish (with figure on the right of Christ on the cross) illustrated in Chami 1973, p.28; Vasseur 1995; Cartier 2001, p.130, nos 419–21; Giguet 2002–3; Lefevre 2004, pp.26–9; Winterbottom 2018, pp.27–8.

This imposing plate is one of a small group of 'plats de la passion' that were made in or near Beauvais in the early sixteenth century. Six other authentic examples are known, all in French museum collections, and all bearing the same dated inscription.[127] Fragments of dishes from the same moulds were excavated in Beauvais during the 1840s, and again during post-war reconstruction. Until the acquisition of this example, there was nothing comparable in any UK public collection. These plates have been the subject of much fierce debate regarding their authenticity and enigmatic iconography.

Until sherds from the same moulds were excavated from sixteenth-century sites, some scholars had believed the plates to be nineteenth-century forgeries. Emile Chami, to whom no.**18** had previously belonged, used archival research and archaeological excavations to prove beyond doubt the authenticity of these plates and to reclaim Beauvais' importance as a centre of ceramic production in the sixteenth century.

The dish is crisply moulded around the rim with the stages of the Passion. Moving clockwise from the actual crucifixion, interspersed by crowned shields bearing the arms of France, the dauphin, Anne de Bretagne (1477–1514), and others, are the following: the pillar at which Christ was scourged, with a cat-o-nine-tails type whip, a birch-type bundle of twigs, and the cock that crowed when Peter denied Christ thrice; the ladder used for the deposition of Christ's body together with a hammer, a pair of pliers, a roll of linen used as his shroud, and a flask for the myrrh used to anoint his body; Christ's seamless garment for which the soldiers diced; the armed troop that captured Christ in the Garden of Gethsemane, together with a lantern and the ear of Malchus, the High Priest's servant, attached to the sword with which Peter cut it off; Judas's 30 pieces of silver, with the lance that pierced Christ's side, and the sponge on a hyssop stick, used to moisten the lips of Christ with vinegar.

The central boss has the *IHS* monogram encircled by tongues of flame. Around this are smaller shields with the monogram of Charles (*Karolus*) VIII (1470–1498) and fleurs-de-lys divided by the letters *AVE MARIA*. The outer rim bears an inscription in Latin and French adapted from Lamentations 1, verse 12:

> *O vos omnes qui transitis per viam attendite et videte si est dolor similis sicut dolor meus pax vobis. Fait en décembre MVCXI*

> (O all you who pass by the way, attend and see if there is any sorrow like my sorrow. Peace unto you. Made in December 1511)

Suspension holes in the back of the dish indicate that it was made to be hung on a wall as an object of veneration. The arms of Anne de Bretagne and the

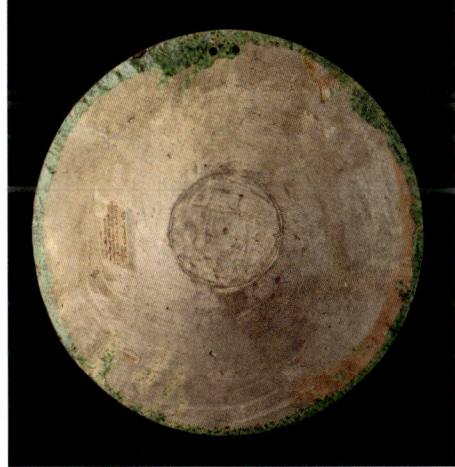
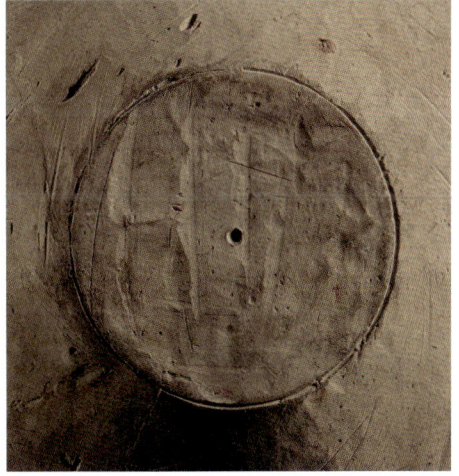

Underside of base photographed in raking light

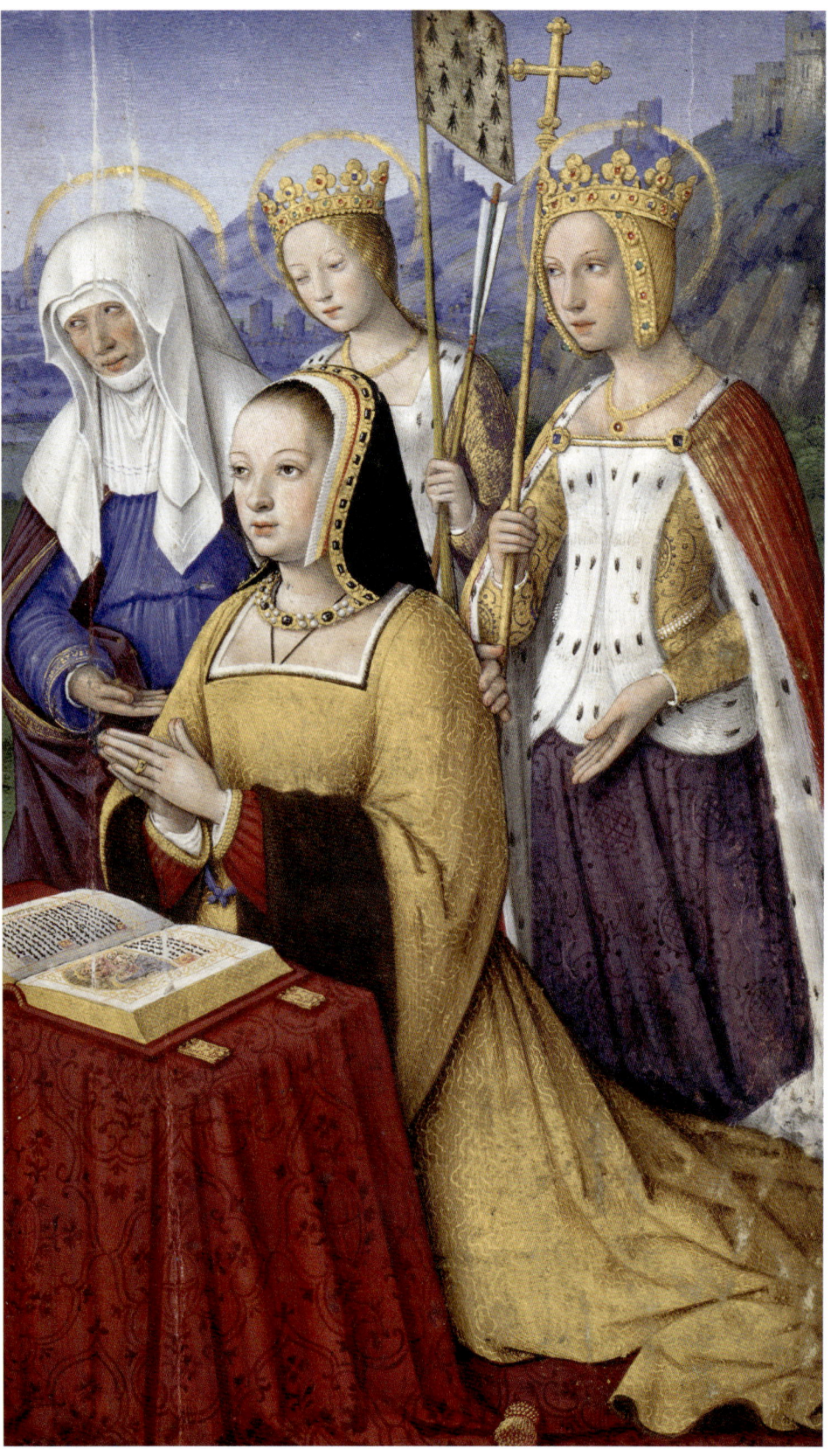

cipher of Charles VIII (King of France from 1483), together with the dated inscription, suggest that the dish may have been commissioned to commemorate what would have been the royal couple's twentieth wedding anniversary. Anne was pregnant in December 1511, and the inclusion of the arms of the Dauphin, who did not exist in 1511, may been a reference to a hoped-for son and heir. The arms may also be a reference to Anne's son, the Dauphin Charles-Orland, who died young on 6 December 1495. Anne and Charles had married in December 1491, initially to Anne's great reluctance. The marriage contract specified that the spouse who outlived the other would retain possession of Brittany. However, it also stipulated that if Charles VIII died without male heirs, Anne would marry his successor in order to secure Brittany for the French crown. Following Charles's death in 1498, Anne therefore married Louis XII after his marriage to Joan, sister of Charles VIII, had been annulled. An important patron of the arts, Anne was admired for her intelligence and shrewdness. She died aged 36, worn out by 14 pregnancies, from which only two children survived.

The dish represents the highest level of Beauvais pottery production in the sixteenth century. The quality of clay from the Pays de Bray and the wide range of objects produced from it made the Beauvais area one of the greatest ceramics centres in France.[128]

127 Two in the Musée National de Céramique, Sèvres 4578 and 4156; Musée départemental de l'Oise, Beauvais, 843.314; Bibliothèque Nationale de France, Paris, 55.445, which was confiscated during the French Revolution on 27 February 1797 from the Cabinet de l'Abbaye de Sainte-Geneviève; Musée de Cluny, Paris, CL 3443; Musée Dobrée, Nantes, 896.1.28.
128 Thanks are due to Aurélie Gerbier for kindly providing bibliographical information.

Fig.9 Anne of Brittany from the *Grandes Heures d'Anne de Bretagne*, by Jean Bourdichon, *c.*1503, Bibliothèque nationale, Paris,

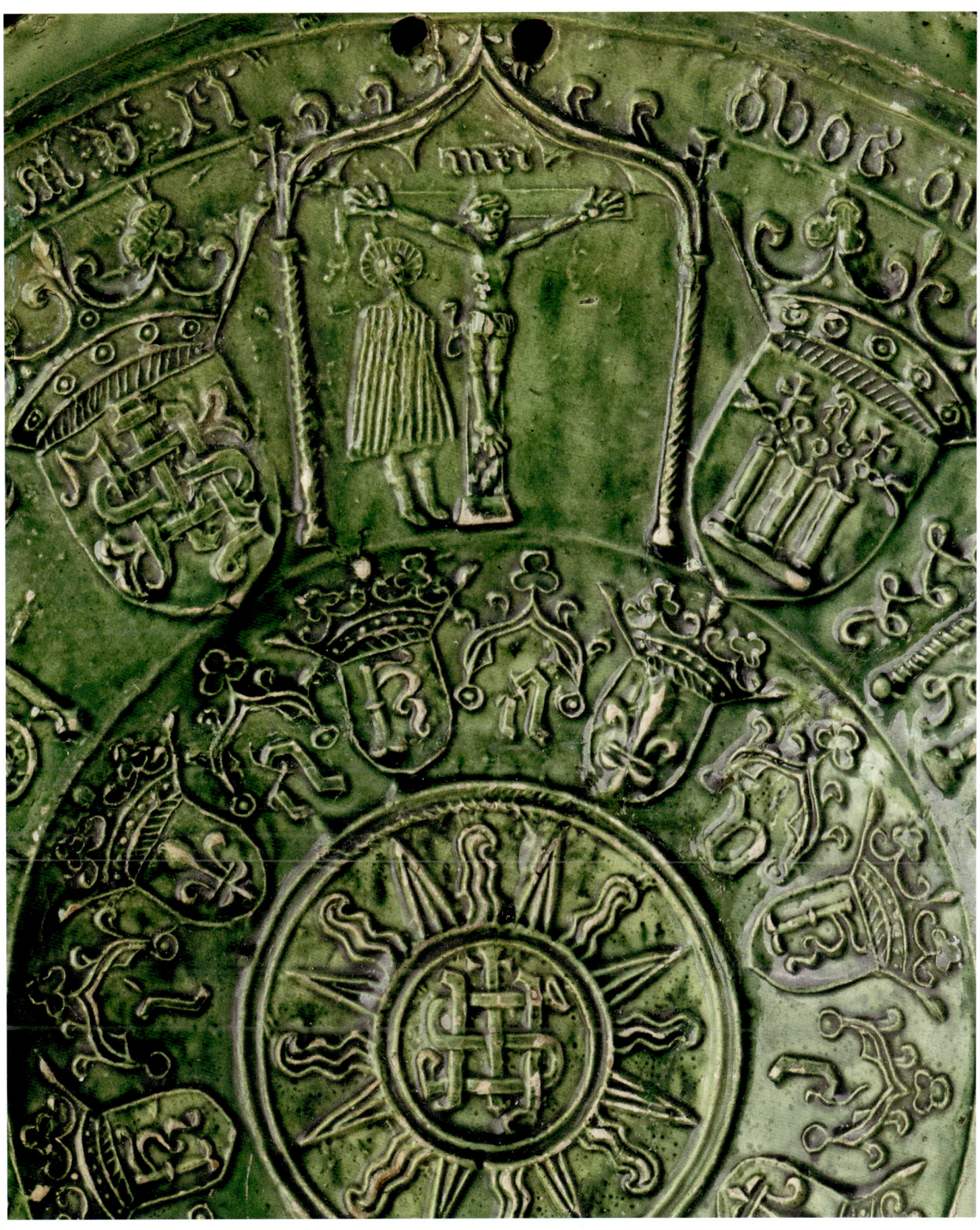

No.**18** (detail)

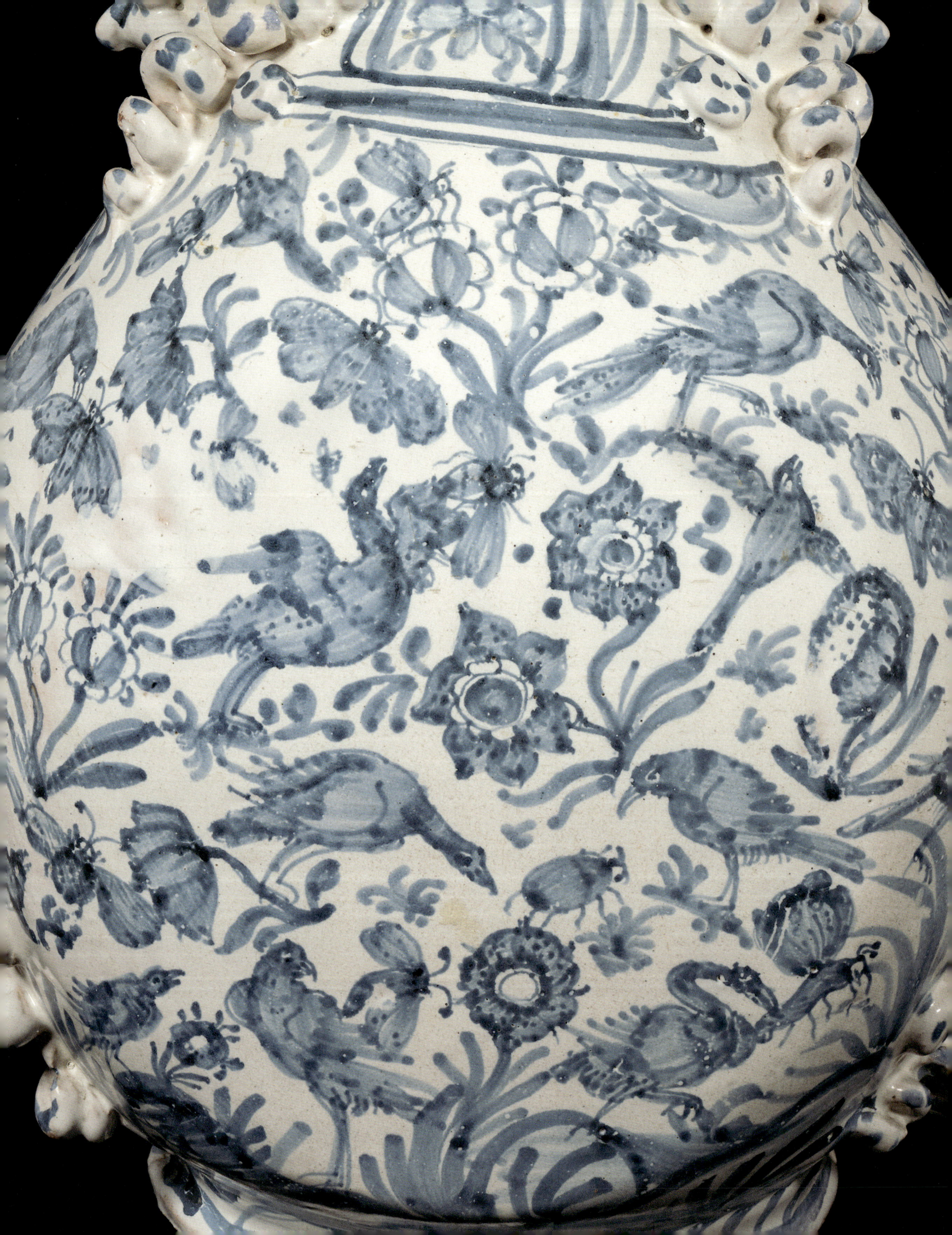

The Sidney R. Knafel bequest of French faience

THE FOLLOWING 24 pieces, nos **19–42**, form part of the near-incomparable collection of French faience formed by Sidney R. Knafel (1930–2021), financier and philanthropist of New York City, and already in his lifetime a supporter of the Ashmolean's ceramic collections. According to the terms of Mr Knafel's will, and through the good will of his widow Londa Weisman, the Ashmolean was permitted to select from the collection, which has transformed the scrappy group of French tin-glazed pottery previously in the Museum. The examples from the three important centres of Nevers, Rouen, and Moustiers are outstandingly good. Other faience from the Knafel collection has found homes in the Frick Collection, New York (the largest group), the Detroit Institute of Arts, and the Davis Museum at Wellesley College, Massachusetts.[129] The collection consists entirely of faience painted in high-temperature (*grand feu*) colours, not the pieces decorated with enamels in a third firing (*petit feu*), which became an important element in French faience, notably at Strasbourg, in the second half of the eighteenth century.

The greater part of the Knafel collection was published in 2016 in a catalogue edited by Christophe Perlès and with texts by various specialists, *French Faïence: The Sidney R. Knafel Collection.* Most of the entries that follow are substantially based on those in the 2016 volume.[130]

129 The faience given in his lifetime by Mr Knafel to the Frick is described in Vignon 2018.

130 We also thank Jody Wilkie, compiler of the appraisal report for the Knafel estate, and Jean Rosen for useful information. The provenances here given have been taken from existing documentation and it has not always been possible to check French sale catalogues. A preliminary account of the bequest was given by Matthew Winterbottom, *Oxford Ceramics Group Newsletter* 59 (June 2024), pp.3–4.

Opposite: detail of no.**22**

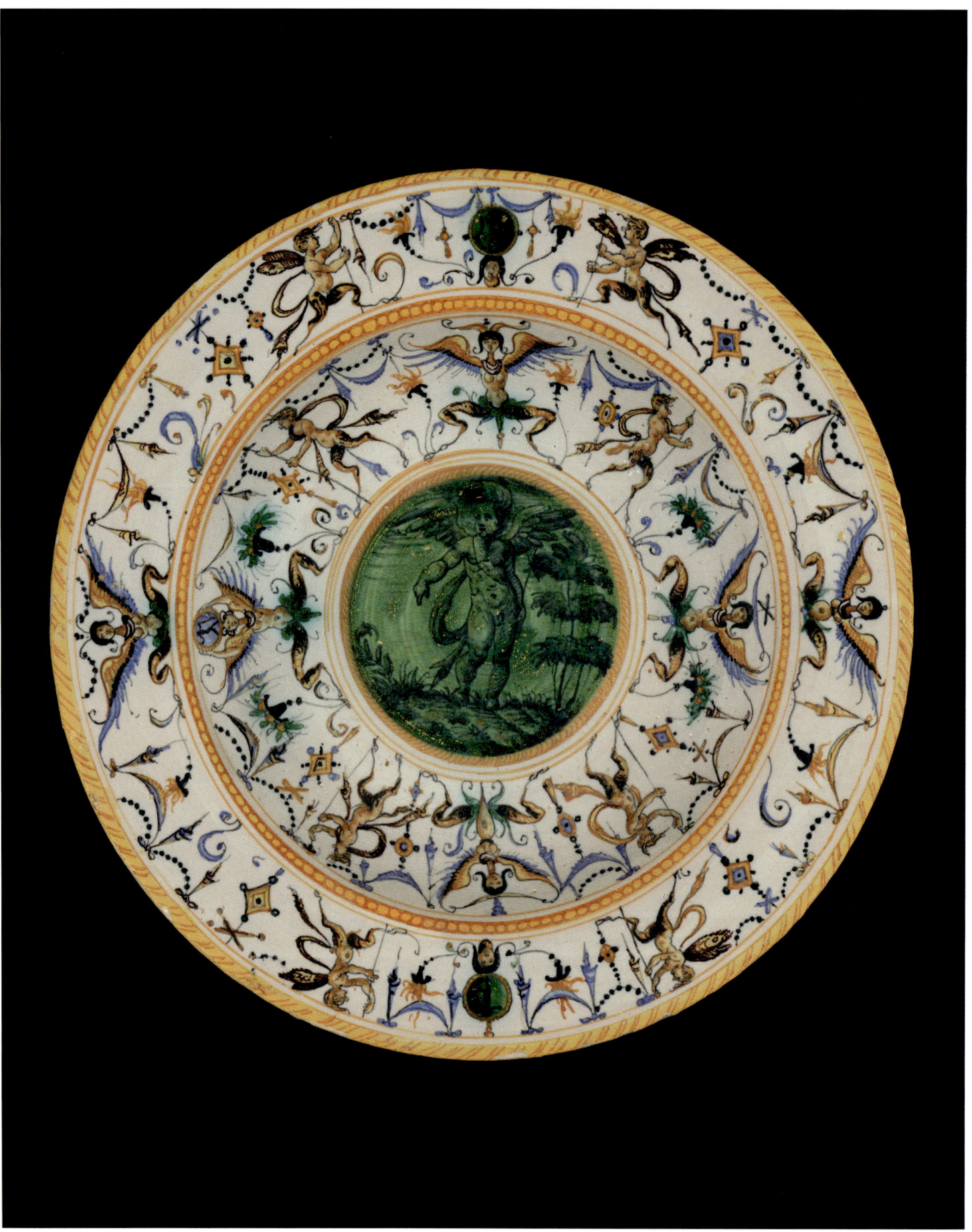

19

Plate with a winged putto and grotesques

Lyon, or possibly in Urbino or Liguria, probably painted by
Gironimo Tomasi of Urbino, *c*.1570–1600
Bequeathed by Sidney R. Knafel, received 2023, WA2023.137.

The plate has a sloping rim with an edge moulding
at the back and a pronounced foot-ring; tin-glazed
front and back. The reverse is undecorated except
for three yellow rings.

Diameter: 32.7 cm

CONDITION: apparently good; the glaze is pock-
marked front and back.

PROVENANCE: Camille Leprince; acquired
by Mr Knafel, 2010, from Voltaire Antiquités-
Vandermeersch, Paris, together with a similar
plate from the same series (now part of the Knafel
bequest to the Detroit Institute of Arts).[131]

BIBLIOGRAPHY: Perlès 2016, no.41B.

The plate is painted in the centre in
manganese, on a ground painted green,
with a winged putto in a somewhat
contrapposto pose in a simple landscape.
On the sides and rim, bordered by narrow
bands of rope pattern, and painted on a
ground heightened with white over the
tin glaze on the wheel, are grotesques
incorporating sphinx-like figures, satyrs,
fictive cameos, cornucopias, braziers, and
swags. On the back are three yellow rings.

This and a companion plate, now
in the Detroit Institute of Arts, are
attributed to the painter Gironimo
Tomasi (or Gironimo di Tommaso) by

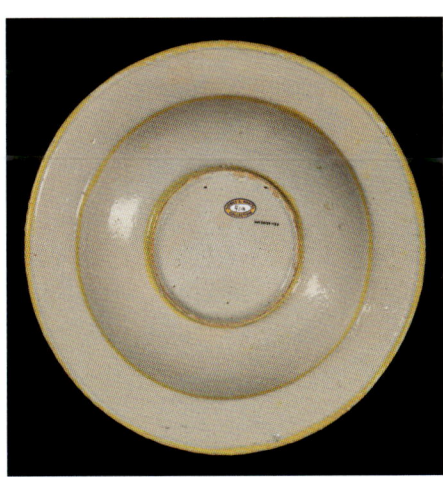

comparison with two signed grotesque-
painted pieces, a plate in the V&A dated
1583, and an undated deep bowl in the
Musée de Beaux-Arts, Lyon.[132] Three
similar plates, unmarked, are in the
Schroder Collection.

Gironimo was trained in Urbino
and, in 1575, signed as made in Urbino
a plate with a view of the Villa d'Este at
Tivoli, formerly in the Berlin museums
but destroyed in 1945.[133] By 1576, he was
in Albisola, near Savona in Liguria,
where he painted, signed as made in
Albisola, and dated a multi-tile panel now
in the church of Nostra Signora della
Concordia, Albisola Marina.[134] By 1582,
he was in Lyon, where he initialled *GTVF
leon* [Gironimo Tomasi Urbinate Fecit,
Lyon] the earliest documentary French
tin-glazed piece made in the Italian
istoriato style, a plate now in the British
Museum. This is dated 1582 and painted
after a woodcut by Bernard Salomon in
the *Quadrins historiques de la Bible* (first
printed in Lyon in 1553), with the Old
Testament subject of a serpent created
by the Israelite priest Aaron devouring,
in front of Pharaoh, a serpent created
by Egyptian magicians.[135] Gironimo
continued to work in Lyon and is the first
identifiable and pivotal character in the
transfer of maiolica style and technology
from Italy to France.

Among other works attributable
to Gironimo are several *istoriato* and
grotesque-painted pieces,[136] as well as two
multi-tile panels at Quinta das Torres,
Azeitão, Portugal,[137] and another such
panel, painted with San Crescentino,
patron saint of Urbino, in the Galleria
Nazionale delle Marche, Urbino.[138] The
signed plate in the V&A mentioned
above is dated 1583, a year or so after

Gironimo's arrival in Lyon, and is of a
form unusual in Italy, so is likely to have
been made in Lyon. The two Knafel
plates may also have been painted there,
but there is no proof that Gironimo did
not make intermittent journeys between
Lyon, Liguria, and Urbino between 1582
and his death in Lyon in 1602, so the
place that these two plates were made
remains uncertain. The shape is not
uncharacteristic of Urbino. The way the
grotesques are painted – over a ground
heightened with white applied on the
wheel – is a technique practised in the
Fontana and Patanazzi workshops in
Urbino, so manufacture in an Urbino
workshop cannot be ruled out.

Since the present entry was drafted,
an innovative book by Anna Falcioni,
Walter Monacchi, and Vincenzo Mosconi
has been published, presenting a wealth
of documentary material in support of
the hypothesis that the pottery painter
Gironimo be identified with a well-
documented individual, Girolamo
di Tommaso Galli of Rancitella, near
Urbino.[139] This intriguing hypothesis
remains to be fully evaluated.

131 Perlès 2016, no.41A.
132 V&A 4354-1857; Wilson 2003, p.92, no.7.;
     Wilson 2003, p.93, no.8.
133 Wilson 2003, p.90, no.5.
134 Wilson 2003, pp.90–91, no.6. The panel is
     additionally marked as made in the workshop
     of a local potter called Agostino.
135 Wilson 2003, pp.90–101, no.1; Thornton and
     Wilson 2009, no.341.
136 Leprince 2009, pp.29–37; Leprince and
     Raccanello 2016, pp.1–27; this article includes
     further attributions to Gironimo of works
     painted in Urbino, probably in the Fontana
     workshop, before he left Urbino in 1575–6.
137 Simões 1946, pp.76–87. I hypothesised the
     attribution to Gironimo, on the basis of the
     inadequate photographs then available to me,

in Wilson 2019, pp.3–9. Subsequent discussion with other specialists leads me to believe the attribution to Gironimo is likely to be correct, though where the two panels were made and fired remains uncertain. I know of no other Urbino-trained maiolica painter who made multi-tile panels of this sort and Gironimo may have learnt the technique in Liguria. A detailed technical study of the important Quinta das Torres panels by Portuguese colleagues is awaited. I thank my friends Alfonso Pleguezuelo and Cecilia Chilosi for advice on this question.

138 Gardelli 1993, pp.39–45; Paolinelli and Wilson 2024, no.30.
139 Falcioni et al. 2024. Among the problems still to be resolved is that *Hyerosmo thomas touppinyer en vesselle de terre* [potter] *natif d'Urbin en Italye au pays de la marche* is apparently recorded as dying in the Hôtel-Dieu in Lyon on 13 July 1602 (Sfeir-Fakhri 2003, pp.104–5). Girolamo di Tommaso Galli of Rancitella was still alive in Urbino in 1627; furthermore, to the best of my knowledge (and subject to correction), no published document describes Galli explicitly as a potter.

20

Shallow bowl with a river god, the moon, and fishermen

Nevers, *c.*1610–40
Bequeathed by Sidney R. Knafel, received 2023, WA2023.131.

Shallow bowl on small, slightly everted foot; tin-glazed front and back; the reverse undecorated.

Diameter: 25.5 cm

CONDITION: apparently good;[140] some wear and chipping to edge.

PROVENANCE: acquired by Mr Knafel from Christophe Perlès, Paris, 2011. A torn, typed label in Italian on the reverse attributes the bowl to Antonio Patanazzi's workshop, Urbino, with inventory number *6168*, and apparently gives a provenance to '… lliam …'.

BIBLIOGRAPHY: Perlès 2014, p.24, no.6; Perlès 2016, no.1.

The bowl is painted with a river god in the traditional ancient iconography of an old man pouring water from an urn. In his arm he holds a cornucopia; beside him is a half-naked female figure with a crescent on her head representing Diana, the moon. Left and right are men fishing from a river and in the background is a town.

The composition is closely after the engraving *Night Fishing* (fig.10) from a series of hunting scenes published 1578–80 by Philips Galle after Stradanus.[141] Another Nevers plate using the same graphic source is in the Musée des Arts décoratifs, Lyon.[142] Both are reminiscent of the contemporaneous work of the Patanazzi family, and the painter may have been trained in the Urbino tradition, though French specialists attribute both to Nevers.

In the first half of the seventeenth century, Nevers was the fulcrum of the transfer of maiolica technology from Italy to France and the cradle of French faience.[143]

140 Items in the Knafel bequest to the Ashmolean have not been subjected to examination by conservators or scientists with specialist equipment and it may be that some of the pieces have restoration that has not been detected by visual examination.
141 *New Hollstein Dutch and Flemish etchings, engravings and woodcuts,* Stradanus, part 3, p.147, no.464; British Museum, P&D, 1957,0413.123.
142 Rosen 2009, II, p.153, fig.154.
143 For the literature see Wilson 2017, pp.22 and 465–6.

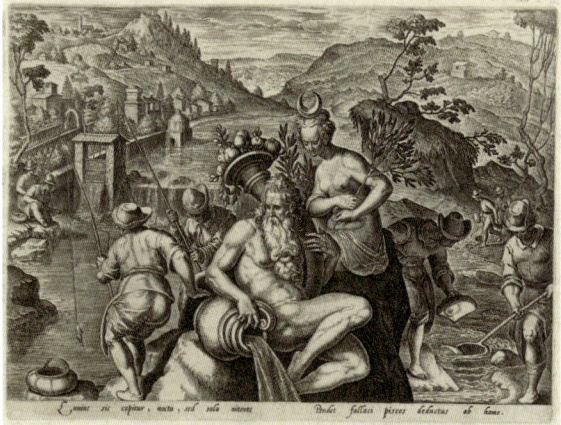

Fig.10 *Night Fishing.* Engraving by Philips Galle after Stradanus, engraving, 1578. Rijksmuseum, Amsterdam

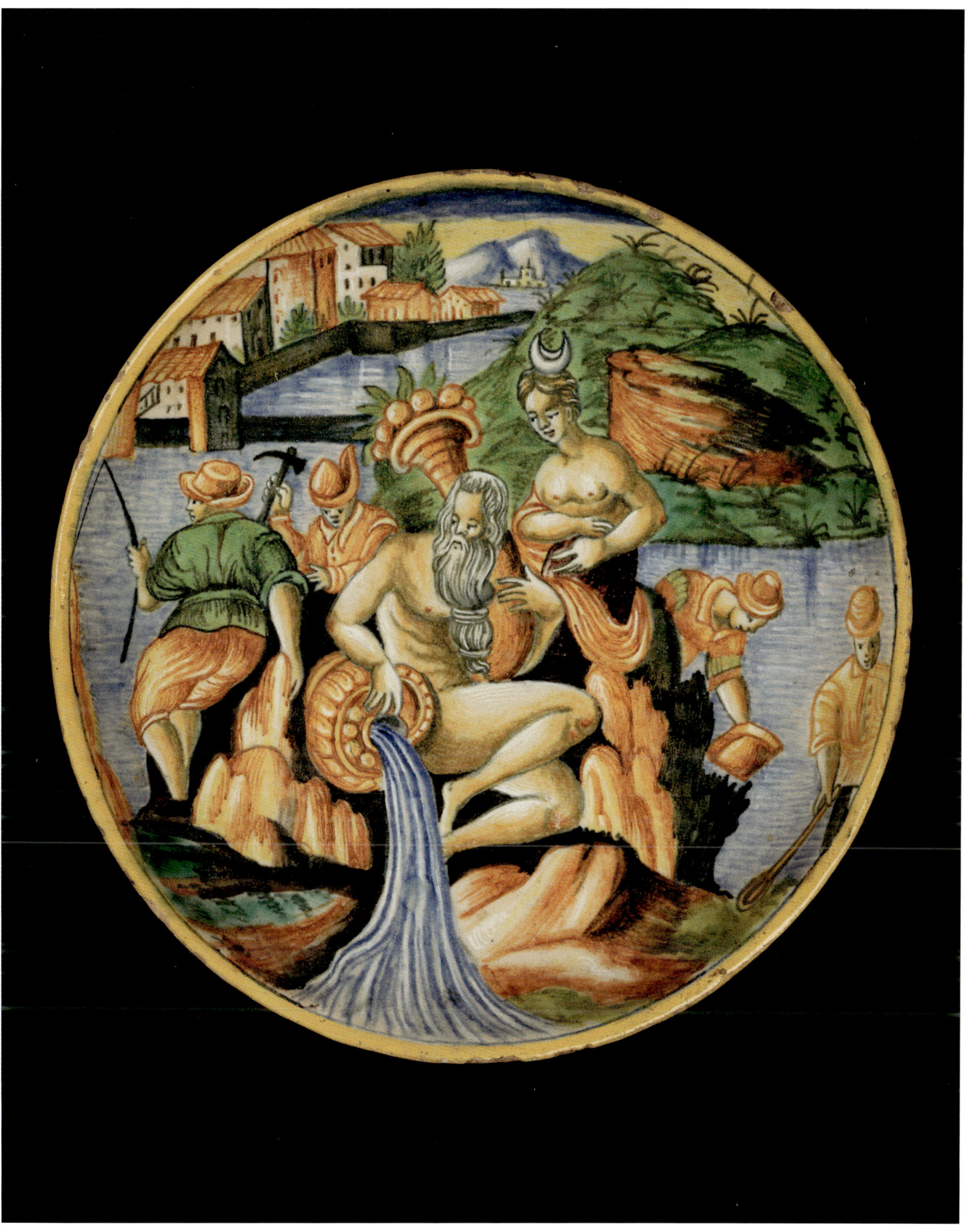

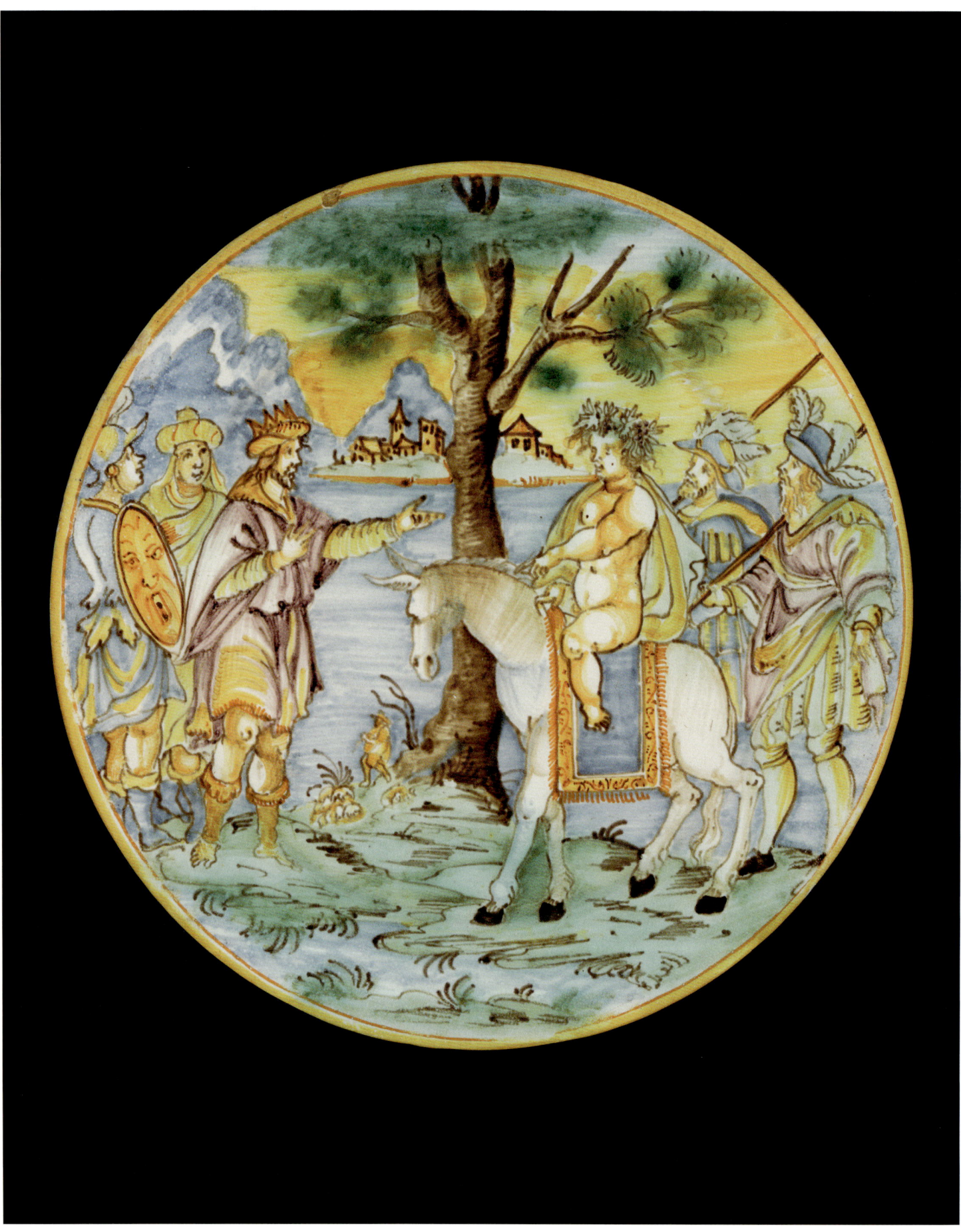

21

Plate, Bacchus approaching King Midas to offer him a reward

Nevers, painted by Denis Lefebvre or an associate, *c.*1635–50
Bequeathed by Sidney R. Knafel, received 2023, WA2023.132.

Tin-glazed front and back.

Diameter: 21.7 cm

CONDITION: apparently good.

PROVENANCE: Charles Louis Meyer; Patrick Leprince; Camille Leprince; from whom acquired by Mr Knafel through Voltaire Antiquités-Vandermeersch AS, Paris. On the reverse a Vandermeersch label and two older labels.

BIBLIOGRAPHY: Chompret et al. 1933–5, II, Nevers, pl.12a, no.2; Leprince 2009, pp.84–5, no.20; Rosen 2009, II, p.156, figs 161–2; Perlès 2016, no.7.

This shallow plate on broad, low footing ring is painted with a watery landscape, centred on a large tree. Bacchus, on a donkey, is approaching Midas (crowned at left). On the back, concentric rings in shades of blue surround the inscription *Midas Roy de phrygie* (Midas, King of Phrygia). There are three kiln scars on the back near the edge.

The scene depicted is from Ovid's *Metamorphoses*.[144] Midas, King of Phrygia, had showed kindness to the aged and drunken Silenus, foster-father of the god Bacchus. In gratitude, Bacchus offered Midas any favour of his choosing. Midas foolishly asked that everything he touched be turned to gold. The wish was granted

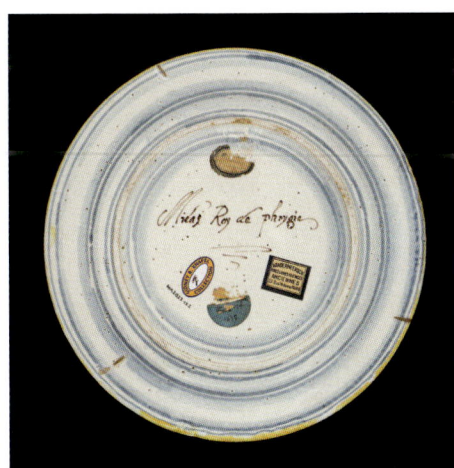

but proved baleful, with even Midas's food being turned to gold before he could eat it. The result was that Bacchus's gift had to be rescinded.

The subject is after an engraving from a series of Ovid subjects known in various versions. One series, published by the Antwerp printmaker Pieter de Jode and dated 1606, was attributed on the title page to, and the prints probably designed by, Antonio Tempesta.[145] However, the scene on the plate is reversed from the Tempesta version, and the maiolica painter doubtless used a version in the other direction such as that engraved by Crispijn de Passe, illustrated here (fig.11).[146]

Denis Lefebvre is first mentioned in Nevers documents in 1619, when he married the daughter of the Nevers-based Italian potter Antoine Salomon (Antonio Salomone). Lefebvre is recorded as a worker in *vesselle de fayance* from 1629, but was dead by 1651. A group of plates with mythological subjects, to which the present plate belongs, some of which were together with this one in the Charles Louis Meyer collection, have been attributed to Lefebvre.[147] However, an *istoriato* plate marked by him, *DLF* (the *L* and *F* conjoined), in the British Museum, does not seem obviously by the same hand.[148] It bears on it handwriting that differs to that on the plate now in the Frick Collection (from the Knafel gift), dated 1635, which forms part of the group assembled by Leprince.[149] An attribution to Lefebvre himself, rather than to a painter in the same workshop, remains hypothetical.

144 Ovid, *Metamorphoses*, XI, 90–104.
145 Bartsch XVII, p.151, no.738; British Museum, P&D, X,3.294. The title page is dated 1606.

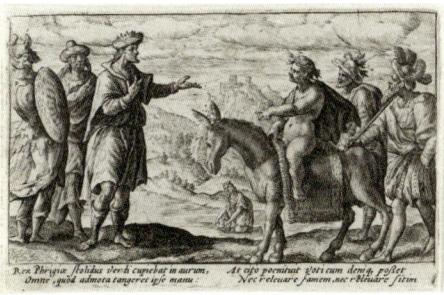

Fig.11 *Bacchus Approaching King Midas to Offer Him a Reward*. Engraving by Crispijn de Passe the Elder. Rijksmuseum, Amsterdam

146 Hollstein Dutch, De Passe, no.852, printed from 1602 onwards, no.98. Neither Hollstein nor the Rijksmuseum website indicate Tempesta as the originator of the *Bacchus and Midas* design. The original designing and the printing history of the various versions of these *Metamorphoses* engravings are problematic. Franken and Laschitzer 1881, pp.253–6, describe the de Passe publication and note that some of the illustrations in the series are signed by Crispijn de Passe as designer (*invenit*) and a few by Maarten de Vos; the *Bacchus and Midas* engraving has no indication of the original artist. We are indebted to An Van Camp for comments on this issue.
147 Leprince 2009, pp.76–87; see also Rosen 2009, II pp.157–9.
148 Thornton and Wilson 2009, pp.708–9, no.RA2.
149 Perlès 2016, no. 6; Leprince 2009, pp. 76–87, pp. 82–3, no. 19. The other recorded *istoriato* piece initialled *DLF* is a covered pot dated 1644 in the Fitzwilliam Museum, Cambridge (C.2314–1928); this is closer in style to the present plate and the group assembled by Leprince than is the British Museum plate.

22

Flask with birds, insects, and flowers

Nevers, workshop of Antoine Conrade, *c.*1640–48
Bequeathed by Sidney R. Knafel, received 2023, WA2023.133.

Tin-glazed earthenware.

Height: 42 cm

CONDITION: probably some repairs, especially on and around the cap, but the extent not clearly ascertained.

PROVENANCE: acquired by Mr Knafel from Camille Leprince, Paris, after 2016.

BIBLIOGRAPHY: none.

A large flask of fat pilgrim-flask shape, with two handles on each side approximating to the form of serpents. The cap is attached by a screw fitting; the body is painted with a dense textile-like pattern of birds, butterflies, insects, and flowers, while the neck is decorated with panels of flowers. The flat, unglazed base has holes in the flange under the handles.

Antoine Conrade, a member of the Corrado family of potters from Liguria, became the most successful member of his family of tin-glaze potters at Nevers and was appointed *fayencier ordinaire* to the young King Louis XIV in 1644. He died in 1648.

Among the production of Antoine's workshop in the 1640s was a series of pieces, mainly plates, densely decorated in blue with naturalistic plants and creatures in a style broadly describable as 'orientalizing'. Similar decoration was practised in Liguria and is known by Italian scholars as *calligrafico naturalistico*.[150] Several plates are marked *de Conrade a Nevers*, the 'de' suggesting they date from after Antoine Conrade was ennobled in 1644.[151] An unusually elaborate plate in this style in the British Museum is unmarked but appears to be dated 1644.[152] This flask is the only piece of the shape with this decoration recorded and one of the most ambitious examples of it altogether.

150 For example Ausenda 2000, nos 368–9. Comparable decoration was carried out in Deruta; see Ausenda 2000, nos 92–3, as by the *Maestro calligrafico.*

151 Rosen 2009, pp.195–200.
152 British Museum, BEP, 1989,0706.1; the authenticity of this plate has been disputed.

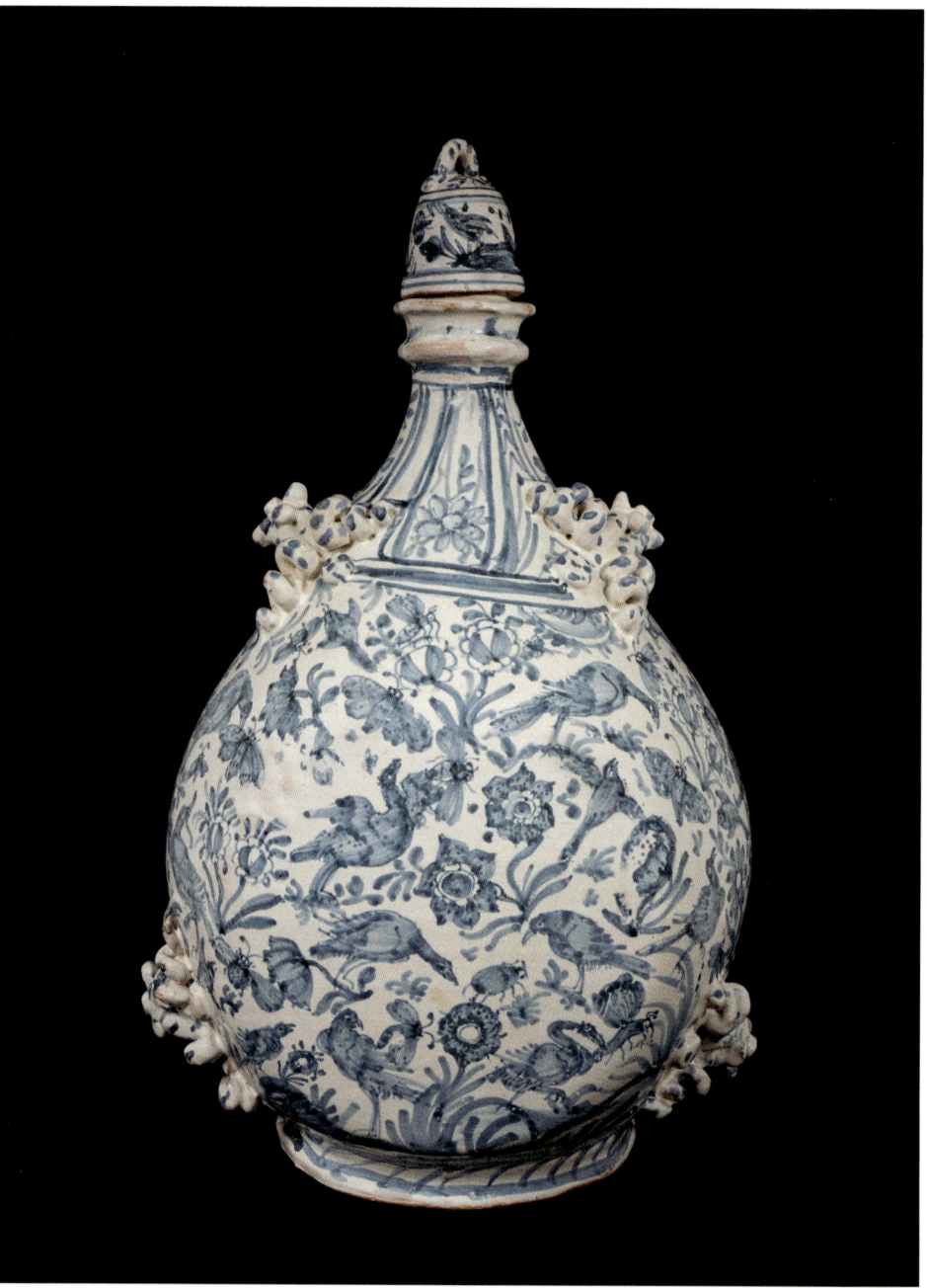

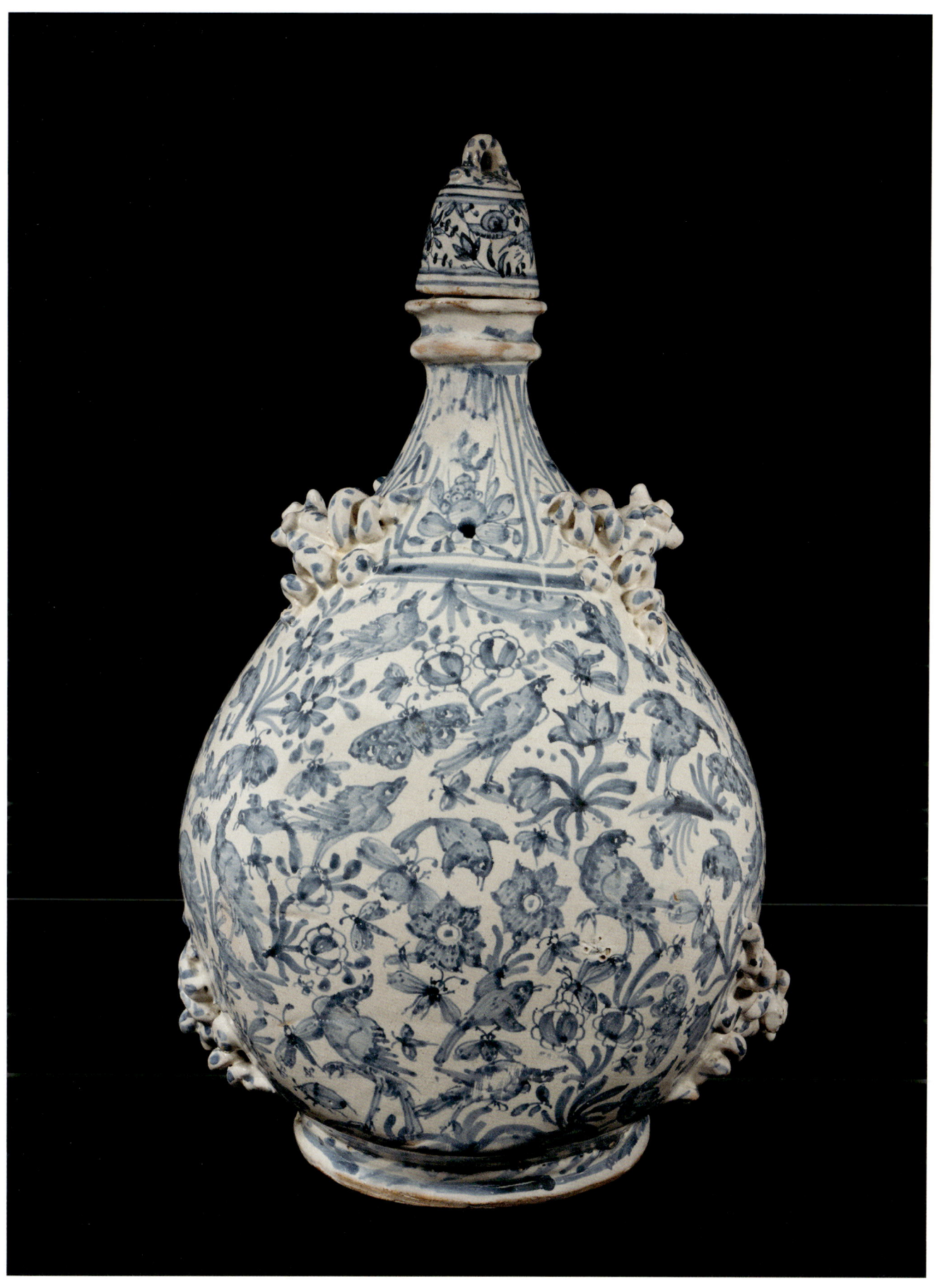

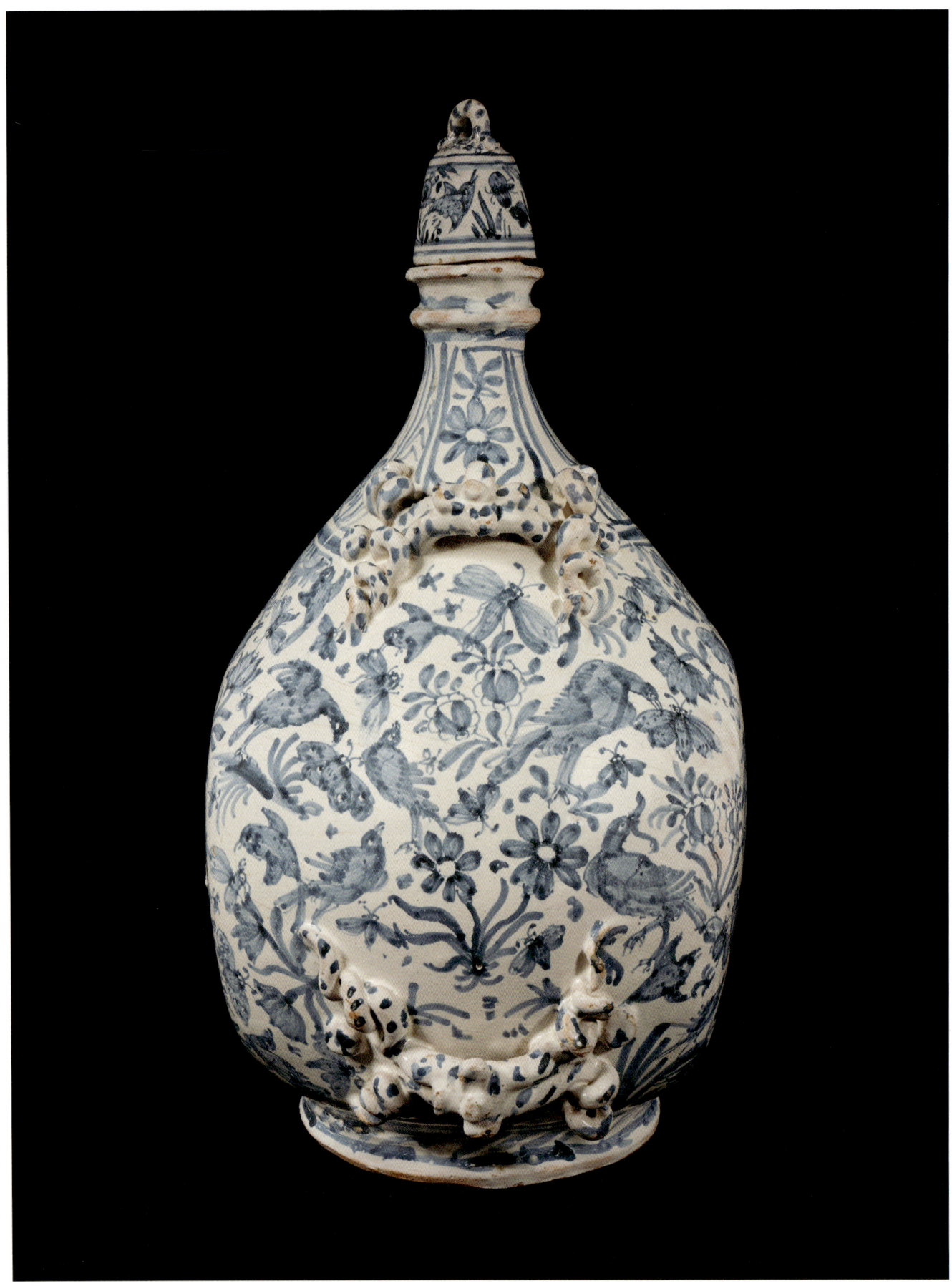

No.22

23

Bowl with a mythological scene

Probably Nevers, *c*.1630–50
Bequeathed by Sidney R. Knafel, received 2023, WA 2023.134.

Tin-glazed front and back.

Diameter: 21.8 cm

CONDITION: formerly on a high spreading foot, now cut away; condition otherwise apparently good.

PROVENANCE: acquired by Mr Knafel from Camille Leprince, 2013.

BIBLIOGRAPHY: none.

In a landscape with water, rocks, and trees, Venus and Cupid walk away to the right. On the left, a young man gestures; he may represent Aeneas, the son of Venus and Anchises.[153] On the back are waves of the sea with four frolicking dolphins.

Flattish dishes on a high foot, like the one this dish once had, are sometimes known by the Italian word *tazza*. Painting the underside of such dishes with waves and aquatic creatures or divinities was made popular in Urbino, probably in the Fontana workshop, around the middle of the sixteenth century.[154] The use of such painted undersides, or reverses, passed to France, and they were still being made in Nevers in the mid-seventeenth century, as shown, among other examples, by an oval plate in the Louvre.[155]

153 We owe this suggestion to Paul Taylor of the Warburg Institute; Venus encounters Aeneas in book 1 of Virgil's *Aeneid*, but Dr Taylor notes that if this is the scene portrayed, Venus should be dressed as a huntress.
154 See, for example, Thornton and Wilson 2009, no.194.
155 Rosen 2009, p.172, figs 215–6.

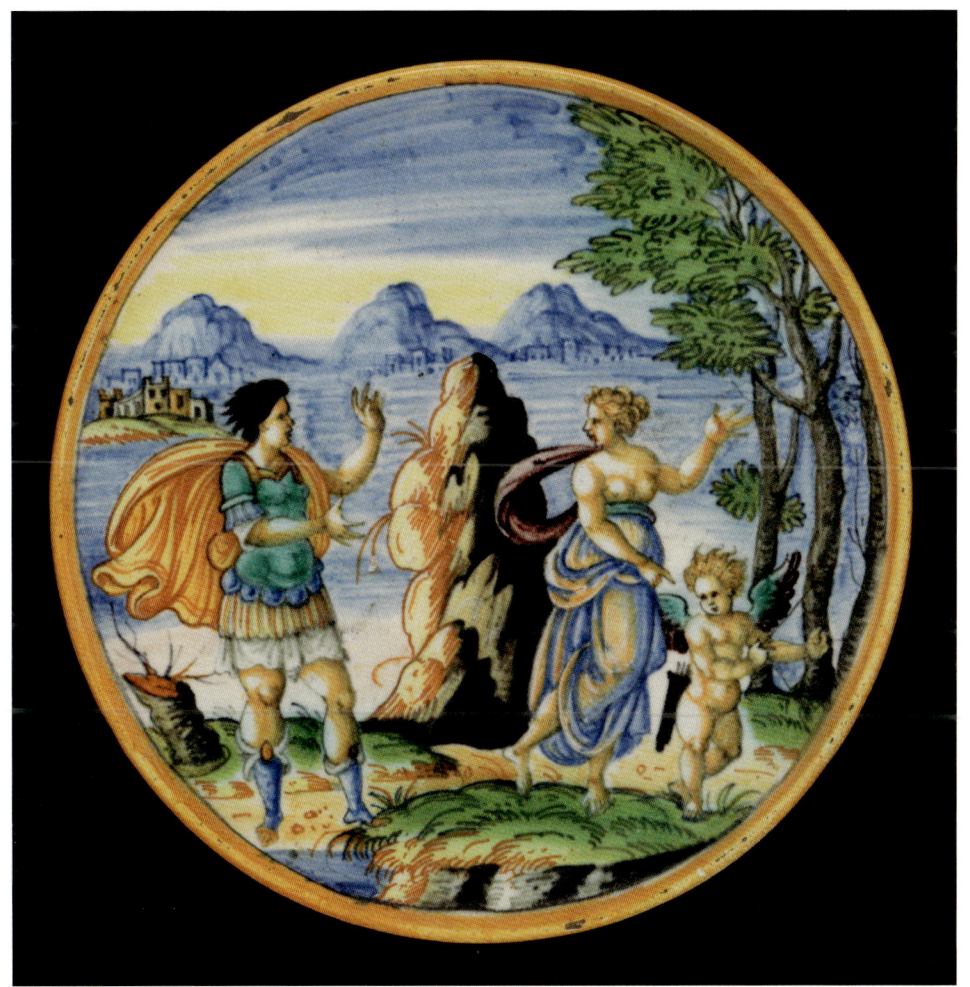

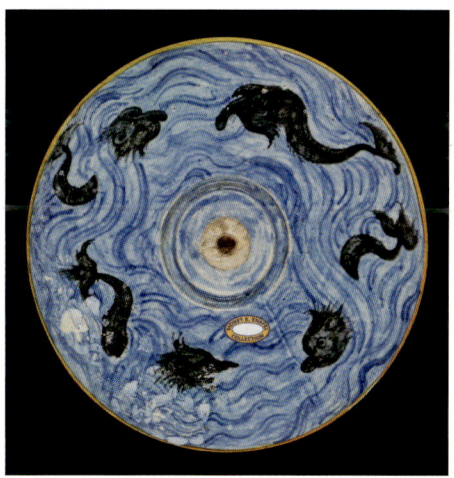

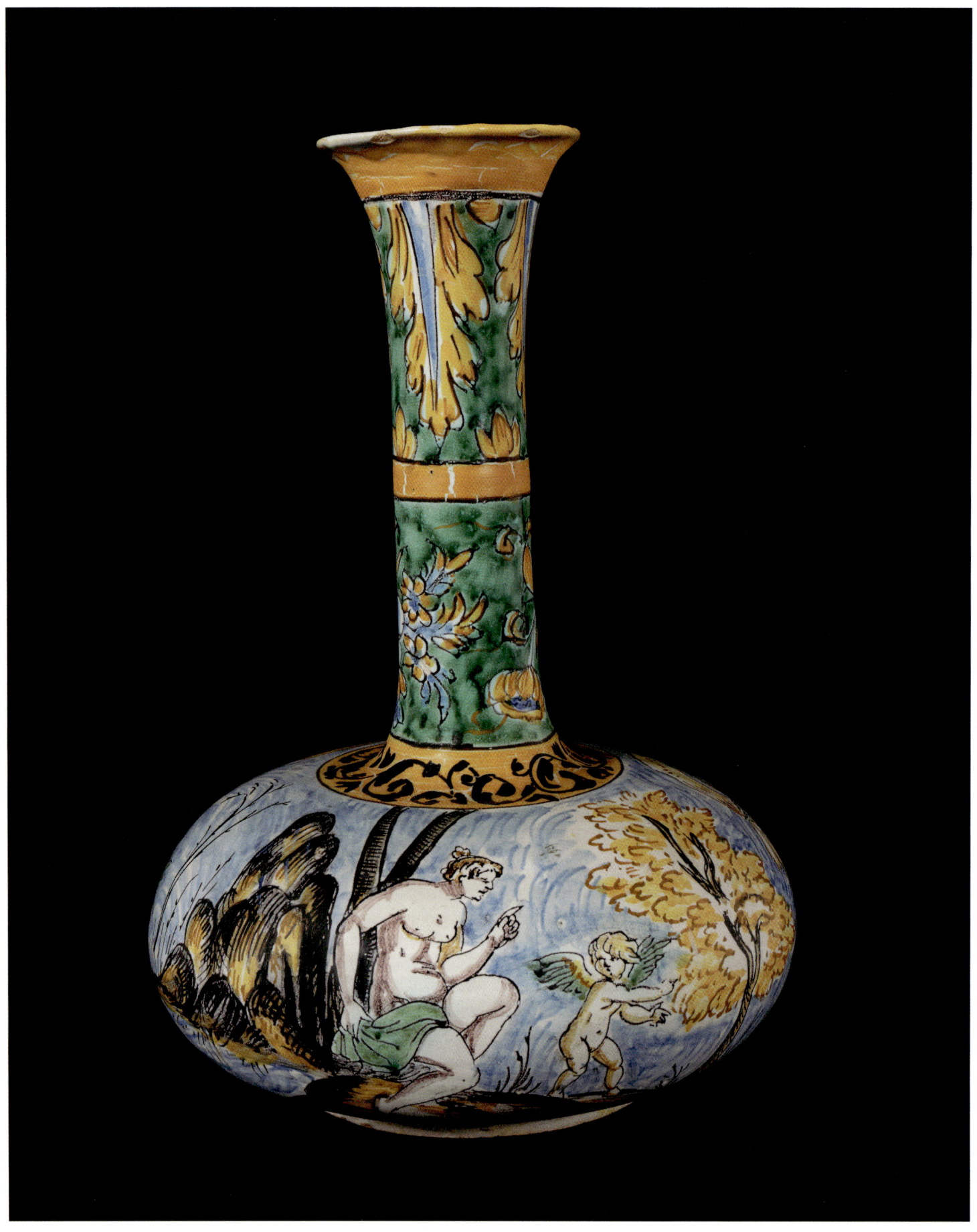

24

Vase

Nevers, *c.*1680–90
Bequeathed by Sidney R. Knafel, received 2023, WA2023.135.

Tin-glazed inside and out.

Height: 29 cm

CONDITION: chipping at rim.

PROVENANCE: acquired by Mr Knafel from
Christophe Perlès, Paris, 2008.

BIBLIOGRAPHY: Rosen 2009, p.285, fig.457; Perlès
2014, (no.8), p.4, no.1; Perlès 2016, no.15.

The vase, of a bottle shape echoing
Chinese porcelain, has a broad, bulbous
body, pronounced foot-ring, and tall neck
flaring at the rim.[156] It is tin-glazed inside
and out and beneath the base.

The body is painted, between two
bands of running foliage in black on an
ochre ground, with Venus admonishing
Cupid, a female figure riding an
apparently female triton, and a child-
triton with a trident. Round the neck are
two bands of flowers on a green ground,
separated by an ochre band; the rim is
painted ochre.

156 For comparable shapes in Nevers faience, see
      Chompret et al. 1933–5, II, Nevers, pls 11B,
      20A, 30A; III, Nevers, 35A and B.

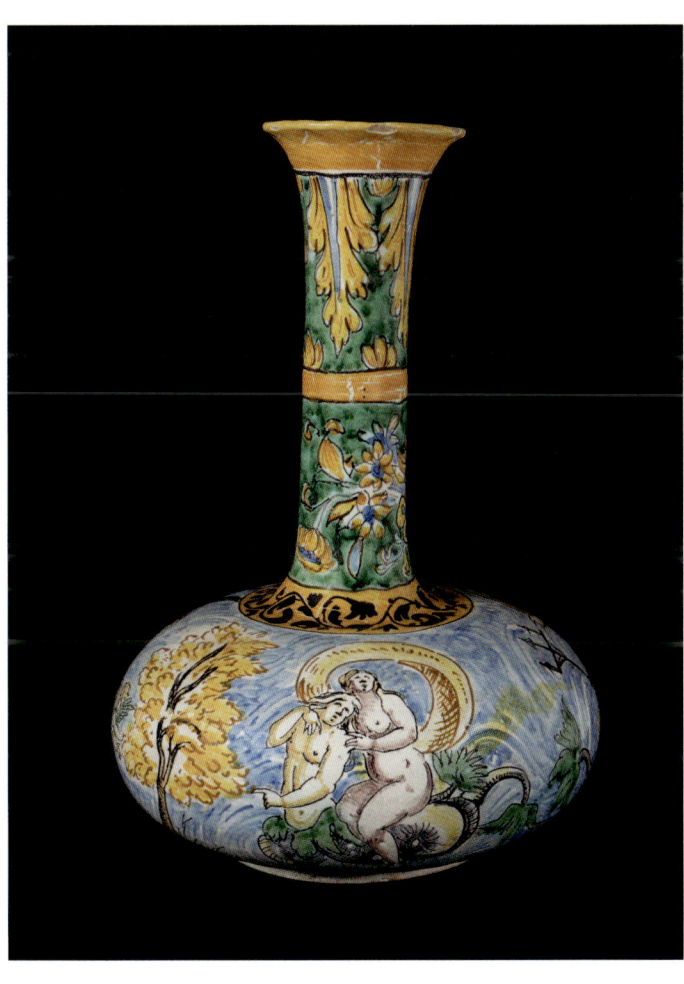
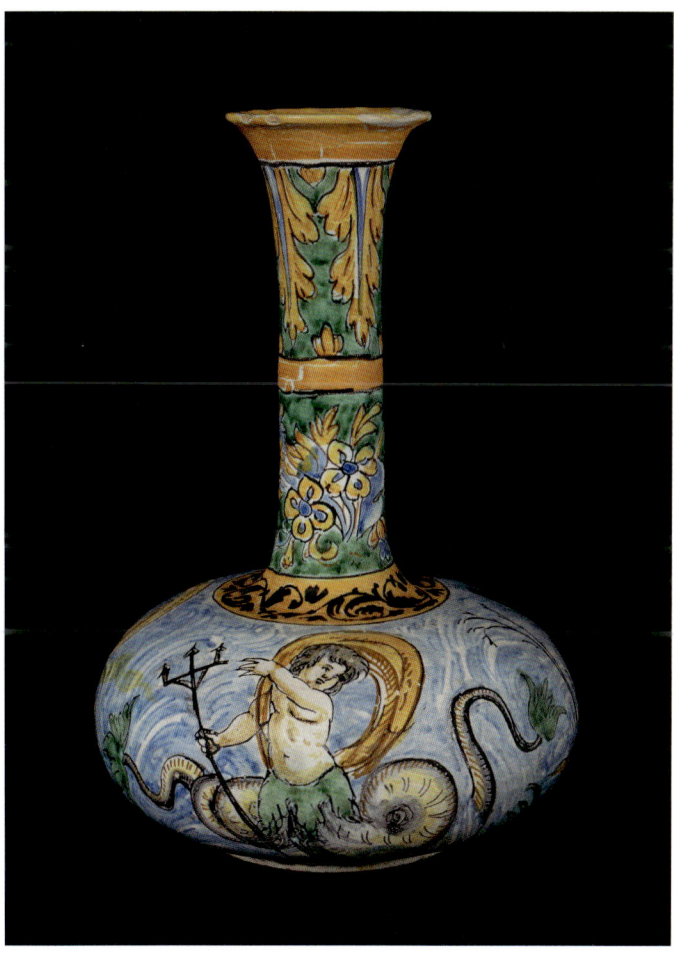

25

Plate, Emperor Vespasian

Nevers, *c*.1670–90
Bequeathed by Sidney R. Knafel, received 2023, WA2023.136.

Tin-glazed front and back. The reverse, which is extensively pock-marked and has a high foot-ring, is decorated with four stylised sprays.

Diameter: 24.1 cm

CONDITION: cracked from the edge at 3 o'clock; retouching to edge at 4 o'clock. Some repairs.

PROVENANCE: Galerie Lefebvre, Paris; Patrick Leprince; acquired by Mr Knafel, 2007, through Camille Leprince, together with another plate from the same series (now part of the Knafel bequest to the Detroit Institute of Arts).[157]

BIBLIOGRAPHY: Perlès 2016, no.17B.

The image is probably based on the engraving of Vespasian in *L'histoire des empereurs romains de Suetone avec leurs porctraits en Taille douce* (1661), published in Paris by Estienne Loyson (1629–1708),

ultimately after a painting by Titian for the Ducal Palace in Mantua, part of a series of Roman emperors. The paintings were later acquired by Charles I, but sold after his execution and destroyed by fire in Madrid in 1734. The image is reversed and reduced from half-length, so there may have been an intermediary or related version.[158]

A comparable plate with Vespasian is at Sèvres, and both are likely to have formed parts of sets of the twelve emperors. Other Nevers sets from the same source are recorded.[159]

157 Perlès 2016, no.17A.
158 Perlès 2016, p.55 and Rosen 2009, II, p.262 say the source is an edition of Suetonius published in 1641. I have found no record of such an edition, but the Bibliothèque nationale online

catalogue mentions another printing of the illustrated French translation of Suetonius, which was also printed by Loyson in 1661 but bears the erroneous date 1641 on the title page.
159 MNC, Sèvres, 4339; others are recorded by Rosen 2009, pp.262–3 and note 205. Six were sold at Normandy Auction, Rouen, 18 March 2018, lots 12–14.

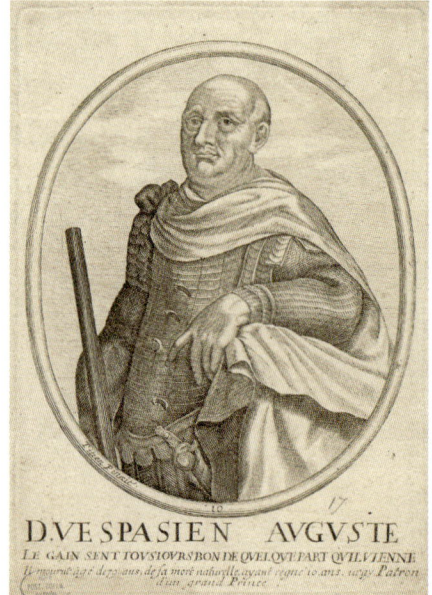

Fig.12 *Vespasian.* Engraving after Titian, perhaps via an engraving by Aegidius Sadeler II, from *L'histoire des empereurs romains de Suetone*, Paris 1661, Ashmolean Museum, Hope Collection, WAHP48975

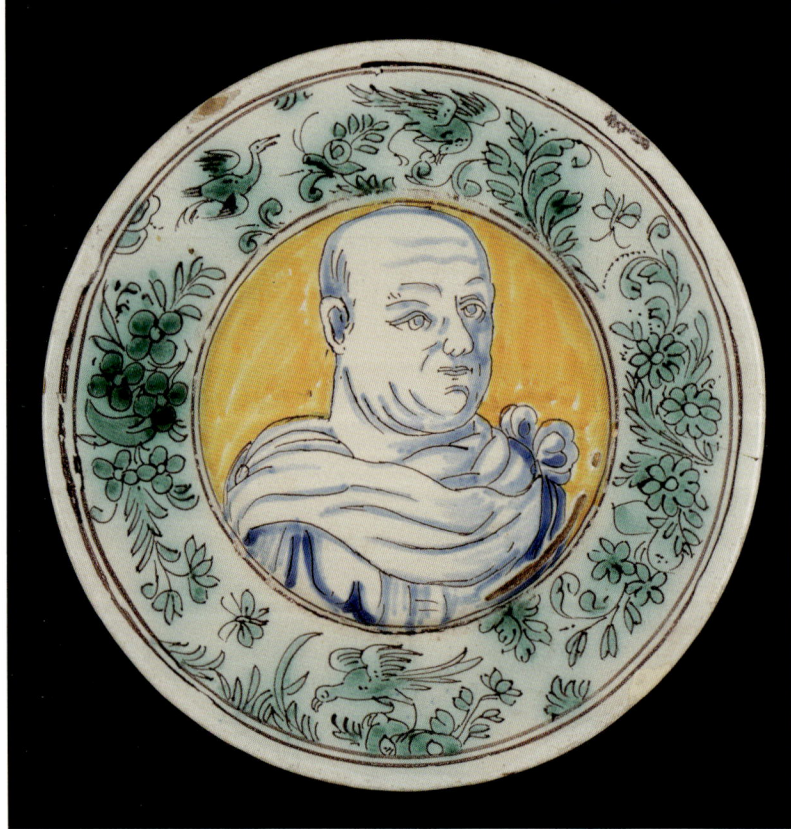

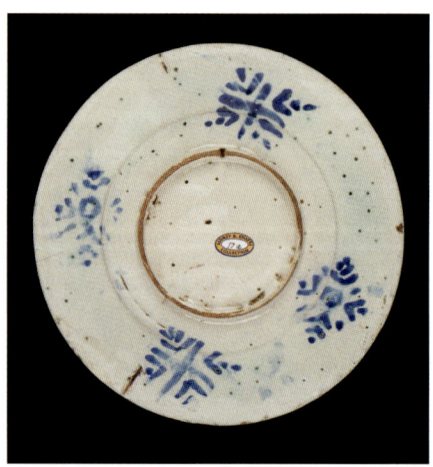

26

Octagonal basin

Rouen, *c*.1710–20
Bequeathed by Sidney R. Knafel, received 2023, WA2023.139.

Tin-glazed front and back.

27.4 × 32.2 × 7.4 cm

CONDITION: cracked from one corner towards
the centre.

PROVENANCE: Galerie Verneuil-Bac, Paris; from
whom acquired by Mr Knafel, 1998. A label on the
back records ownership by J.-G. Peyre and J.-C.
Sieberth, 17 rue du Bac, Paris.

BIBLIOGRAPHY: Perlès 2016, no.51.

The deep, finely potted basin is painted
in shades of blue with floral garlands and
panels with lambrequins. A simple band
of plant ornament runs round the exterior.
Within the foot-ring is a blurred mark,
probably *M*.

After a brief period of brilliance in the
hands of Masséot Abaquesne (died by
1564) in the middle of the sixteenth
century, the manufacture of artistically
ambitious tin-glazed pottery in Rouen
was re-established by the Poterat family in
the 1640s, supported by royal patronage.[160]
The earlier pieces are mainly decorated
in blue and white. In the first half of the
eighteenth century, the golden age of
Rouen faience, workshops multiplied, and
a range of brilliantly executed decorative
ornament, from a variety of design
sources, was carried out.[161]

Lambrequins, described as 'a term
meaning pendent draperies, later
extended to include all kinds of formal
pendent lace-like decorations', were a
favourite element in the decoration of
Rouen faience in its finest period.[162]

160 Wilson 2017, pp.28, 470, with references.
161 Among the literature: Chompret et al. 1933–5,
     IV, Rouen; Grandjean 2001; Perlès 2014;
     Leprince 2020.
162 Honey 1952, p.357.

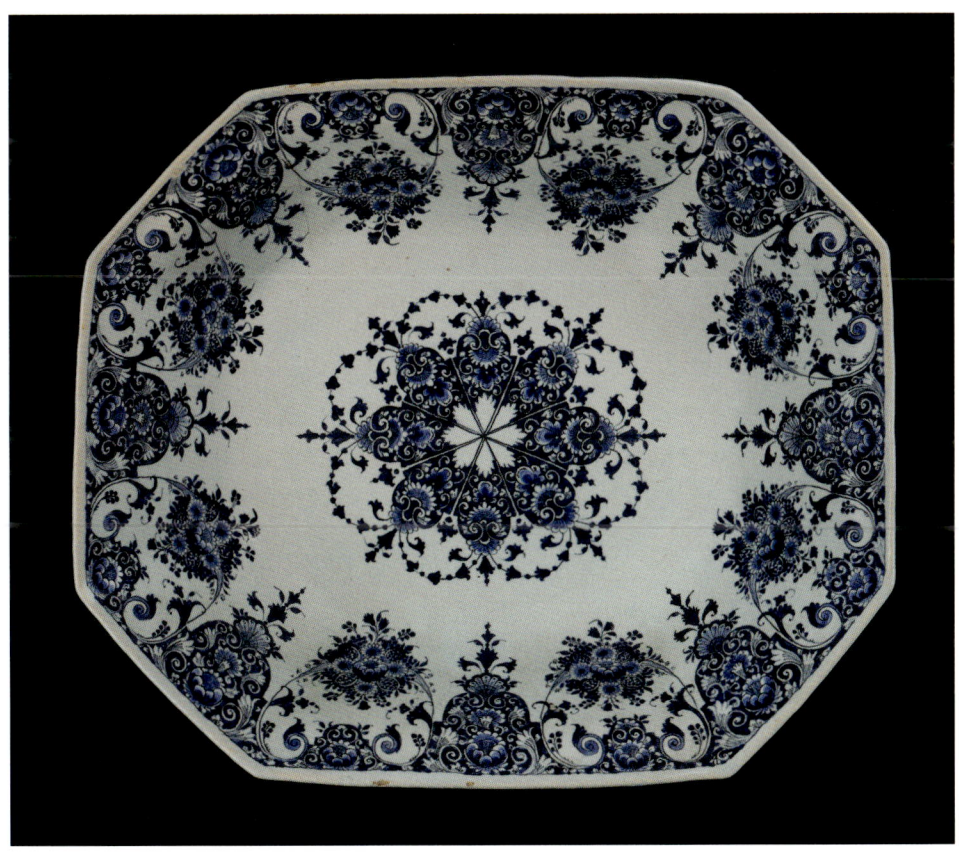

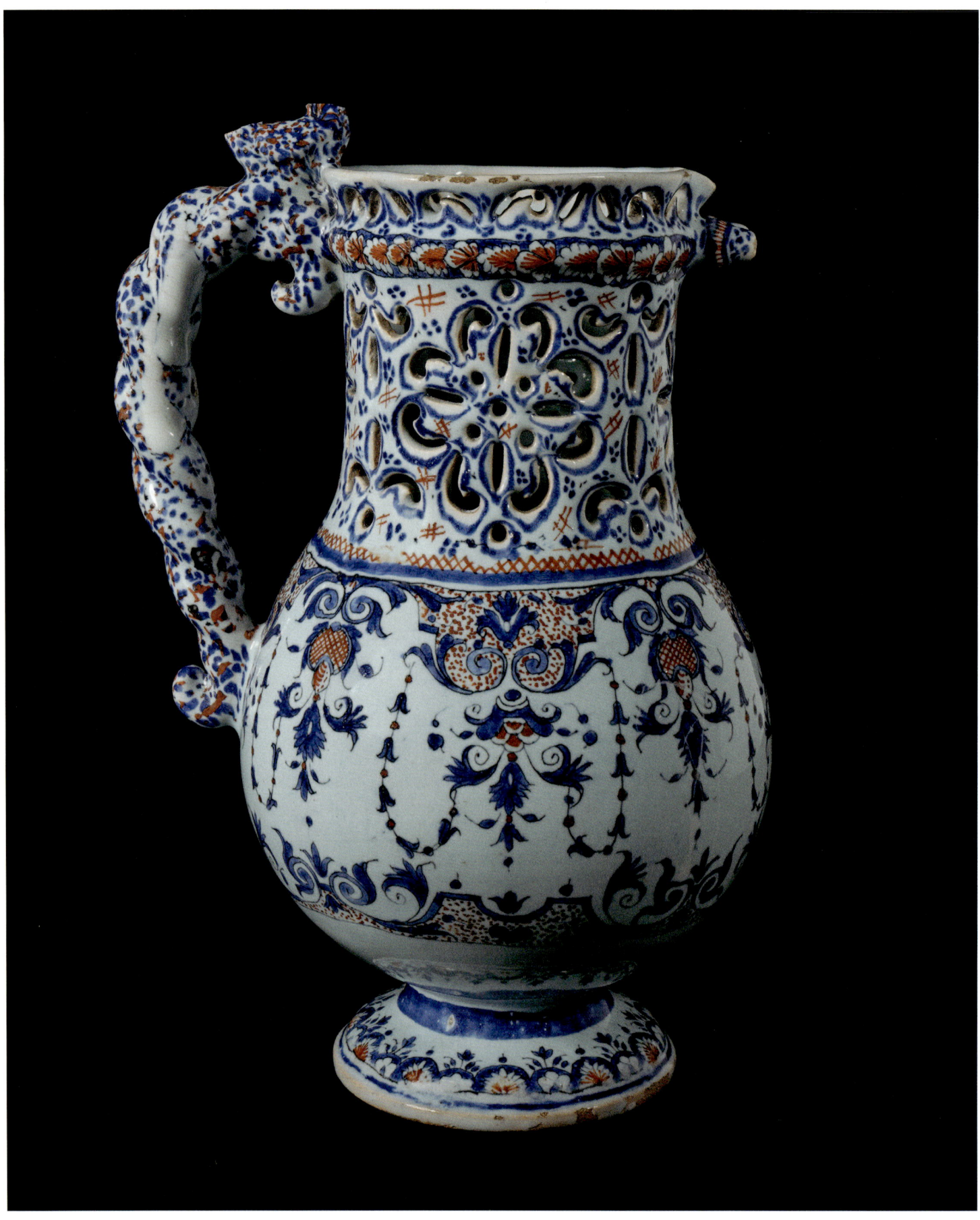

27

Puzzle jug

Rouen, *c.*1710–20
Bequeathed by Sidney R. Knafel, received 2023, WA2023.140.

Tin-glazed outside and in.

Height to rim: 20.1 cm

CONDITION: upper part of both spout at top of handle broken off; minor chipping round base; otherwise apparently good.

PROVENANCE: Dupont Auberville collection; Laniel collection; Jameson collection; sale, *Anciennes faïences de Rouen,* Paris (Galliéra), 18 June 1964, lot 50; Boucheron collection; sale, *Collection d'un amateur: Rouen 1680–1740,* Sotheby's, Paris, 18 June 2008, lot 561; Christophe Perlès, Paris; from whom acquired by Mr Knafel before 2016. Label on the base for the Paris 1932 exhibition.

BIBLIOGRAPHY: Paris 1932, no.337; Chompret et al. 1933–5, IV, Rouen, pl.117B; Perlès 2014, no.46; Perlès 2016, no.55.

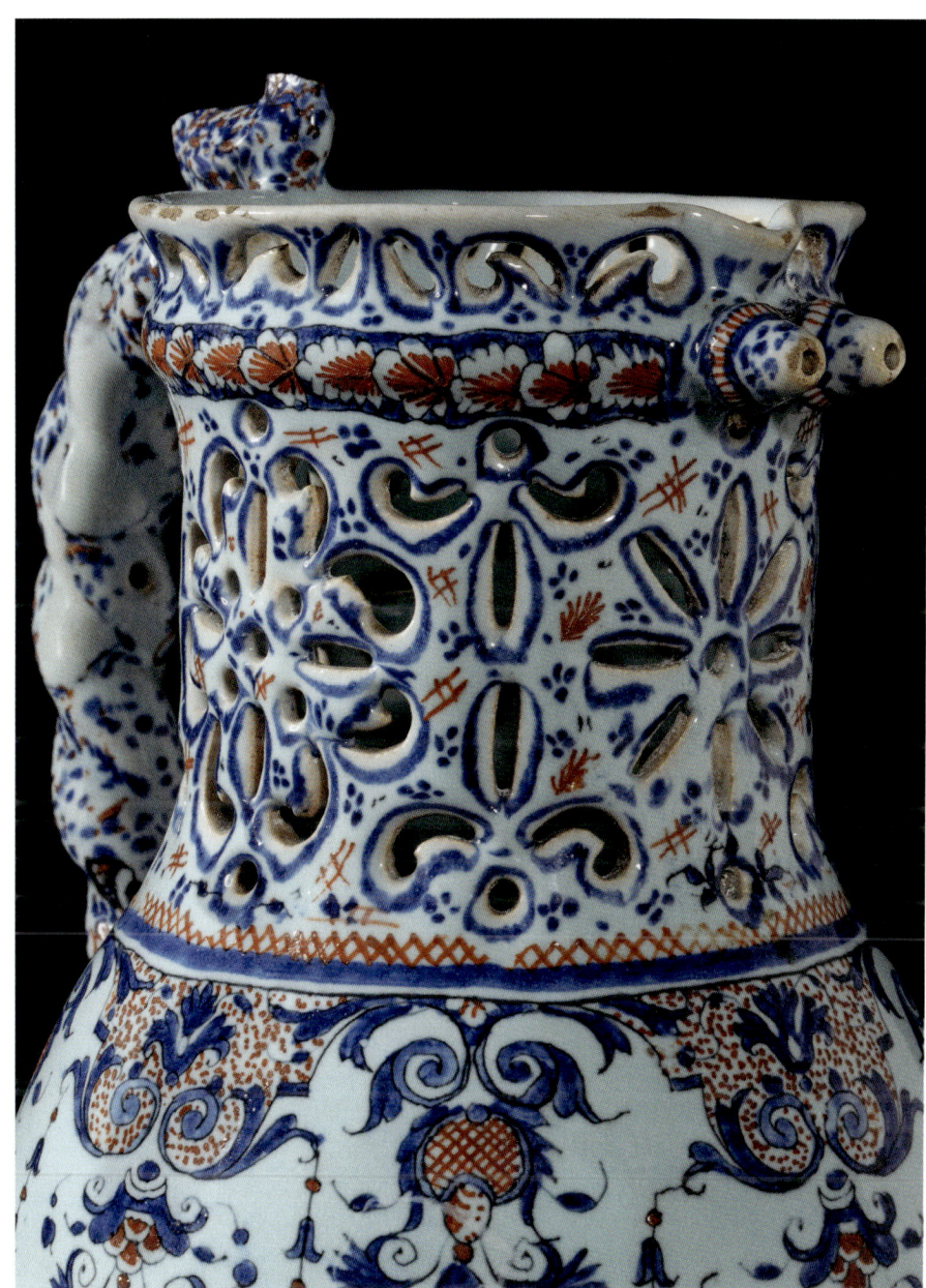

Pear-shaped jug, tin-glazed inside and out and beneath the hollow base; slightly flaring at the rim; the upper part pierced. The twisted handle has a bird finial (partly broken off) and both are hollow, connecting with a hollow tube running round below the rim; from this tube two spouts project under the small lip. Decorated in shades of blue and red with characteristic Rouen decoration, including scrolls and lambrequins.

Puzzle jugs like this – which can only be drunk from by one of the spouts if you know how to block both the others and one or more hidden holes – have a long tradition in European ceramics, from medieval pottery and Italian Renaissance maiolica onwards.[163] This is one of the finest Rouen examples.

163 For Italian Renaissance puzzle jugs and cups, see Hollein et al. 2022, no.35; for English delftware examples, Ray 1968, no.114.

28

Bust, Mark Antony

Rouen, *c*.1725–40
Bequeathed by Sidney R. Knafel, received 2023, WA2023.141.

Tin-glazed earthenware. The interior is tin-glazed with some patches of bare clay.

Height: 35.5 cm

CONDITION: minor restorations.

PROVENANCE: Anonymous sale, Binoche and Giquello, Hôtel Drouot, Paris, 21 October 2013, lot 117; Christophe Perlès, Paris; from whom acquired by Mr Knafel before 2016.

BIBLIOGRAPHY: Perlès 2016, no.71.

Well-modelled bust of a Roman-style figure in armour, crowned, looking to his right. The armour on his right shoulder is formed as a lion mask, the left shoulder is covered with drapery. Part of the top of his head is left unglazed. The front and sides of the flaring, hollow base are painted with characteristic Rouen floral decoration enclosing lobed compartments, the front one containing an elaborate interlaced monogram incorporating the letters *P*, *C*, and perhaps *J*. Simple gadroons adorn the base. The upper part is linked to the base at the back by a slender strut.

Rouen potters in the decades after 1700 produced the finest large-scale polychrome sculpture in tin-glazed earthenware made in Europe since the Della Robbia workshop in the fifteenth and sixteenth centuries.

The identification of this crowned figure as the Roman soldier Mark Antony (who was never a king or emperor) is based on the existence in the Musée municipal at Louviers, France, of a slightly smaller version of the same figure paired with a Cleopatra, Antony's lover, identified by a serpent at her breast.[164] Some other versions of both Antony and Cleopatra are identified on the plinths by monograms moulded in relief of *MA* interlaced with *C*. There are considerable variations both in size, facture, and palette between the various versions.[165] It has been suggested that the earliest versions of the couple were made at Nevers and that the models were then copied at Rouen.[166]

164   Rouen 1999, p.97, nos 22–3. We are indebted to Cédric Pannevel, Director of the Louviers museum, for courteous information on these and related busts.
165   Some versions of the Mark Antony are larger, 53–5 cm high.
166   For various versions of both him and her, see Rouen 1999, pp.90–97.

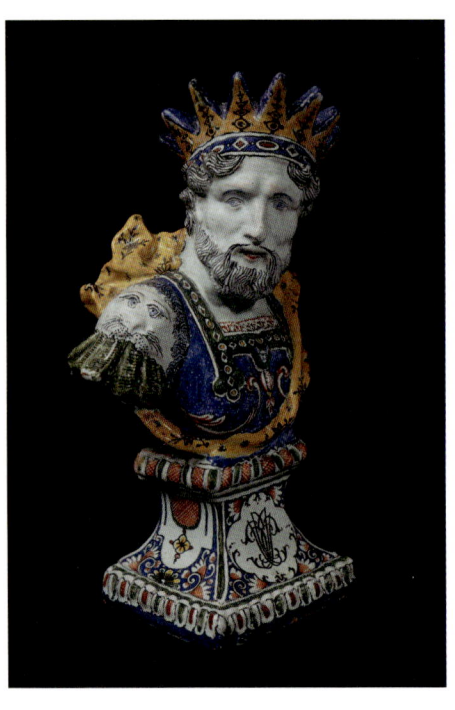
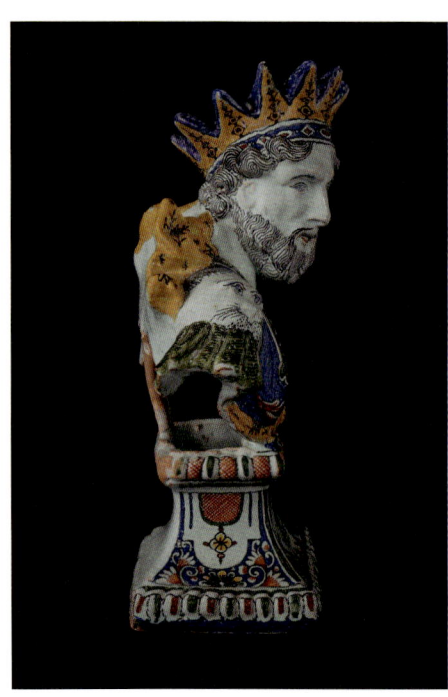
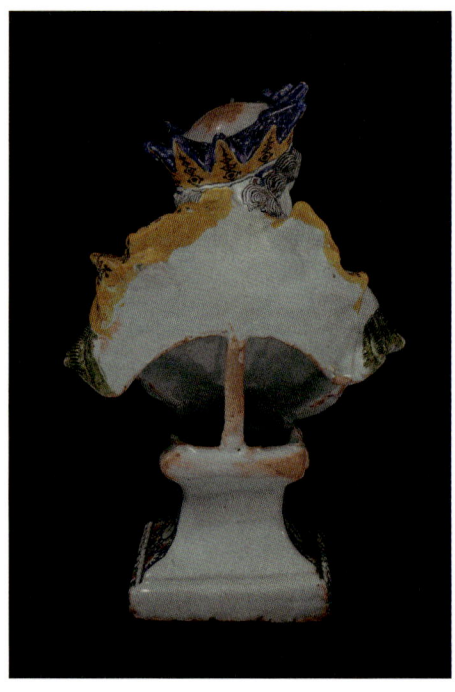

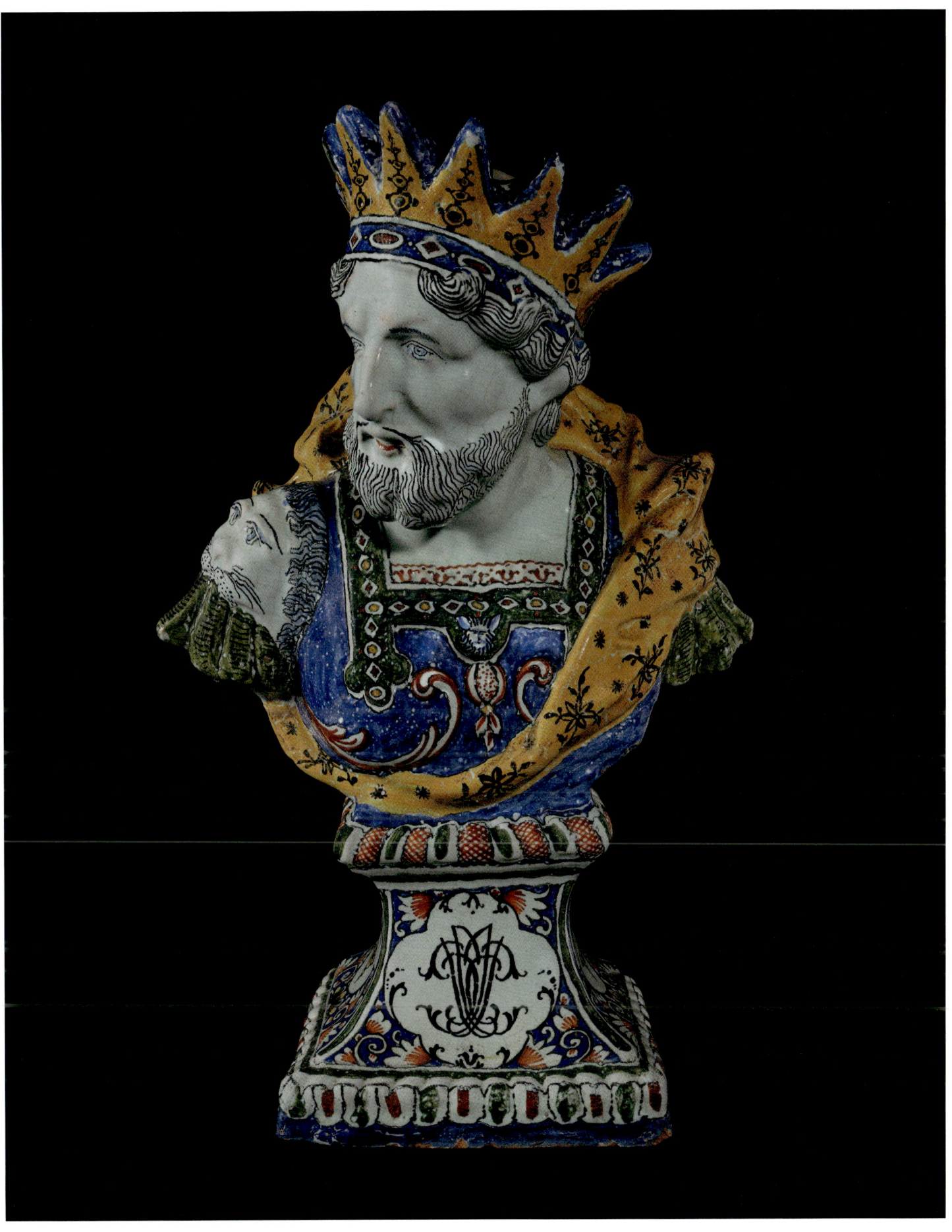

29

Octagonal tray with Chinese figures

Rouen, *c.*1730–50
Bequeathed by Sidney R. Knafel, received 2023, WA2023.142.

Tin-glazed front and back.

26.2 × 40 cm

CONDITION: apparently good.

PROVENANCE: stated to be from the Loisel collection, sold in 1891; Papillon collection; sale, Paris (Drouot), 10–12 March 1919, lot 228; Jacques Guerlain (in 1932); Christian Bonnin, Béziers; Christophe Perlès, Paris; from whom acquired by Mr Knafel 2014. Papillon, Guerlain, and Bonnin labels on the back; also painted numbers *N°. 275* and *54 PAS.*

BIBLIOGRAPHY: Paris 1932, no.644; Chompret et al. 1933–5, IV, Rouen, pl.133B; Perlès 2014, no.68; Perlès 2016, no.75.

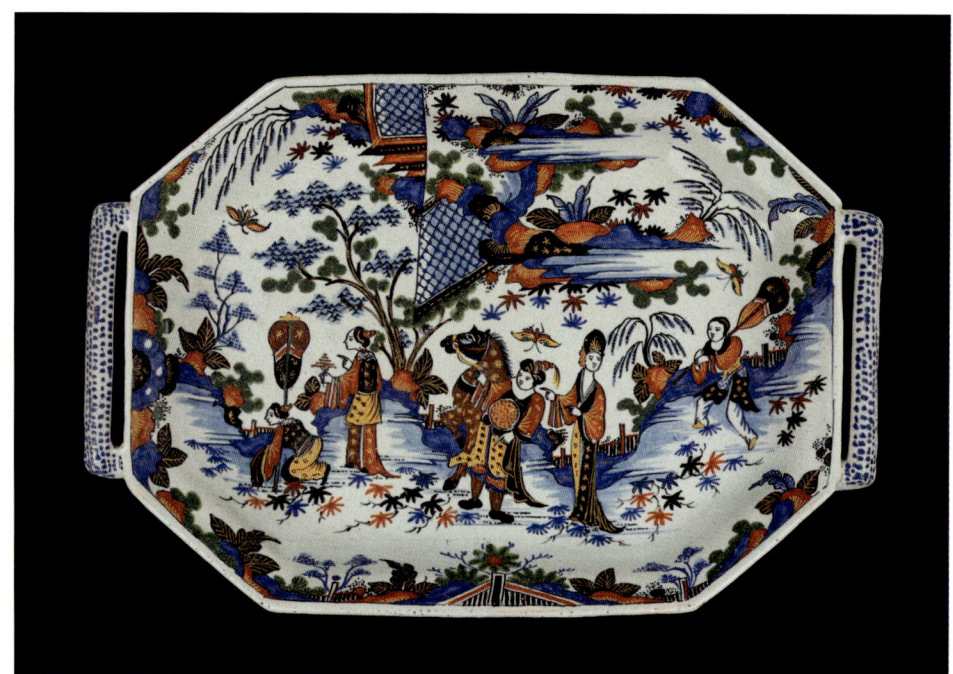

The octagonal tray has handles at each end and a pronounced foot-ring. Painted in colours, among which, blue and red are prominent, are chinoiserie figures, including a tall lady, other attendant ladies, and a figure holding a demi-horse, as well as trees, plants, and insects.[167] On the underside, a band of simple plant ornament runs round below the edge.

The ornament is known to French specialists as *aux chinois noirs*.[168] The tall lady on Chinese porcelain and its European derivatives has been known to generations of collectors in the English-speaking world as a 'long Eliza'. There are Chinese prototypes from the reigns of the emperors Kangxi (1662–1722) and Yongzheng (r.1722–35) in both blue and white and polychrome.[169]

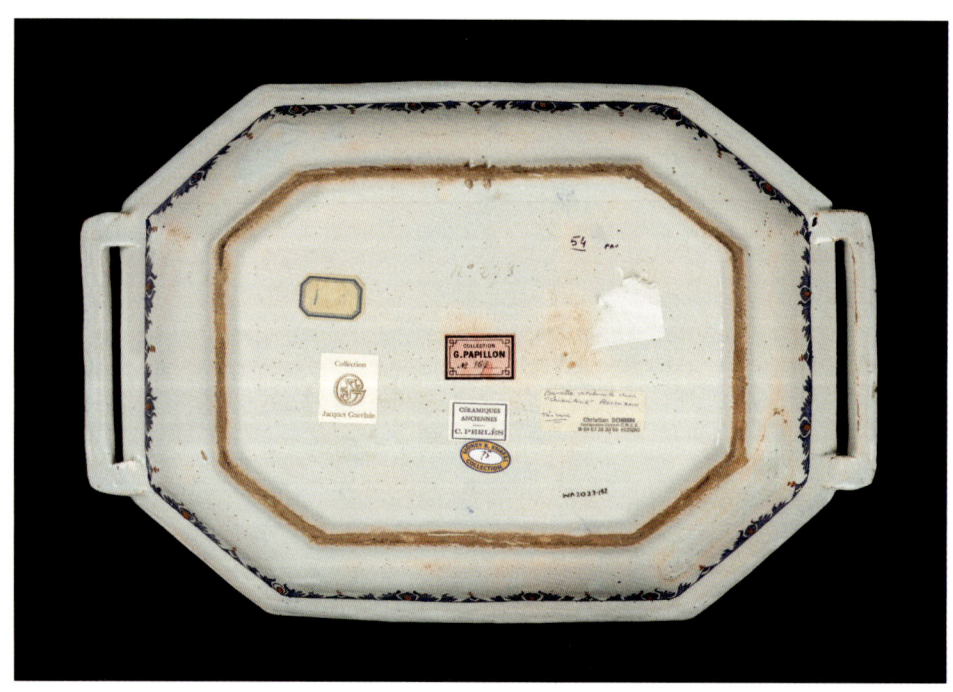

167 Described in Perlès 2016, no.75, as a warrior.
168 For closely analogous decoration, see Chompret et al. 1933–5, IV, Rouen, pls 131–3; Grandjean 2001, p.125. For a Chinese prototype, see Du Boulay 1984, pp.266–7, no.1.
169 We thank Shelagh Vainker for comments on the relationship between chinoiserie faience and Chinese porcelain.

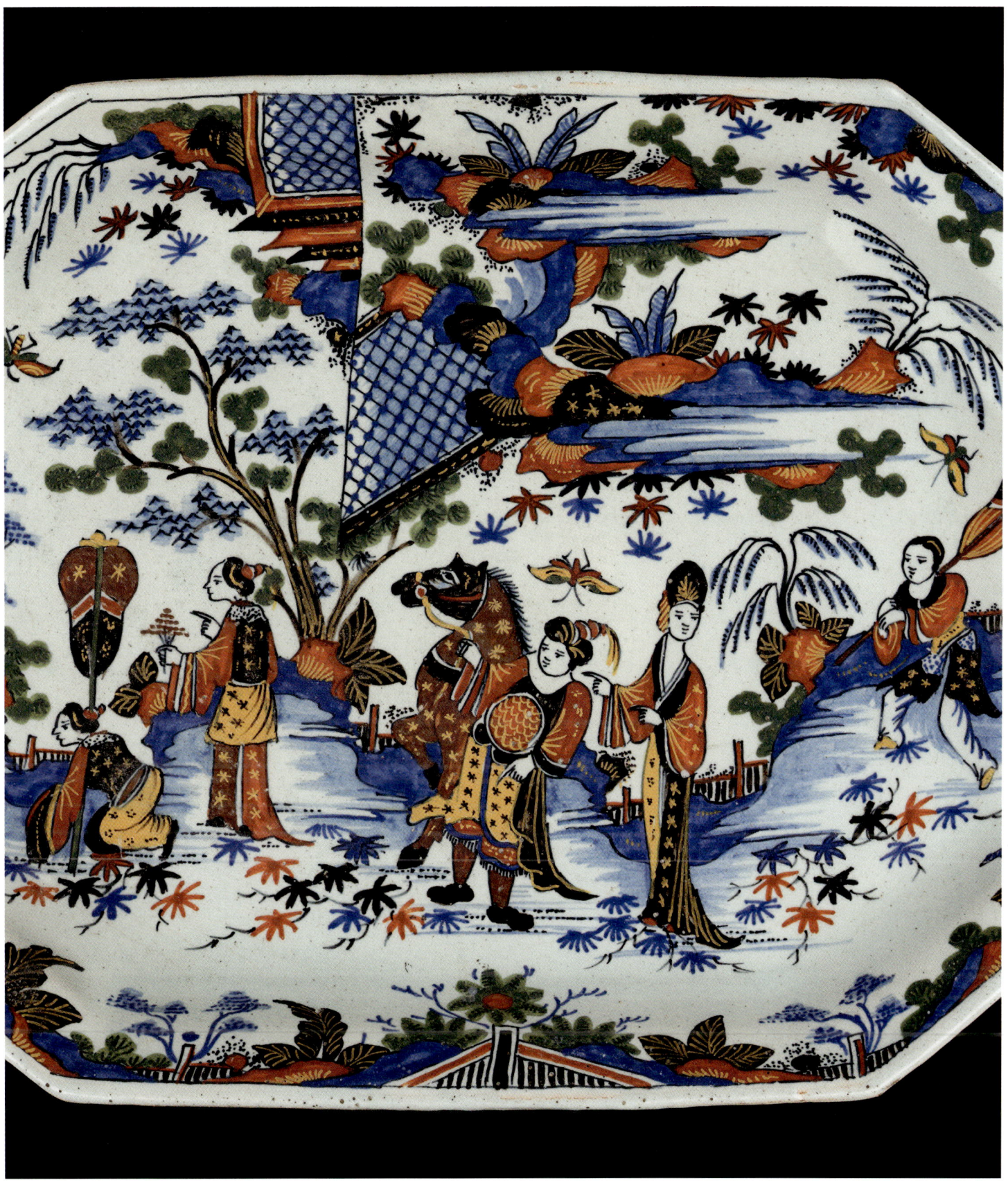

30

Dish

Rouen, workshop of Jean-Baptiste Guillibaud, *c.*1720–39
Bequeathed by Sidney R. Knafel, received 2023, WA2023.143.

Tin-glazed front and back.

30.5 × 42.2 cm

CONDITION: some cracking to glaze.

PROVENANCE: Galerie Nicolier, Paris; Boucheron collection; sale, Sotheby's, Paris, 18 June 2008, lot 564; Galerie Vandermeersch, Paris; from whom acquired by Mr Knafel. Nicolier and Vandermeersch labels on the back.

BIBLIOGRAPHY: Perlès 2016, no.77.

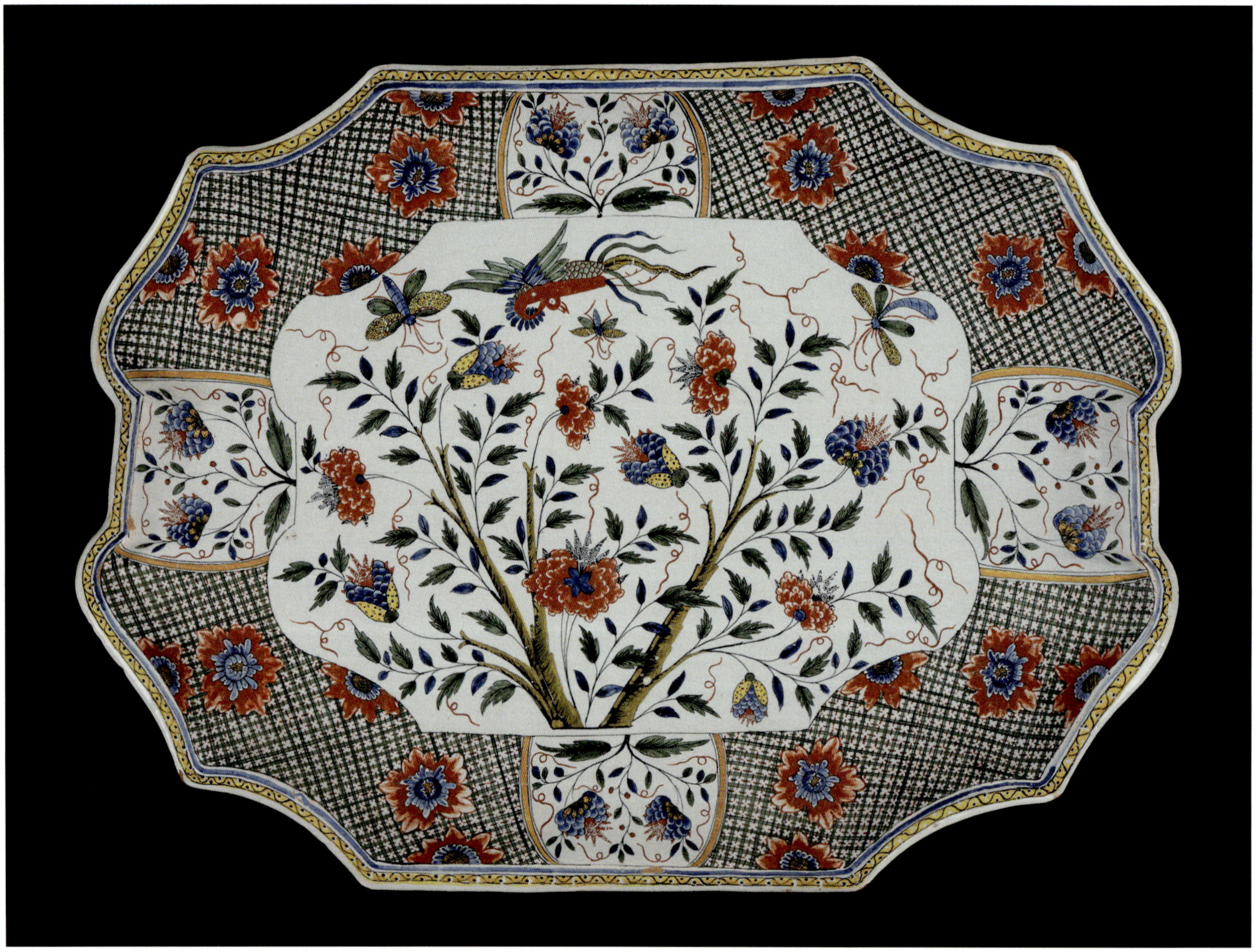

Lobed dish on low, spreading foot. The centre is painted with a large spray of flowers (possibly peonies or chrysanthemums) with a fabulous bird and insects. Around this is a border of trellis panels, with rosettes alternating with panels of flowers. Painted on the back, which has a patch wiped clean of glaze in the centre, is a mark that looks

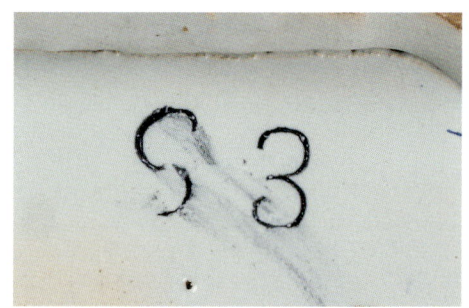

like *G3* or *S3*, but may in fact be intended for *GB*, for Guillibaud. Jean-Baptiste Guillibaud (1687–1739) ran a successful workshop in Rue Tous-Vents, Rouen.

A similarly decorated dish of the same shape in the the Musée de la Céramique in Rouen has a similar *G3/GB* mark and also the full signature of Guillibaud. It bears the arms of Charles-François II, Duke of Montmorency-Luxembourg,

who made a formal entry into Rouen, having succeeded his father as Governor of Normandy, in 1728.[170]

The floral ornament owes something to Chinese porcelain, but the shape and border are not from Chinese models. In a pleasing circularity, a Rouen dish of this sort was closely copied by Chinese porcelain makers (fig.13).[171]

170 For this dish and the set of which it formed a part, see Grandjean 2001, pp.116–17; see also the up-to-date account of Rouen faience in Leprince 2020, especially no.18.

171 The tureen and stand illustrated were sold at Sotheby's New York 22 January 2016 lot 1106. Thanks to Margi Schwartz for the image. See also Du Boulay 1984, p.261, no.10 (Christie's, London, 31 March 1969, lot 25).

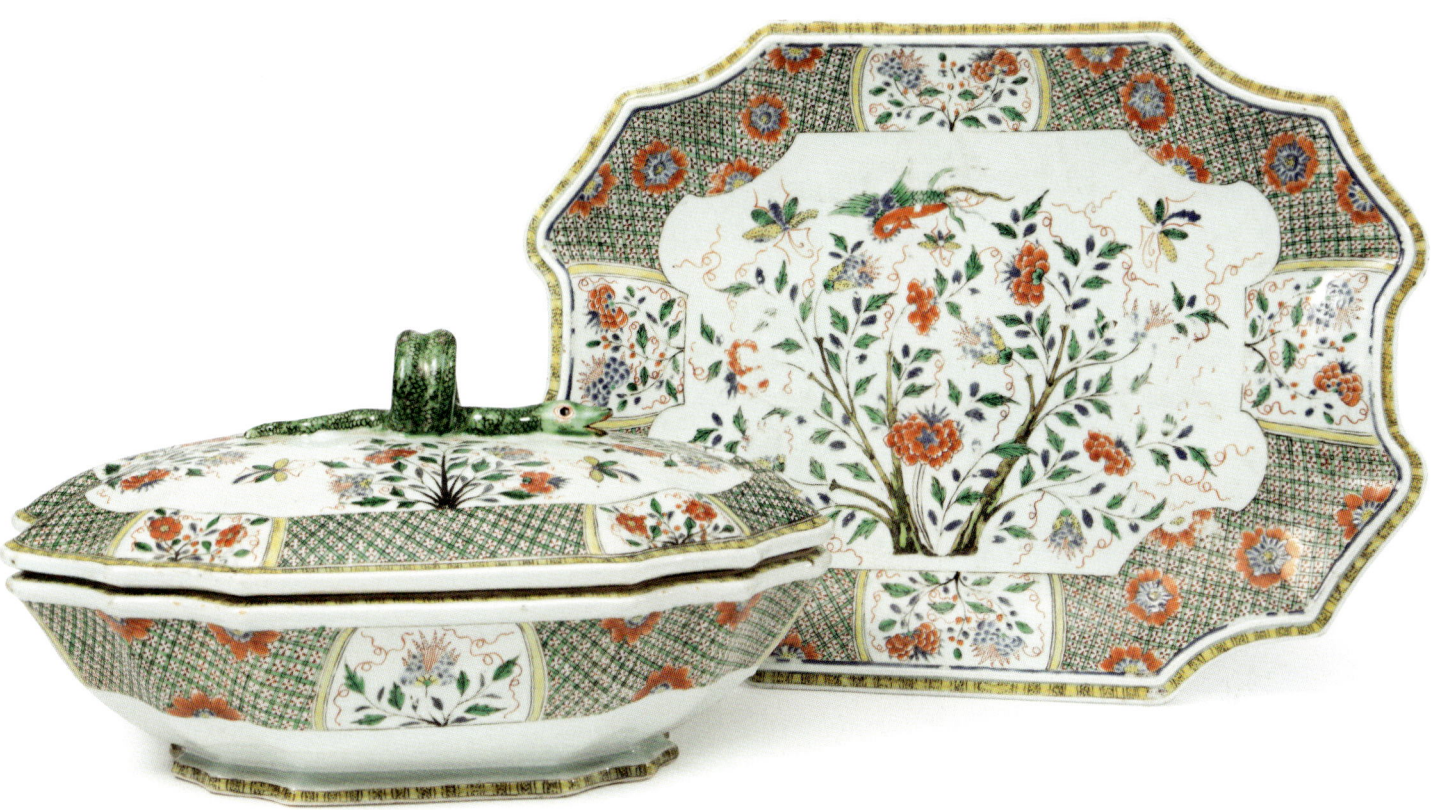

Fig.13 Chinese porcelain tureen and stand copying Rouen faience. Photo: Courtesy Sotheby's

31

Bowl with Chinese figures

Rouen, *c.*1730–40
Presented by Londa Weisman from the collection of Sidney Knafel, WA2023.155.

Tin-glazed front and back.

Diameter: 27.2 cm; depth: 7.6 cm

CONDITION: some wear and chipping.

PROVENANCE: Christophe Perlès, Paris. Painted on the underside, but worn, *500* (a price?) and perhaps *S50*.

BIBLIOGRAPHY: Perlès 2014, no.80; Perlès 2016, no.84.

Deep, lobed bowl on thick foot-ring. Painted with two chinoiserie figures with parasols, a man rowing a boat, a large exotic insect, trees, and ornamental panels. On the exterior, in green, are plant sprays and an unidentified mark, perhaps a painter's signature, *W Fn*.

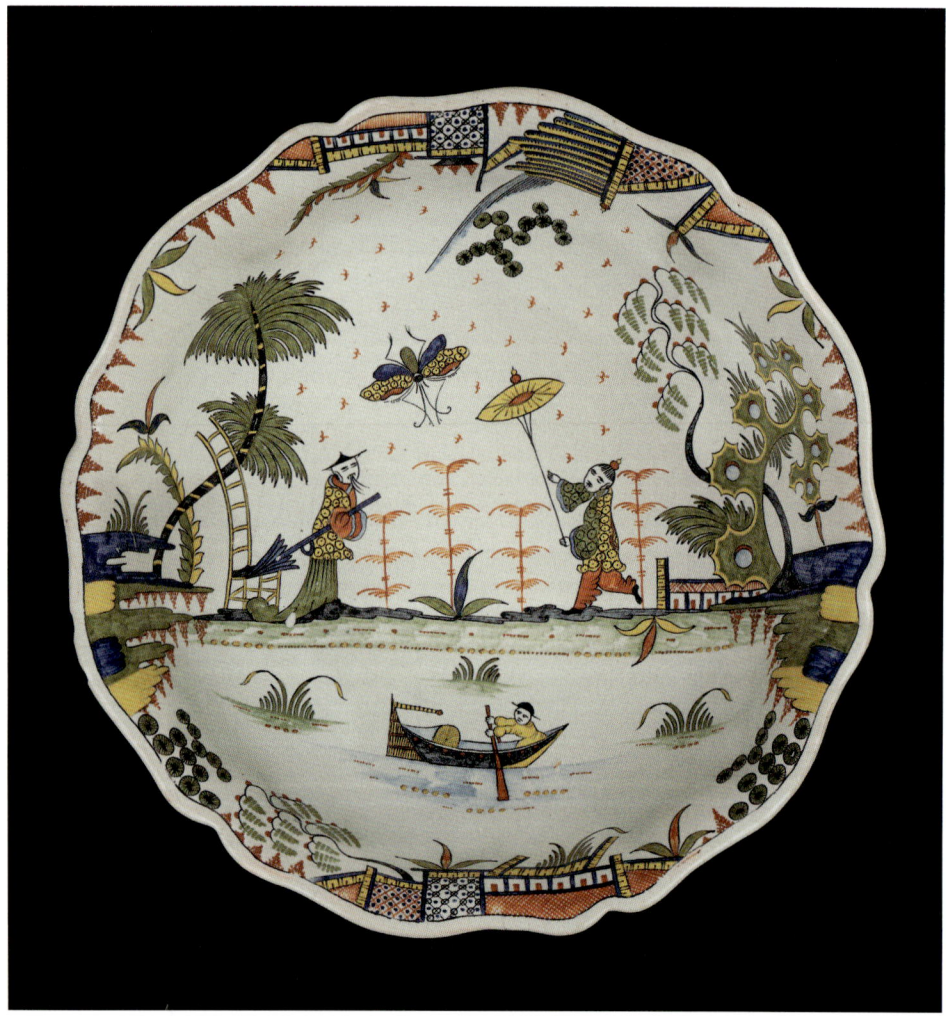

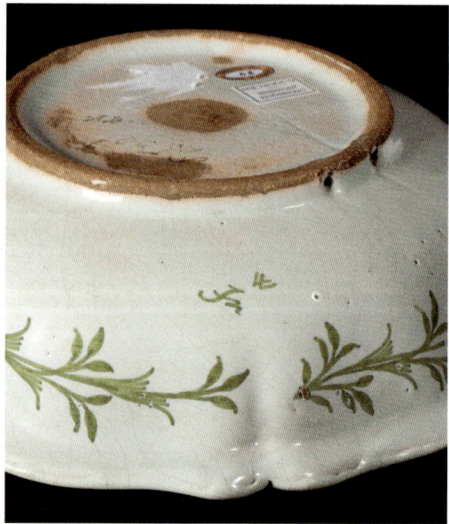

32

Platter

Moustiers, Clérissy workshop, *c.*1730
Bequeathed by Sidney R. Knafel, received 2023, WA2023.144.

Tin-glazed front and back.

26.5 × 37 cm

CONDITION: wear and chipping to the edge.

PROVENANCE: Reynaud collection; sale, *Faïences anciennes*, Paris (Drouot), 31 March 1971, lot 59 (one of two); sale, Versailles, 17 July 1978, lot 215 (one of two); sale, Étude Tajan, Paris (Drouot), 10 March 1997, lot 263 (with the companion platter, now part of the Knafel bequest to the Detroit Institute of Arts). Labels on the back include a Reynaud collection label and ones recording its display at the 1952 and 1957 exhibitions.

BIBLIOGRAPHY: Aix 1952, no.33; Nyon 1957, no.489; Perlès 2016, no.91B.

The platter is painted in shades of blue. In a central cartouche with an ornamental edge, an infant Bacchus is seated on a barrel and holding a wine-cup. Near him are three winged putti, also holding wine-cups. An ornamental border runs round the edge. The reverse is undecorated.

A companion platter, now in the Detroit Institute of Arts, has Mercury and a shepherd.[172]

Moustiers-Sainte Marie is a small town in a mountainous part of Provence.[173] The faience industry there was established by Pierre Clérissy who set up a workshop in 1679, making mainly monochrome blue wares.

172   Perlès 2016, no.91A.
173   See Chompret et al. 1933–5, II, Moustiers; Mompeut 1980; Collard-Moniotte 1988; Julien 1991.

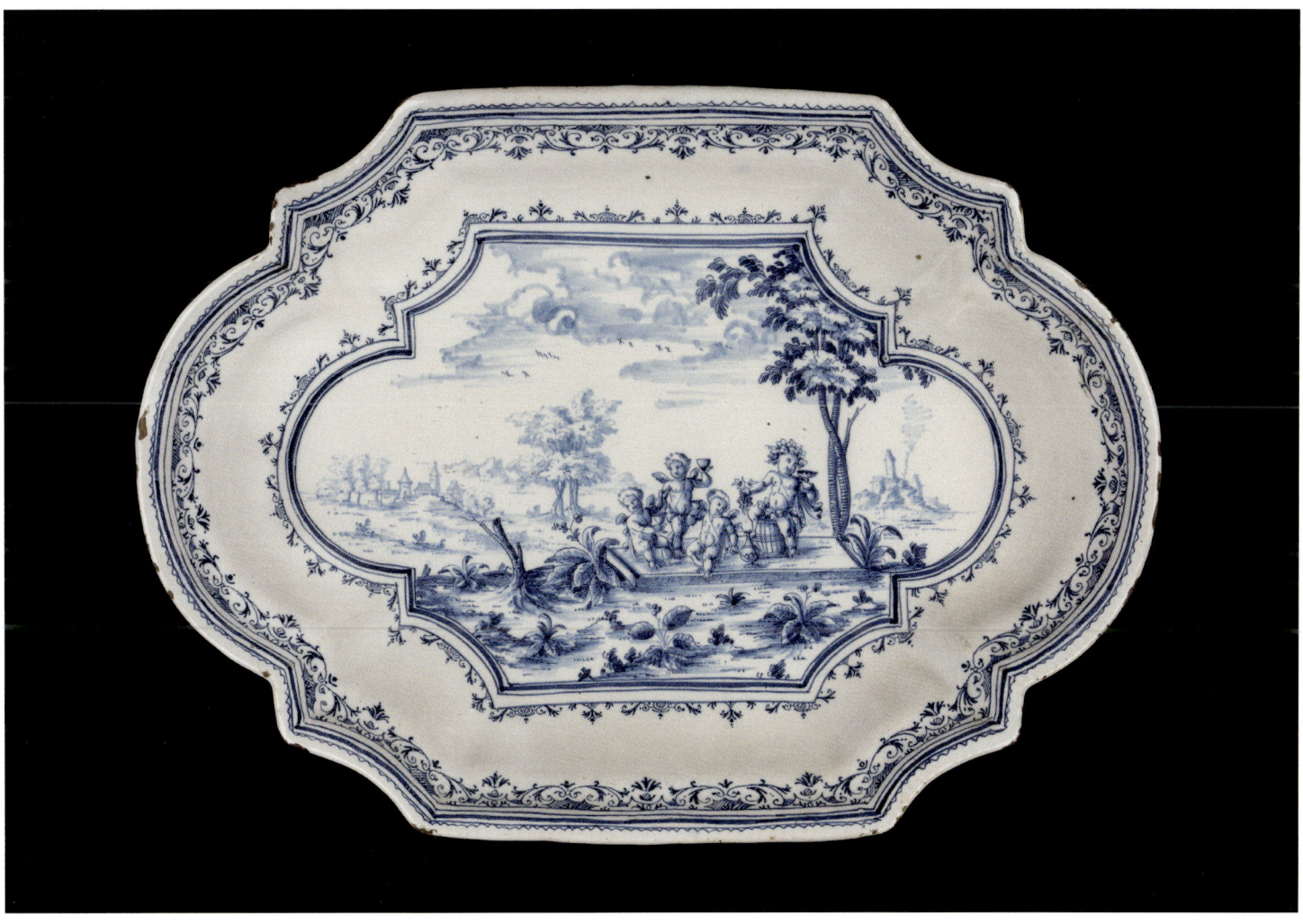

33

Armorial plate

Moustiers, probably Clérissy workshop, *c.*1750–60
Bequeathed by Sidney R. Knafel, received 2023, WA2023.147.

Tin-glazed front and back.

Diameter: 25.4 cm

CONDITION: good; minor chipping.

PROVENANCE: A. Chevet collection; sale, Paris (Drouot), 5–6 November 1951, lot 243; sale *Collection Monsieur et Madame S.*, Étude Tajan, Paris, 14 June 1995, lot 116 (one of two); acquired by Mr Knafel through Michel-Witold Gierzod, from Voltaire Antiquités-Vandermeersch AS, Paris, 1999 (with another, now part of the Knafel bequest to the Detroit Institute of Arts).[174]

BIBLIOGRAPHY: Perlès 2016, no.105A

The plate, with slightly scalloped outline, is painted with three main figures: a standing donkey playing a tambourine, a black man in an elaborate headdress and long robe, and an exotic bird. Three floral swags spread from the border to the well of the plate. At the top are two shields of arms conjoined beneath a coronet. The back is undecorated.

The arms have been identified as those of François Deschamps and his wife Marie Reine Constant.[175] About a dozen other pieces of the service are recorded, including another plate from the Knafel collection which is now in the Detroit Institute of Arts.

The series is attributed by French specialists to the Clérissy workshop, but the design comes close to pieces marked as made in the Olérys-Laugier workshop, including no.**36**.[176]

174 Perlès 2016, no.105B.
175 Perlès 2016, pp.248–9. A different identification of the right-hand (sinister) shield as being the arms of the Gilli or Gilly family, originally of Languedoc, is given by Collard-Moniotte 1988, p.157, where others with the arms are listed. A larger platter from the set was given by Mr Knafel to the Frick Collection: Perlès 2016, no.104.
176 See also Chompret et al. 1933–5, II, Moustiers, pl.21, for another similar example marked as made by Olérys-Laugier.

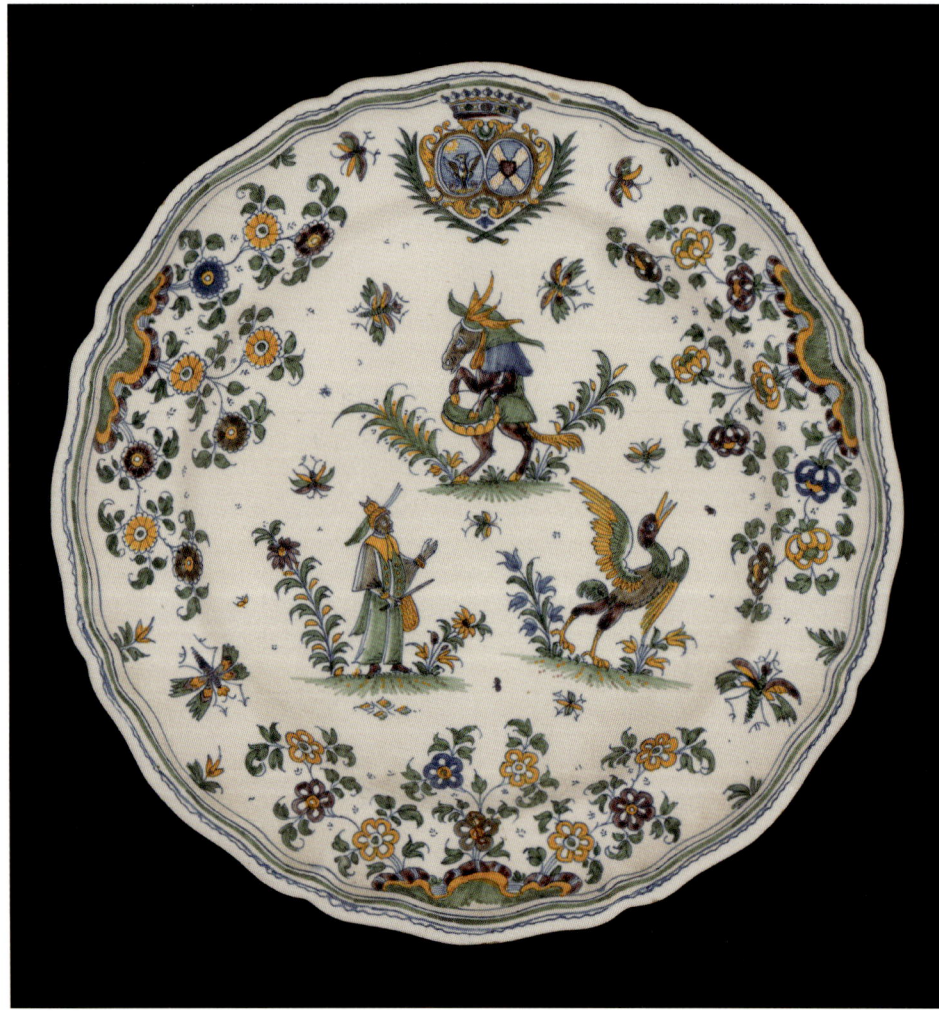

34

Plate

Moustiers, Olérys-Laugier workshop, *c.*1750
Bequeathed by Sidney R. Knafel, received 2023, WA2023.148.

Tin-glazed front and back.

Diameter: 21.8 cm

CONDITION: good.

PROVENANCE: Galerie Verneuil Bac, Paris; from whom acquired by Mr Knafel, 1998.

BIBLIOGRAPHY: Perlès 2016, no.109.

The plate is of scalloped outline and has no foot-ring. Painted in slightly greenish manganese with a naked male and female couple, perhaps Adam and Eve or possibly a wild man and his consort, together with exotic birds, a flying insect, and floral sprays. On the back is a mark *G* with *OL* in monogram and +… below. The *G* (which resembles an *S*) is probably a painter's mark for Pierre Giroud or [Jean-]François Guiot.[177]

For the Olérys-Laugier workshop see no.**35**.

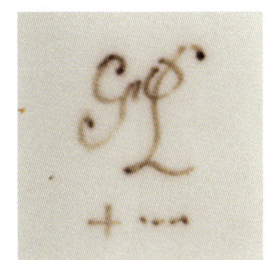

177 Collard-Moniotte 1988, pp.106, 222.

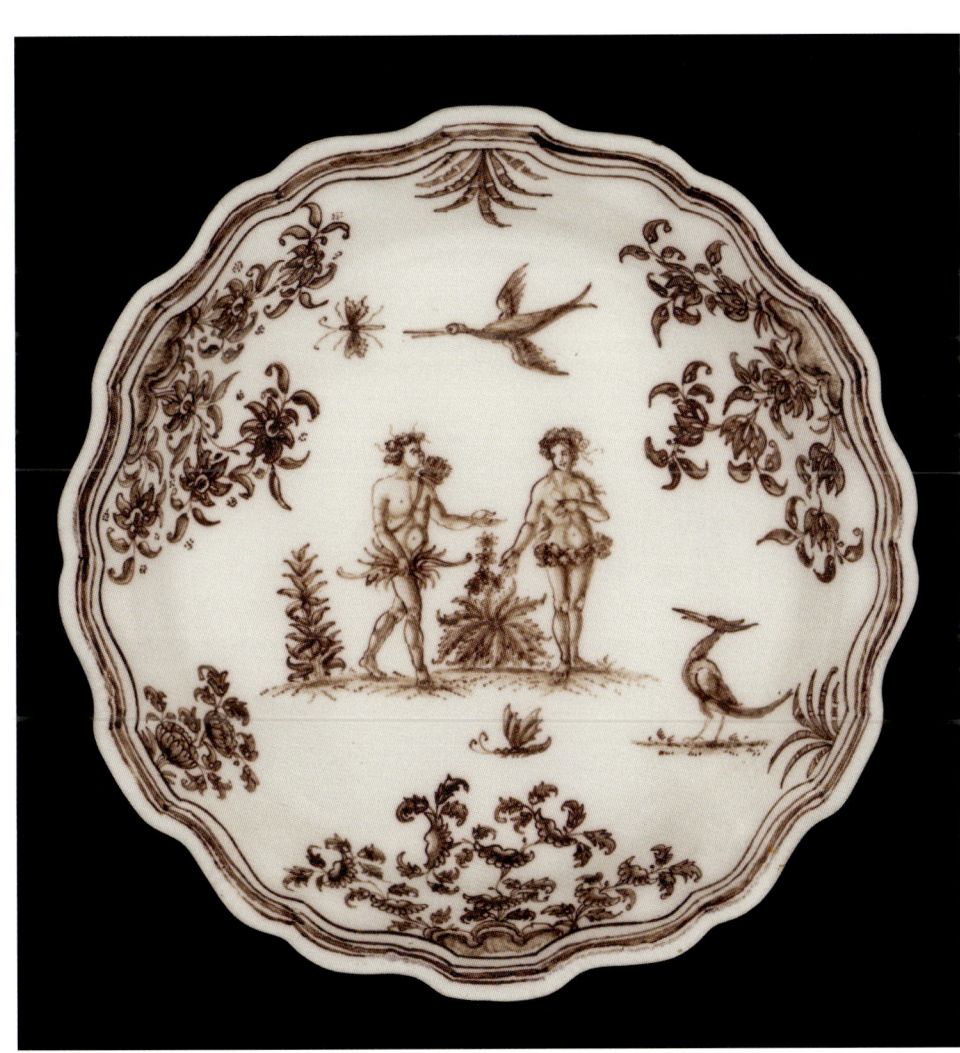

35

Bowl (*écuelle*) with stand and cover

Moustiers, Olérys-Laugier workshop, painting by Jean-François Pelloquin, *c.*1750
Bequeathed by Sidney R. Knafel, received 2023, WA2023.145.

Tin-glazed outside and in.

Width of bowl to handles: 26.5 cm

Diameter of plate: 24.7 cm

CONDITION: apparently good.

PROVENANCE: Gaudry collection; Bape collection; private collection, Canada; acquired by Mr Knafel through Michel-Witold Gierzod, from Voltaire Antiquités-Vandermeersch AS, Paris, 1999.

BIBLIOGRAPHY: Godefroy 1922, no.202; Perlès 2016, no.99.

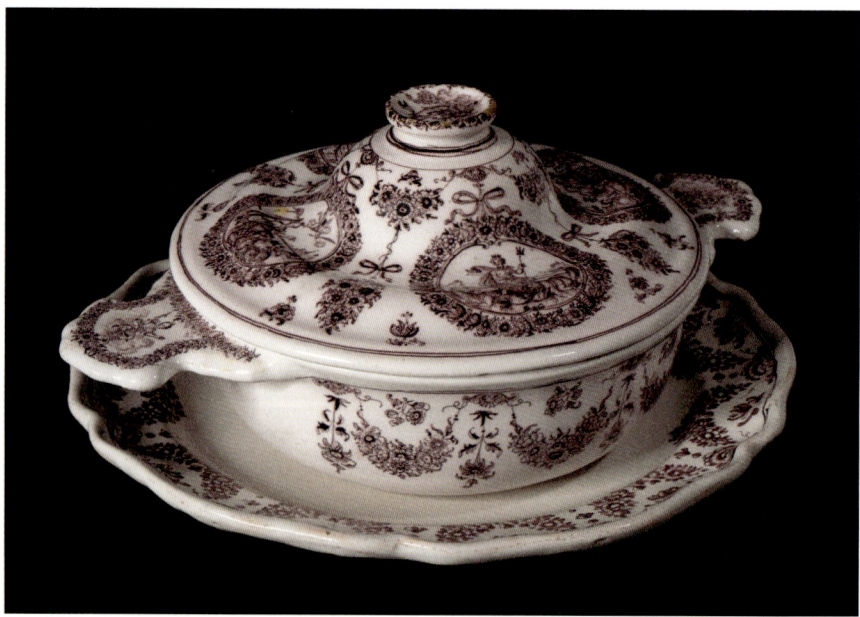

The bowl, cover, and stand are finely painted in manganese, in a manner that recalls the best painting on German or Austrian porcelain, with occasional touches of yellow-gold. On the finial of the cover is Juno(?). In wreathed roundels below, between pendent swags, are Greco-Roman deities: Neptune, Amphitrite or Venus(?) with Cupid, Apollo(?), and Bacchus with Ceres. On the handles of the bowl are Apollo and Diana; around the exterior are more pendent swags. The stand is painted with a flower spray and swags. Painted beneath the cover is *OL* in monogram for Olérys and Laugier; and *P* for the painter Jean-François Pelloquin (d.1775).[178]

After Clérissy, the other pre-eminent Moustiers workshop was set up in 1738–9 by Joseph Olérys, partly financed by his brother-in-law, Jean-Baptiste Laugier. Olérys had previously worked in Spain, helping establish the Alcora manufacture. At Moustiers, he popularised faience painting in polychrome, with products sometimes resembling Alcora wares.

178   See Collard-Moniotte 1988, nos 79, 80 and p.222.

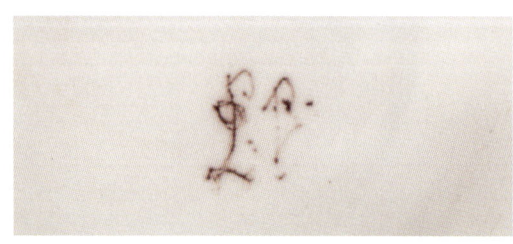

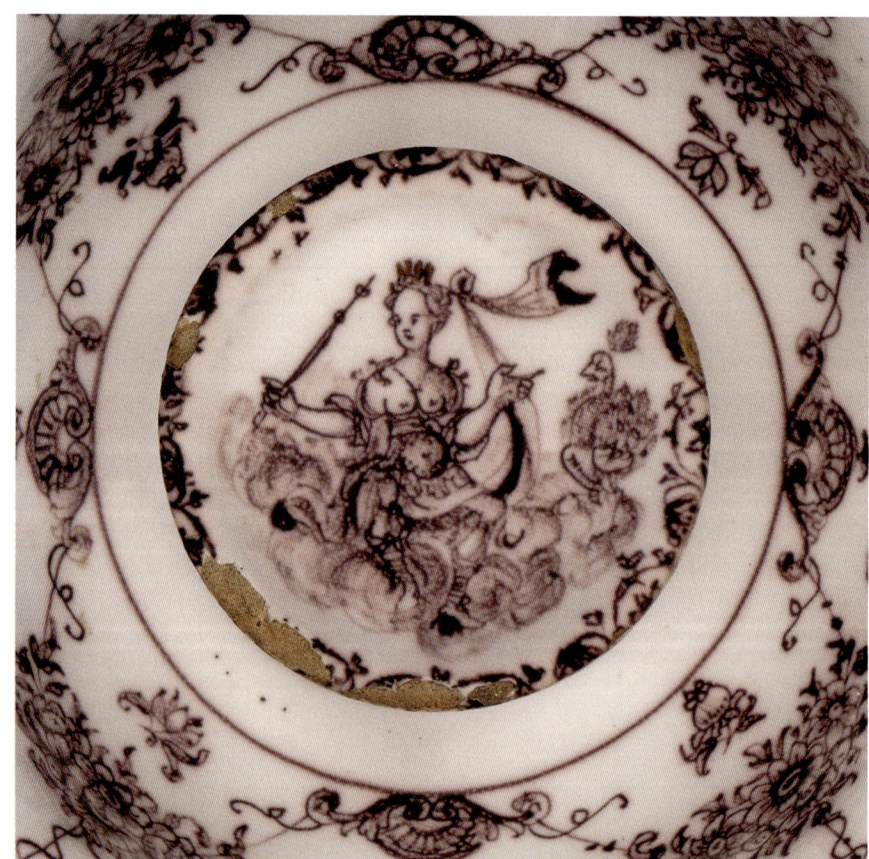

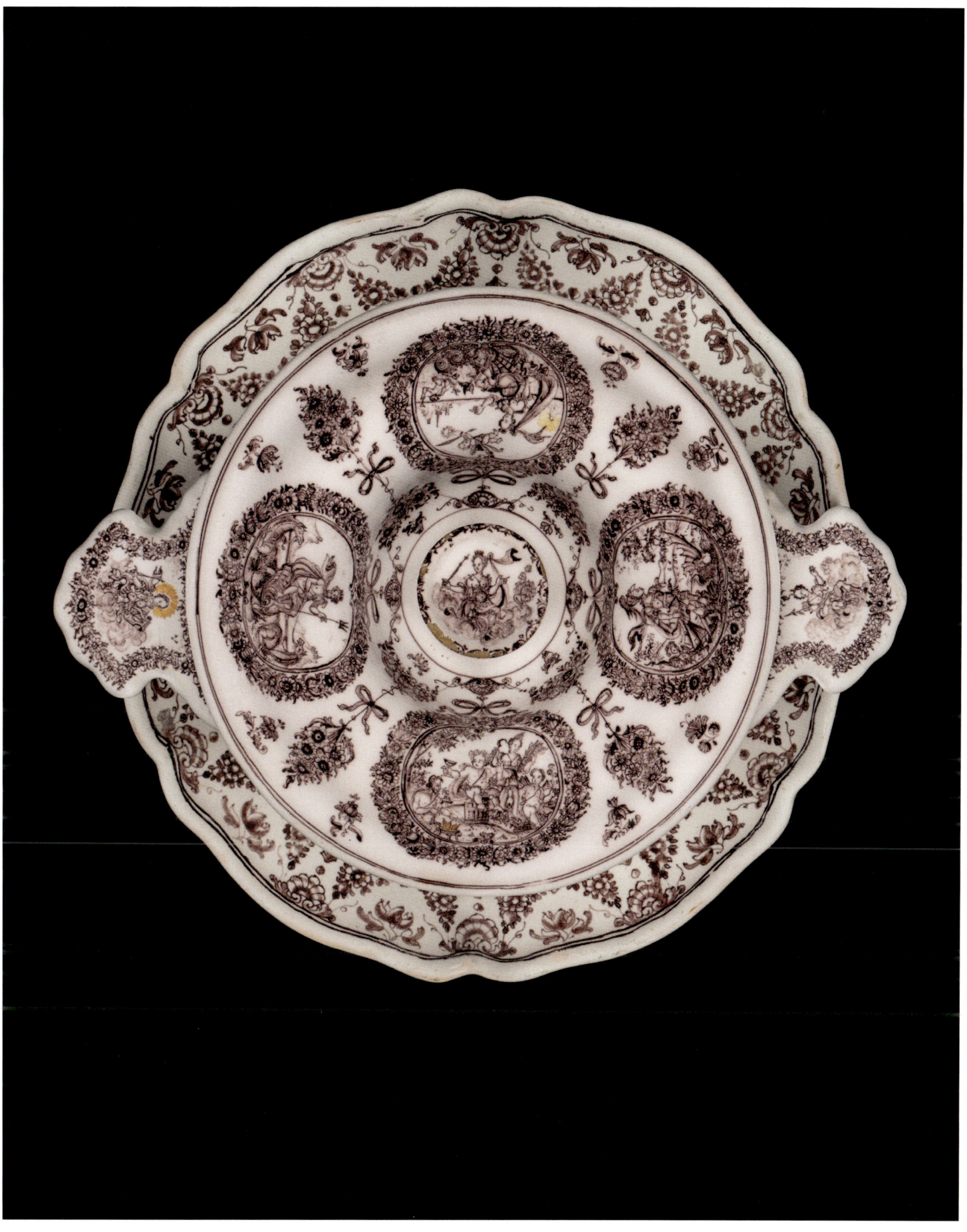

36

Dish

Moustiers, Olérys-Laugier workshop, *c.*1750
Bequeathed by Sidney R. Knafel, received 2023, WA2023.149.

Tin-glazed front and back; there is no foot-ring.

28 × 38.5 × 28 cm

CONDITION: good.

PROVENANCE: sale Paris (Drouot), 21 March 1977, lot 168, together with the companion dish; Galerie Verneuil Bac, Paris; from whom acquired by Mr Knafel, 2000, together with the companion dish, now part of the Knafel gift to the Frick Collection, New York.[179]

BIBLIOGRAPHY: Perlès 2016, no.112B.

This scalloped dish is painted in manganese and green with fantastical and comic figures between plant and flower sprays. In the centre, a donkey plays a keyboard instrument with a faun(?) holding up the music. At right, another donkey strums a bass viol(?); above are two dwarves, a dog, and insects. At left, two men ride a boar, one holding a banner, the other firing a gun. Below is a long-beaked bird and a sheep-like creature with long horns. On the back is the mark *OL* in monogram followed by what is probably an *f*.[180]

The figure of a donkey at the keyboard recurs on a polychrome plate given by Mr Knafel to the Frick Collection.[181]

179 Perlès 2016, no.112A.
180 For the mark, see Collard-Moniotte 1988, pp.152, 222. The last letter may possibly be a maker's mark, but is perhaps simply for *fecit*, 'made'.
181 Perlès 2016, no.106.

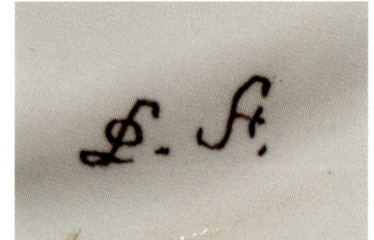

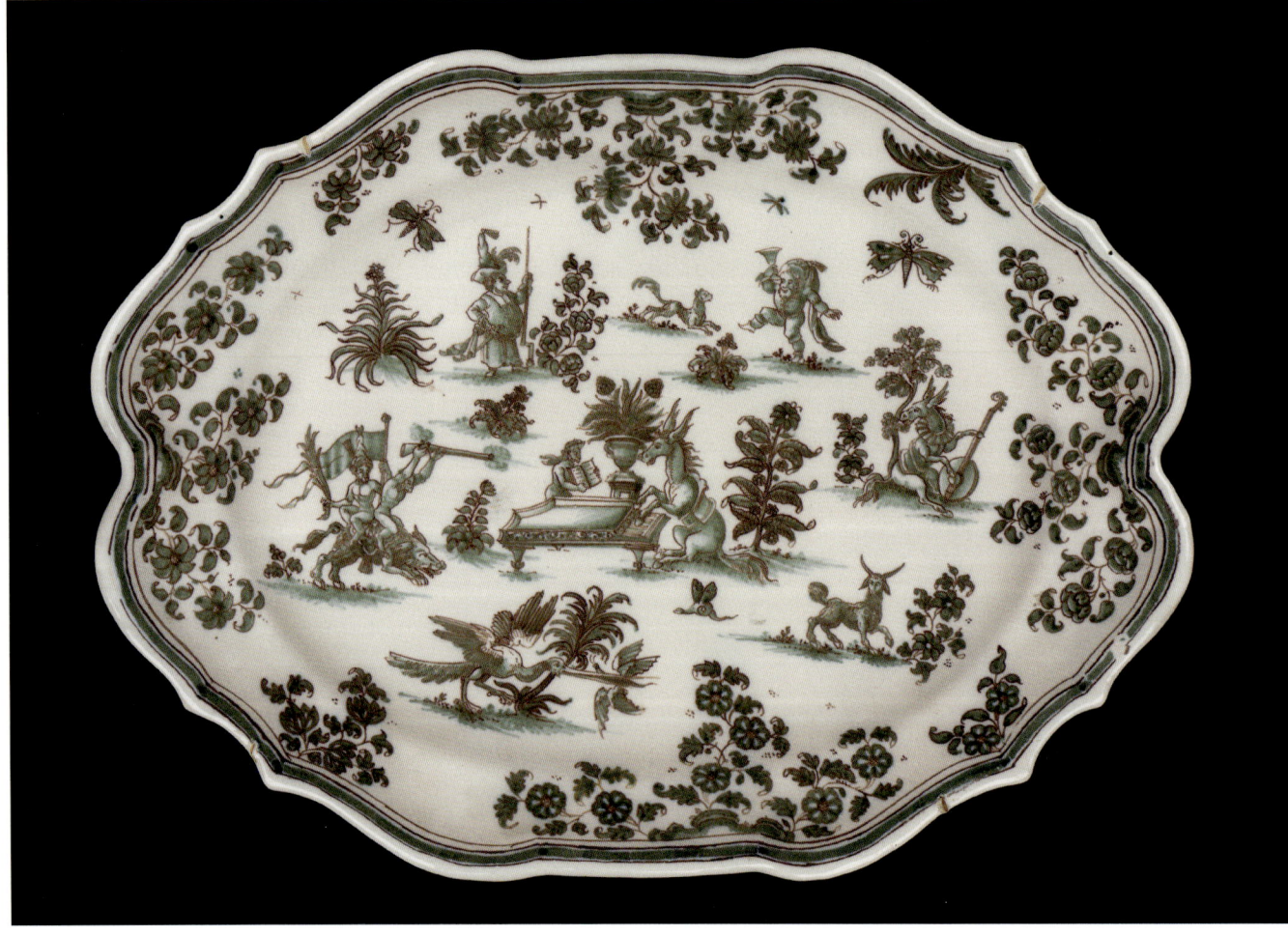

37

Plaque with a pastoral scene

Moustiers, *c.*1750
Bequeathed by Sidney R. Knafel, received 2023, WA2023.146.

Tin-glazed front and back.

21.8 (to top of finial) × 20 cm

CONDITION: good.

PROVENANCE: Perrot collection; sale, *Faïences anciennes françaises et étrangères*, Paris (Drouot), 20 March 1923, lot 60; sale Ader Trajan, Paris (Drouot), 25 October 1993, lot 86.

BIBLIOGRAPHY: Perlès 2016, no.103.

The plaque, which has an integral frame in three dimensions, is painted with an animated pastoral scene with a shepherd (Acis?) playing a flute accompanied by two other shepherds and various animals. An integral finial has the letter *A*.

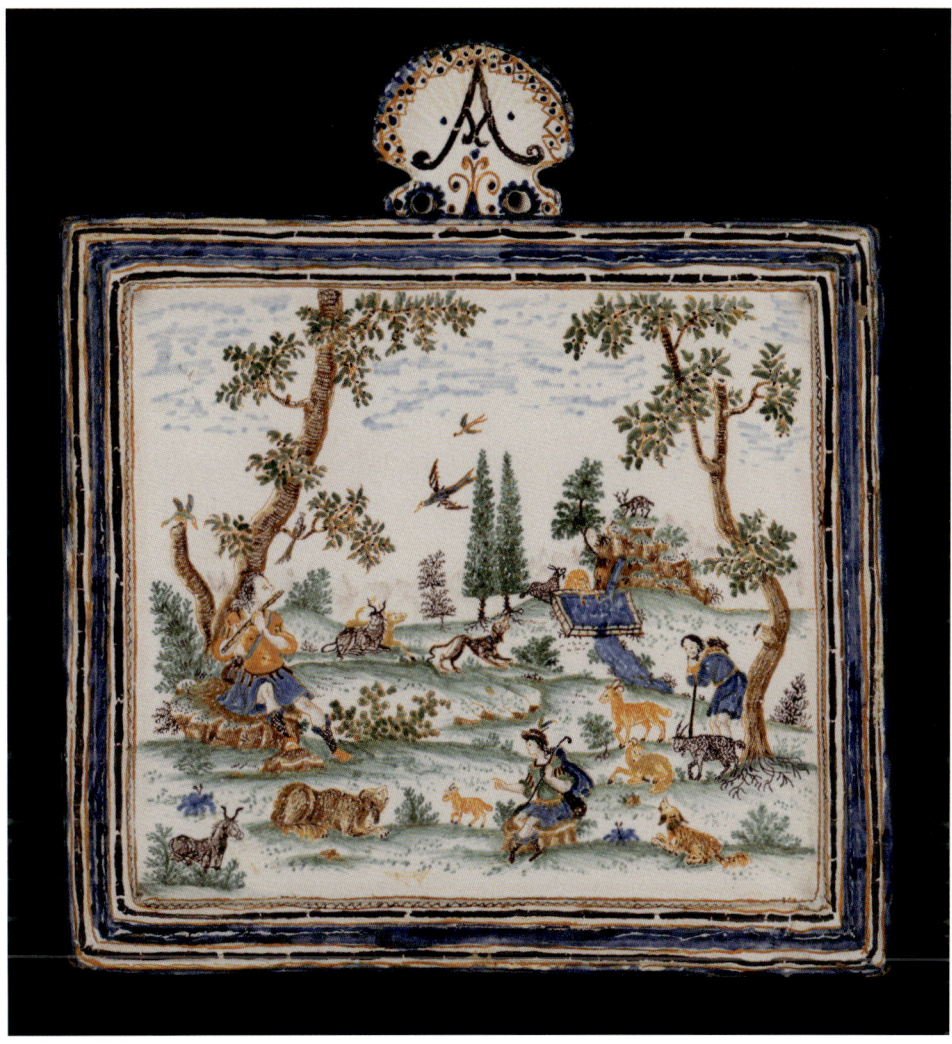

38

Bottle cooler

Marseille, Fauchier workshop, *c.*1730–40
Bequeathed by Sidney R. Knafel, received 2023, WA2023.151.

Tin-glazed overall.

Height: 19.4 cm

CONDITION: chipping at rim.

PROVENANCE: anonymous sale, *Faïences et porcelains …*, Paris (Drouot), 10 March 1999, lot 73 (with another, now part of the Knafel bequest to the Detroit Institute of Arts).[182]

BIBLIOGRAPHY: Perlès 2016, no.132A.

Bottle cooler on spreading foot, of a form derived from silver prototypes, with two lion-mask handles. The lower part is bulbous with vertical flutings; the upper part has recessed arched compartments. Round the lower part is a band of foliate scrollwork. Between the handles are two multi-lobed compartments fringed by foliate scrollwork. Within these compartments, on one side, painted in orange-yellow, is a reclining Venus with two Cupids, a building, and a tower. On the other, a figure representing Diana, with a quiver, bow, and dog, reclines between a tree and a building. She is accompanied by a Cupid and represented in an unusually erotic way for this chaste goddess.

Successive members of the Fauchier family at Marseille ran one of the most successful of French faience factories between 1710 and 1795.[183]

182 Perlès 2016, no.132B.
183 For Marseille faience in general, see Maternati-Baldouy 1997.

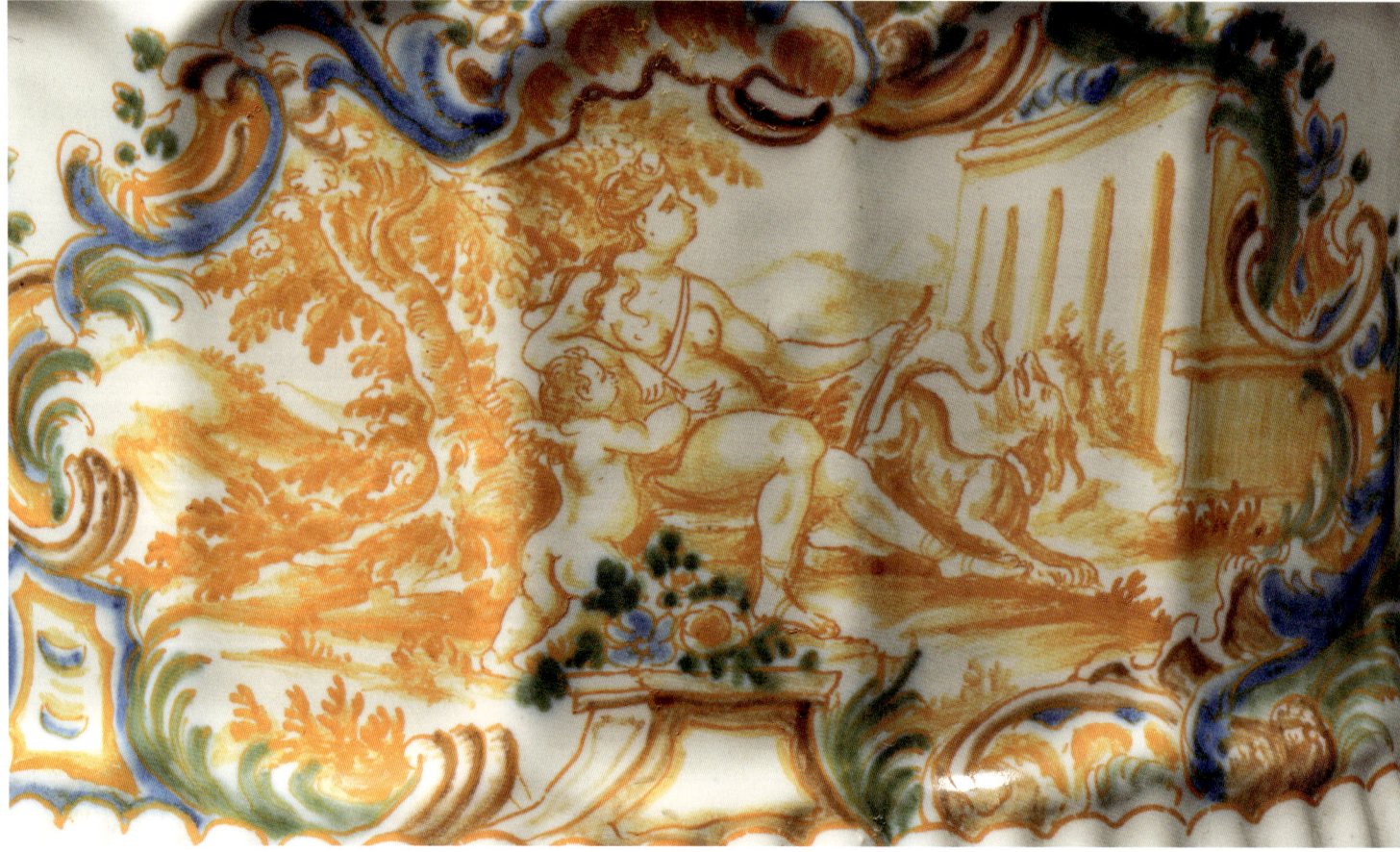

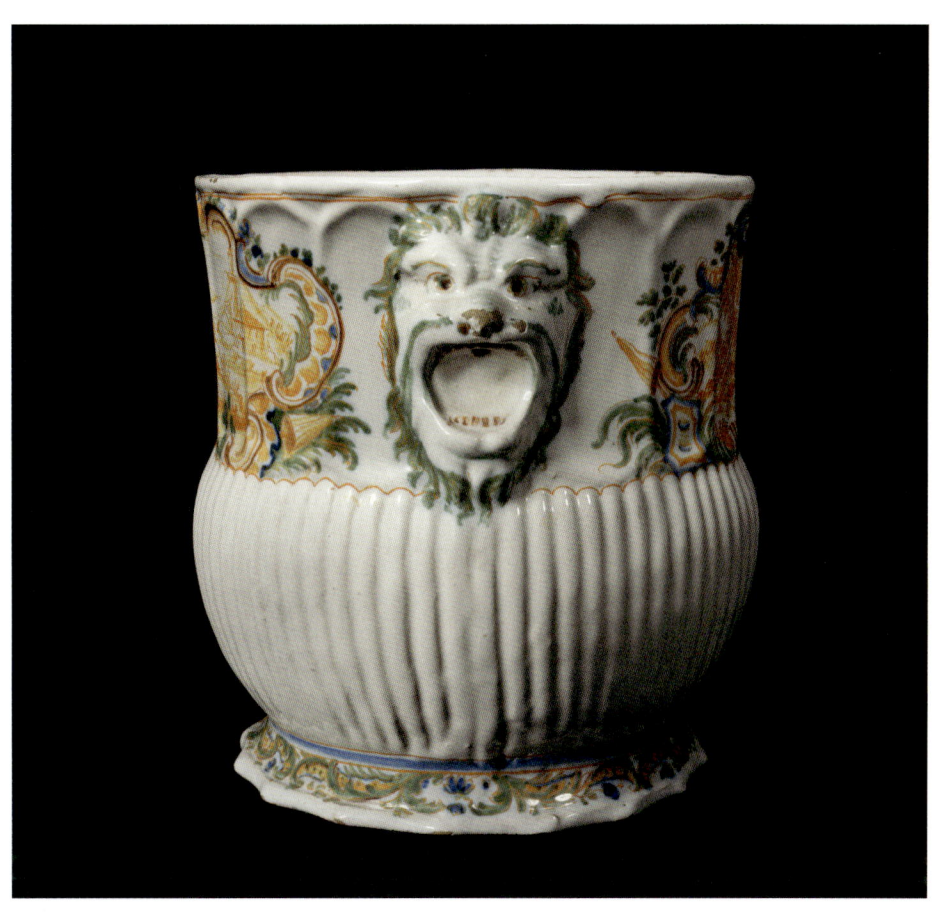

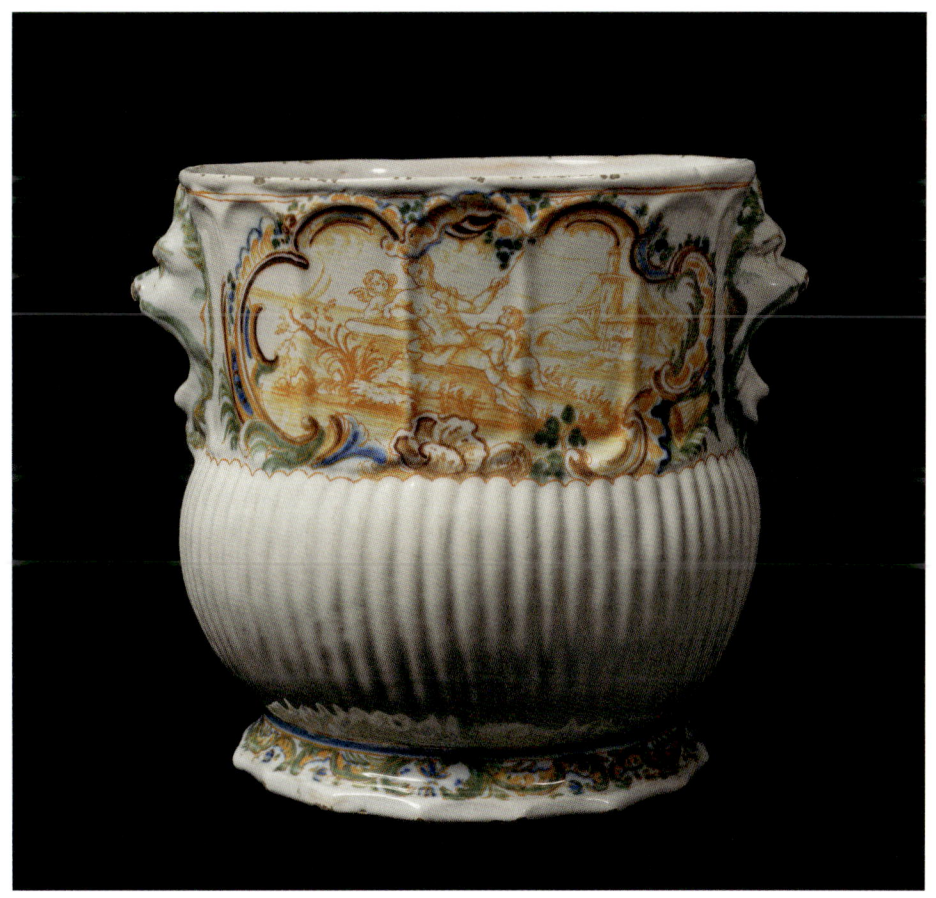

39

Plaque painted with a vase of flowers

Marseille, attributed to the Leroy workshop, mid-eighteenth century
Bequeathed by Sidney R. Knafel, received 2023, WA2023.150.

Tin-glazed front and back.

37.7 × 23.5 cm

CONDITION: apparently good.

PROVENANCE: acquired by Mr Knafel, 2010, from
Christophe Perlès, Paris, with a companion plaque
now part of the Knafel bequest to the Detroit
Institute of Arts.[184]

BIBLIOGRAPHY: Perlès 2014 (no.11), no.30 and
cover illustration; Perlès 2016, no.124A (suggesting a
surprisingly early date of *c.*1730).

The octagonal plaque is bordered with
openwork foliage and has a shell finial
above. It is painted with a vase of flowers
on a terrace.

The faience industry in Marseille was in
great part established by Joseph Clérissy,
from the potting family in Moustiers, who
arrived at Marseille in 1677 and set up a
workshop at the suburb of Saint-Jean-du-
Désert. In the first half of the eighteenth
century, numerous workshops in the city
included those run by several families
who sometimes intermarried: Clérissy,
Héraud, Fauchier (see nos **38** and **40**),
and Leroy.

In 1749, following the death of his
mother Madeleine Héraud-Leroy, with
whom he had worked since 1731, Louis
Leroy set up a successful independent
workshop; he died in 1778, and the
workshop's production ceased in 1780.

Plaques of this type are more often
found supporting holy water stoups or
candles. According to the catalogue of
Mr Knafel's collection, the pair made up
of this and the companion plaque now
in Detroit is 'the only known example of
this sort and represents the height of the
Leroy production in Marseille'.[185]

184 Perlès 2016, no.124B.
185 Perlès 2016, p.287.

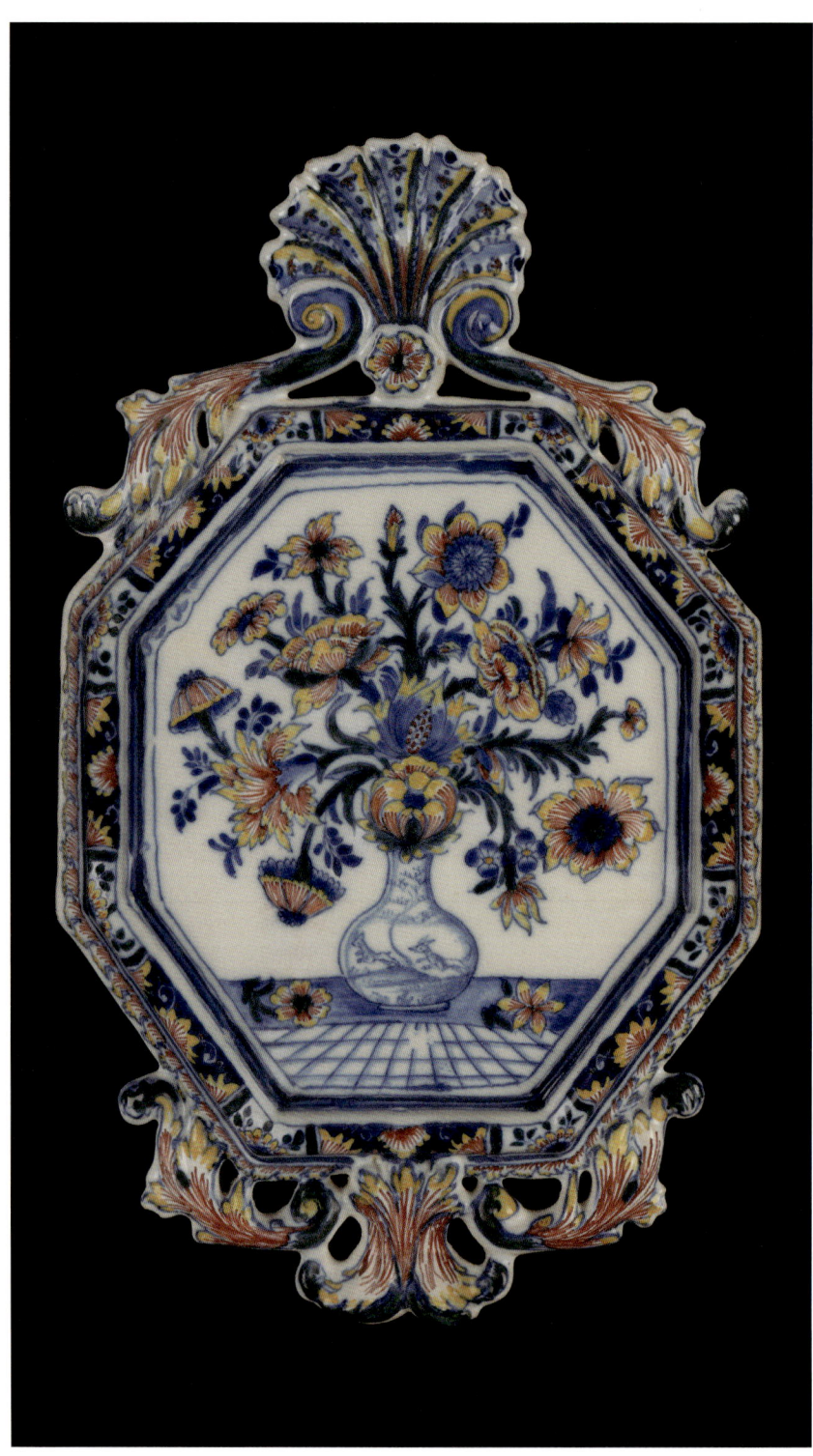

40

Ewer and basin

Marseille, Fauchier workshop, *c.*1750–60
Bequeathed by Sidney R. Knafel, received 2023, WA2023.152.

Tin-glazed overall.

Basin: 24.5 × 37 × 11.6 cm

Ewer: height: 26.3 cm

CONDITION: minor chipping and scuffing; a crack near the lip of the ewer.

PROVENANCE: unrecorded.

BIBLIOGRAPHY: Perlès 2016, no.137.

The deep basin is of wavy outline; it has two handles and is set on four stubby feet. The ewer has a scrolling handle and a hollow foot. Both are painted with sprays of roses and other flowers, with the addition on the ewer of a butterfly or moth.

The catalogue of Mr Knafel's collection describes this set as 'a beautiful example of floral *grand feu* decoration at its height in Marseille'.

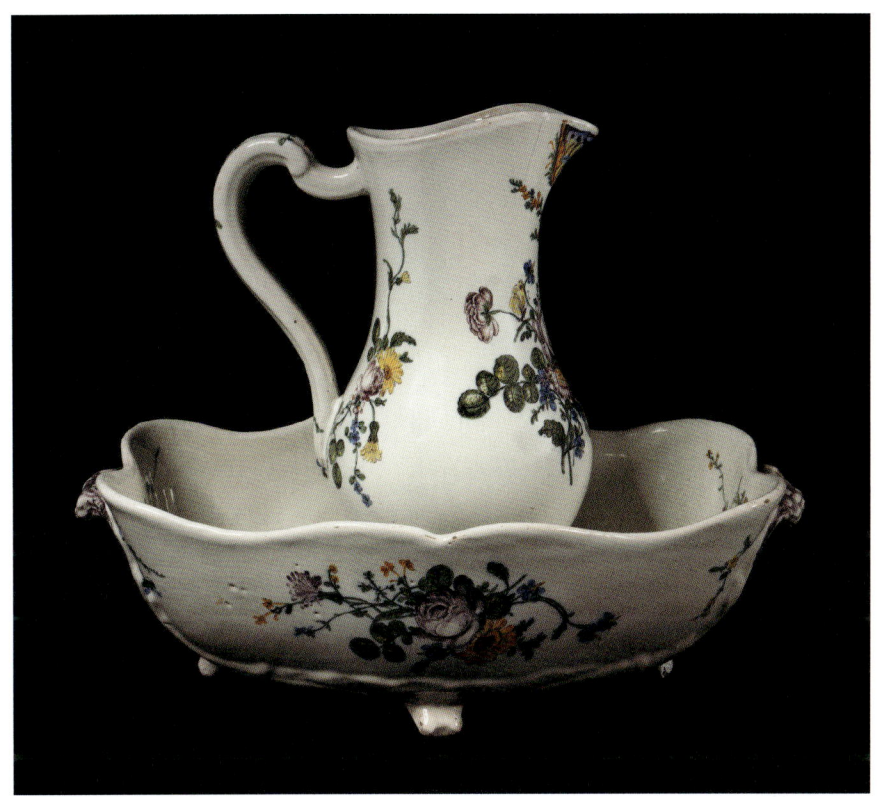

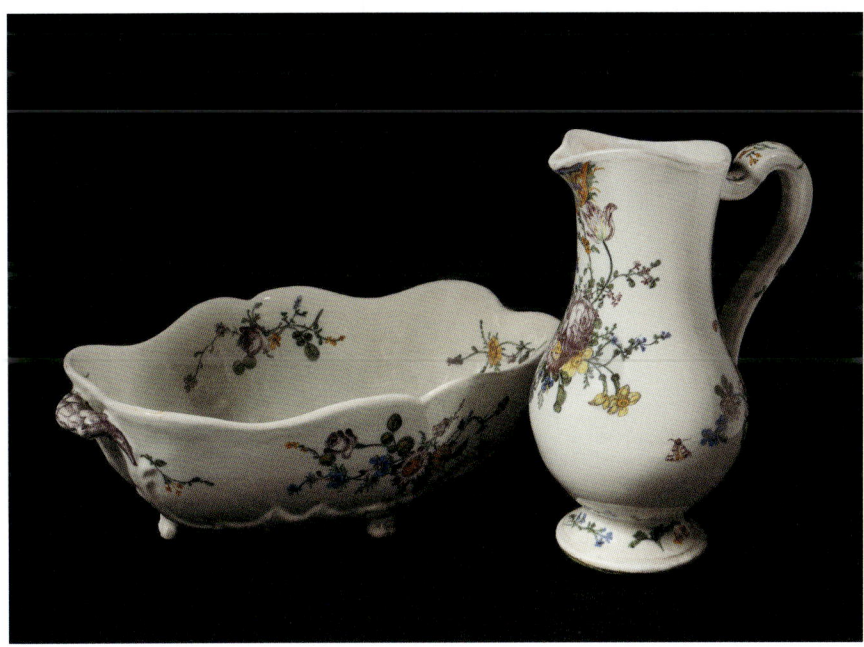

41

Plate with Chinese musicians

Moulins, *c.*1750–60
Bequeathed by Sidney R. Knafel, received 2023, WA2023.153.

Plate with flat well, no foot-ring; there are two long kiln-support marks on the back.

Diameter: 24.3 cm
CONDITION: apparently good.
PROVENANCE: Galerie Vandermeersch, Paris.
BIBLIOGRAPHY: Perlès 2016, no.143.

The plate is painted with two figures playing the horn (left) and guitar (right) amidst energetic rococo scrollwork, with birds, insects, a dragon, and a parasol.

The design is known to French specialists as *aux chinois musiciens,* and echoes figures on Chinese porcelain, but the two figures here seem as European as Chinese.

Moulins is a town in central France that had several faience workshops during the eighteenth century. This plate shows Moulins chinoiserie wares at their best.

A virtually identical plate is included in the monumental *Répertoire de la faïence française* and others of the same model are known.[186]

186 Chompret et al. 1933–5, II, Moulins, pl.IIB; Perlès 2016, no.143, mentions two other plates 'of this model'.

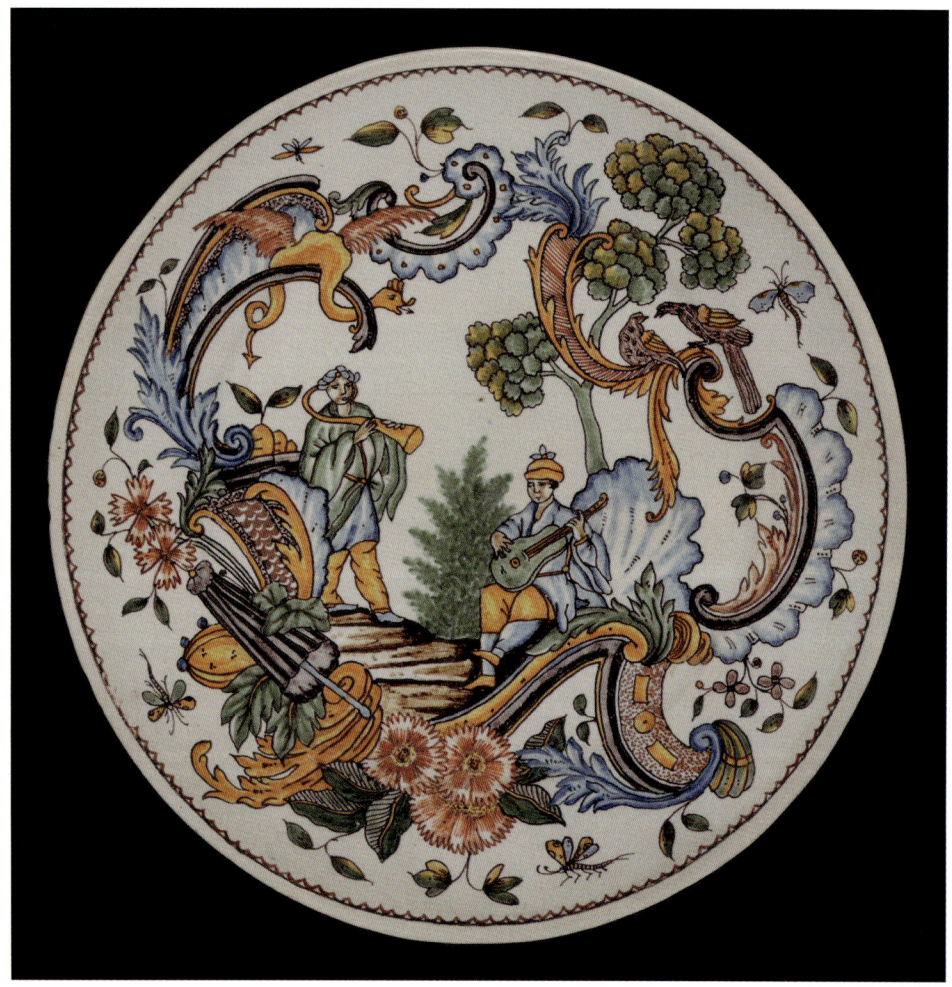

42

Lobed dish

Attributed to the workshop of Pierre-Marie Mongis, Lyon, *c.*1740–50
Bequeathed by Sidney R. Knafel, received 2023, WA2023.138.

Lobed dish without foot-ring; the glaze is pockmarked on the back.

34.8 × 46.8 cm

CONDITION: minor wear.

PROVENANCE: sale, *Faïences & porcelaines anciennes,* Paris (Drouot), 20 November 1978, lot 51; Galerie Verneuil-Bac, Paris; from whom acquired by Mr Knafel, 2002. Among labels on the back are two old labels attributing the dish to Pierre Mongis and a label with the handwritten number *113.*

BIBLIOGRAPHY: Perlès 2016, no.46.

The dish is of a form derived from silver. Painted with various figures in contemporary dress, a cupid carrying what seems to be a gun, and a prancing child in theatrical costume; with flowers and exotic birds.

After playing an important role as conduit between Italy and France in the sixteenth and early seventeenth centuries, Lyon declined as a centre of artistic faience until the establishment in 1733 of a workshop by Joseph Combe, a *faïencier* from Moustiers. Among the few identifiable artists in the city was Pierre Mongis, who had been born in Turin in 1712; he married in Lyon in 1741 and was still alive in 1756.

Lyon-eighteenth-century faience is rarely marked and is internationally eclectic in its stylistic sources, including Turin, Milan, Moustiers, and Marseille.[187] The attribution of this dish by French specialists to '*l'atelier di Pierre Mongis*' remains to be proven.

187 See Deloche 1994, especially fig.300 on p.150 and the shape chart on p.148; Guillemé Brulon 1994, pp.21–37.

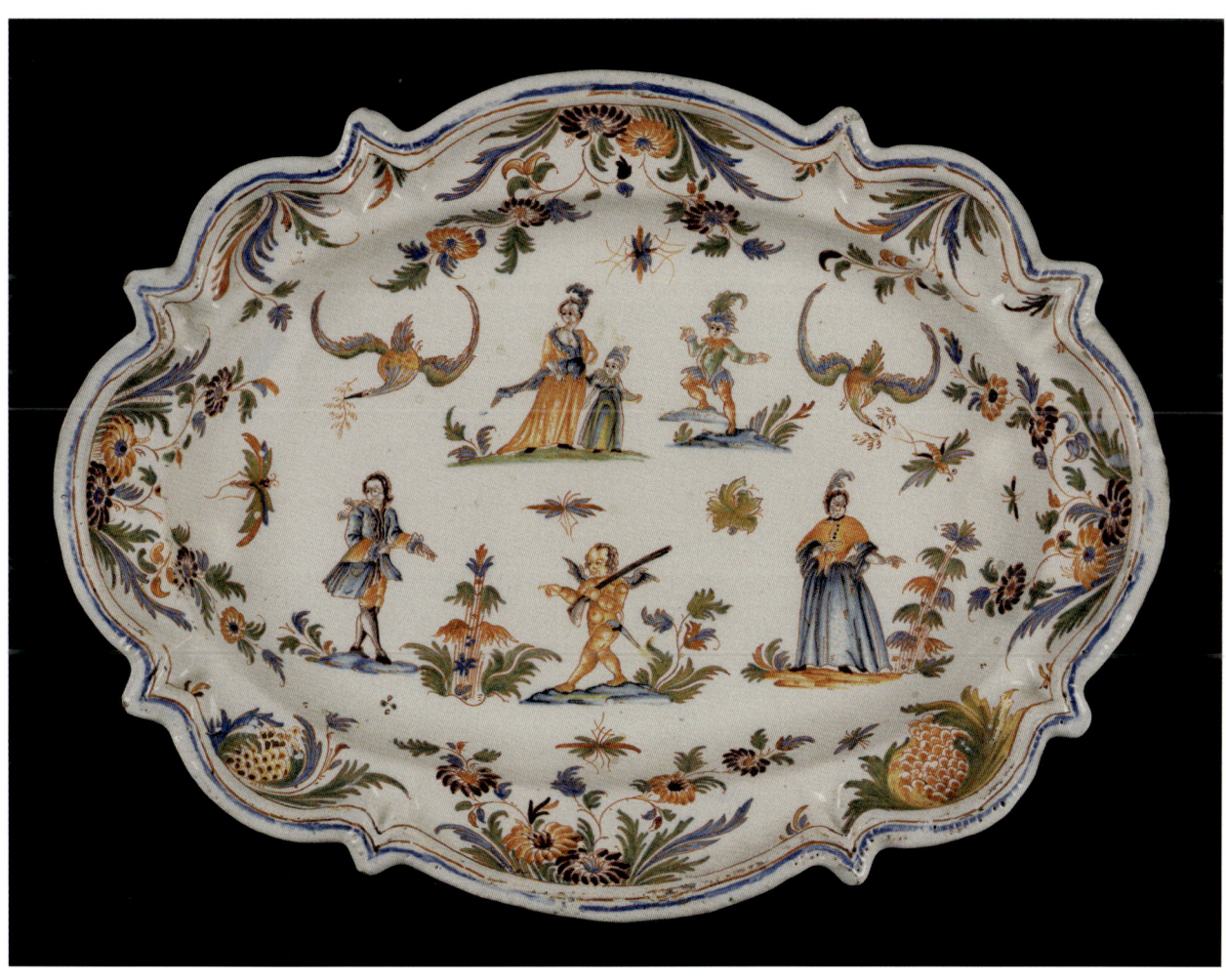

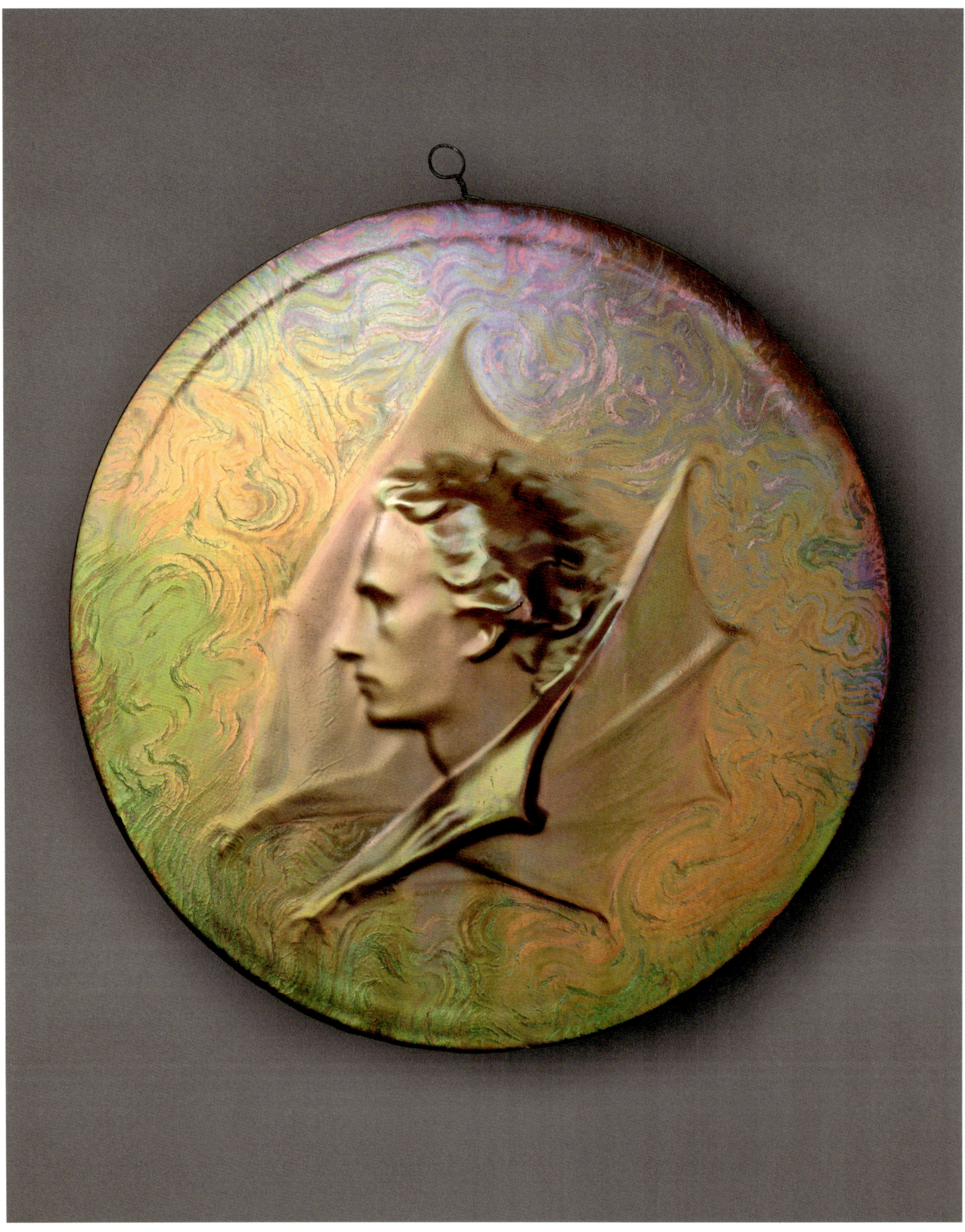

43

Portrait head of Walter Carruthers with bat wings

Golfe-Juan, France, Clément Massier, after Alexander Munro, *c.*1890
Purchased, 2022, from Allan Chinn European Sculpture, Brussels, with the assistance
of the ACE/V&A Purchase Grant Fund and the late Martin Foley, WA2023.57.

Earthenware, glazed, and lustred, in moulded relief.
Inscribed in lustre: *Clement Massier Golfe Juan
AM* and impressed: CLEMENT MASSIER GOLFE
JUAN AM and incised with what looks to be a large
letter 2.

Diameter: 33 cm

CONDITION: good.

PROVENANCE: private collection, France; Galerie
Mathieu Néouze, Paris.

BIBLIOGRAPHY: Winterbottom 2023, pp.27–8.

The plaque shows the profile head of
Walter Carruthers (1829–1885) with a
pair of bat's wings. Carruthers was a
parliamentary reporter for the *Morning
Chronicle*, and consequently worked late
nights in the reporters' gallery of the
House of Commons. The bat's wings are
a light-hearted reference to Carruthers's
nocturnal schedule and flying back and
forth to Fleet Street to meet newspaper
deadlines. This portrait plaque, originally
called *Ye Bat Friend—a portrait of WC,*
was modelled in the early 1850s by
Carruthers's friend and eventual brother-
in-law, Alexander Munro (1825–1871).
Versions in marble or plaster are depicted
in a photographic album belonging to the
Munro family.

Munro was a Scottish sculptor closely
associated with the Pre-Raphaelites,
although not an official member of the
Brotherhood, unlike his friend, Thomas
Woolner (1825–1892). Munro produced
work that upheld Pre-Raphaelite ideals of
naturalism and medievalism. However,
his career was built on a series of relief
portrait medallions of various friends and
patrons. This type of portrait sculpture
became increasingly popular in the
mid-nineteenth century, inspired by
the Della Robbia ware exhibited at the
South Kensington Museum, and Munro

was considered a stylistically innovative
practitioner and sensitive portraitist.

The Ashmolean has two exceptional
relief portraits by Munro of John Everett
Millais (1829–1896) and the Revd Dr
Henry Wellesley (1794–1866) in its
collections. However, this lustred ceramic
plaque is of a very different character
from Munro's plaster and marble
reliefs. It was made in the late 1880s or
early 1890s in the pottery workshop of
Clément Massier (1844–1917) at Golfe-
Juan on the fashionable Côte d'Azur in
the South of France. Munro suffered
from chronic lung disease and had
moved to the Côte d'Azur in the 1860s
to improve his health. There, he met
Clément Massier, a brother-partner in
the pottery firm Jerôme Massier et Cie.
Munro gave Massier several casts of
earlier works, which the latter reproduced
in red terracotta. Massier continued to
reproduce Munro's work long after the
sculptor's death in 1871. During the 1880s,
Massier introduced experimental metallic
lustre glazes to the firm's wares, inspired
by medieval Hispano-Moresque pottery.
The combination of silver- and copper-

oxide glazes, enriched with etching
and painting, produced kaleidoscopic,
iridescent effects. Although this was a
notoriously difficult technique to master,
Massier would win a gold medal at the
1889 Paris World's Fair for the exceptional
quality and beautiful colours of his
lustrewares.

During the 1880s and 1890s, Massier
employed Symbolist artists and sculptors,
such as Lucien Lévy-Dhurmer (1865–
1953), Jules Scalbert (1851–1933), and
James Vibert (1872–1942), to design and
decorate avant-garde lustred ceramics.
However, *Ye Bat Friend—a portrait of
WC* uniquely combines a closely studied
mid-Victorian portrait with colourful
lustres that shows a fascinating and wholly
original connection between British
Pre-Raphaelite art and the burgeoning
French Symbolist movement in the late
nineteenth century.[188]

188 Another version with different lustred
     decoration was recorded in a private collection
     in Virginia in 2023; a lustred version with
     additional stars, inscribed *La Nuit* is in the
     Musée Magnelli, musée de la céramique,
     Vallauris.

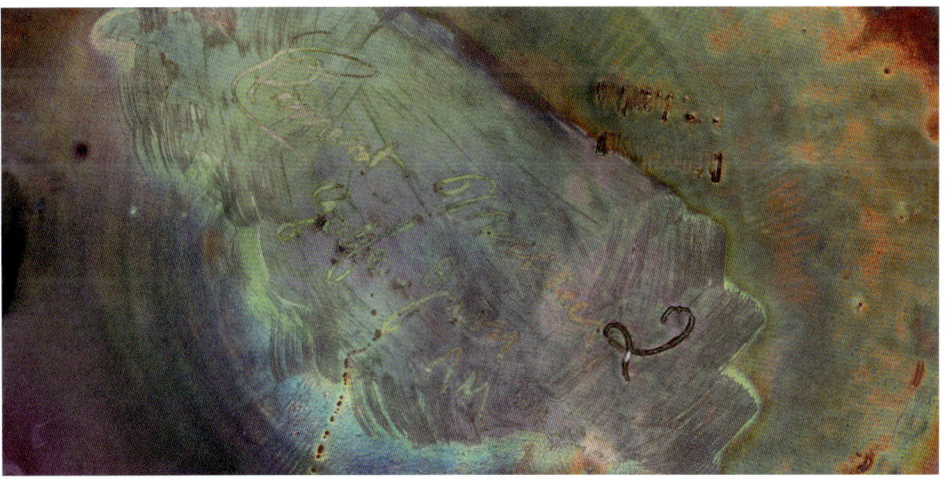

44

Lustred teasel vase

Golfe-Juan, France, workshop of Clément Massier, c.1890
Bequeathed by Peter Rose and Albert Gallichan, 2021, WA2021.28.

Earthenware vase of flattened oval form painted in lustre with teasels. Inscribed in faint lustre: *Clement Massier Golfe Juan AM* and impressed: CLEMENT MASSIER GOLFE JUAN AM.

30 × 16 × 14 cm

CONDITION: good.

PROVENANCE: unrecorded.

The ethereal silhouettes of teasel heads painted in iridescent lustre on the sides of this vase are probably the work of Symbolist artist Lucien Lévy-Dhurmer, who worked as a ceramic decorator and later artistic director for Massier between 1887 and 1895. For Clément Massier see no.**43**.

Peter Rose (1927–2020) and Albert Gallichan (1930–2001) assembled, at their home in Brighton, one of the finest private collections of Victorian fine and decorative arts. In 2003, Peter Rose established the Albert Dawson Educational Trust to promote the study of British nineteenth-century fine and decorative art. Under his will, several UK museums received works from the collection.[189]

189   See https://www.albertdawsontrust.org.uk/ biography

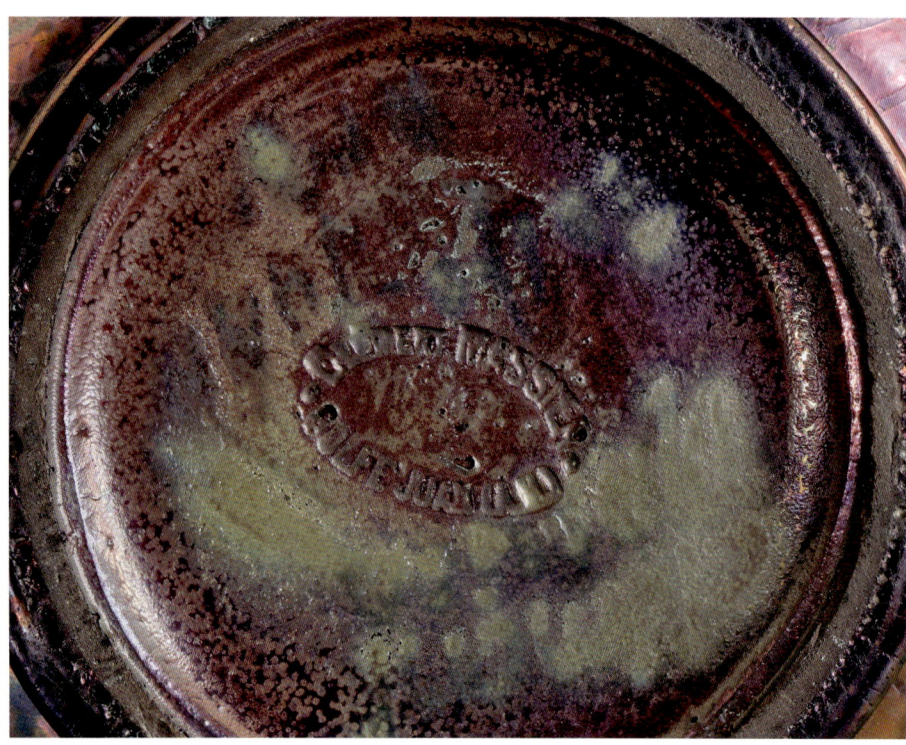

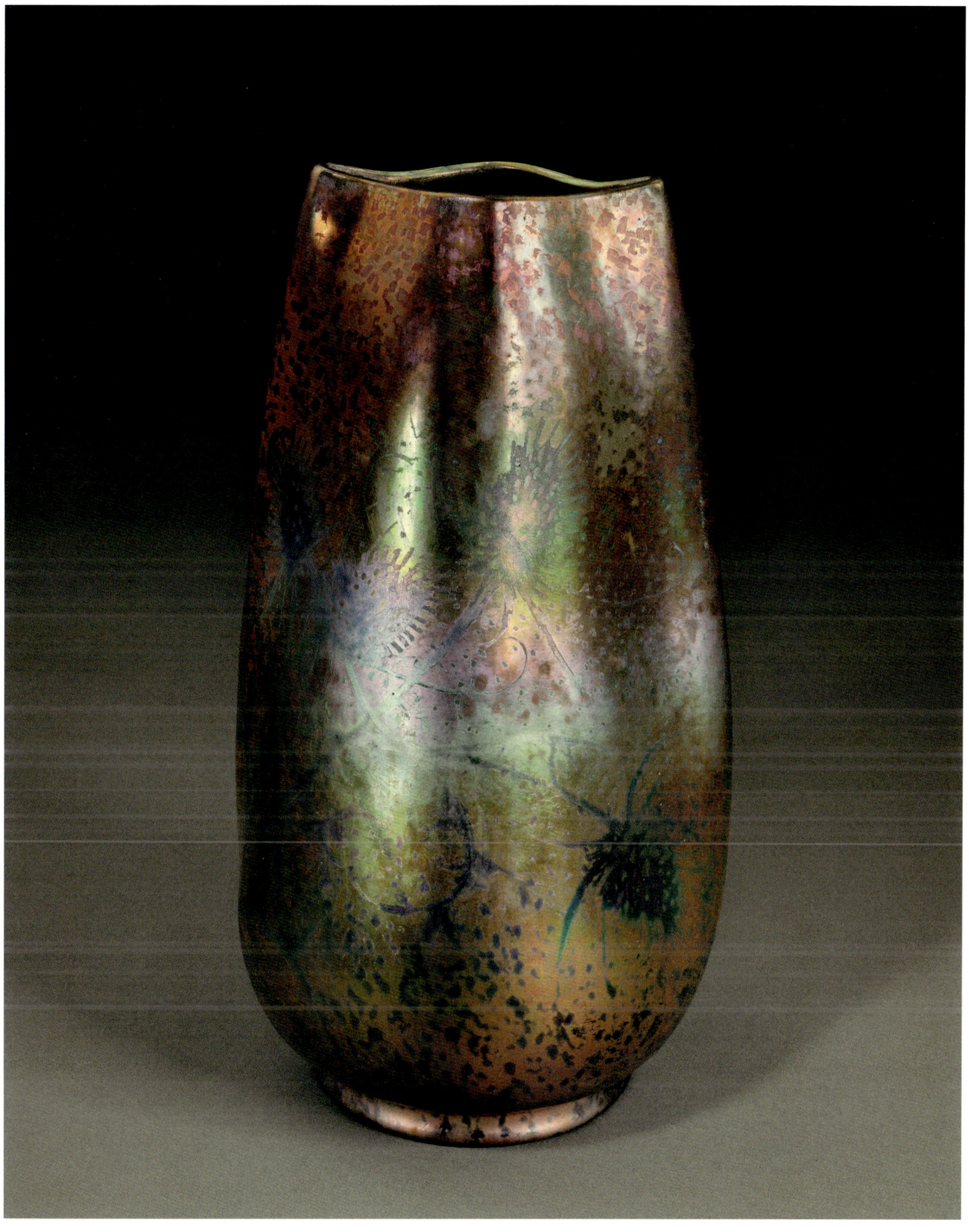

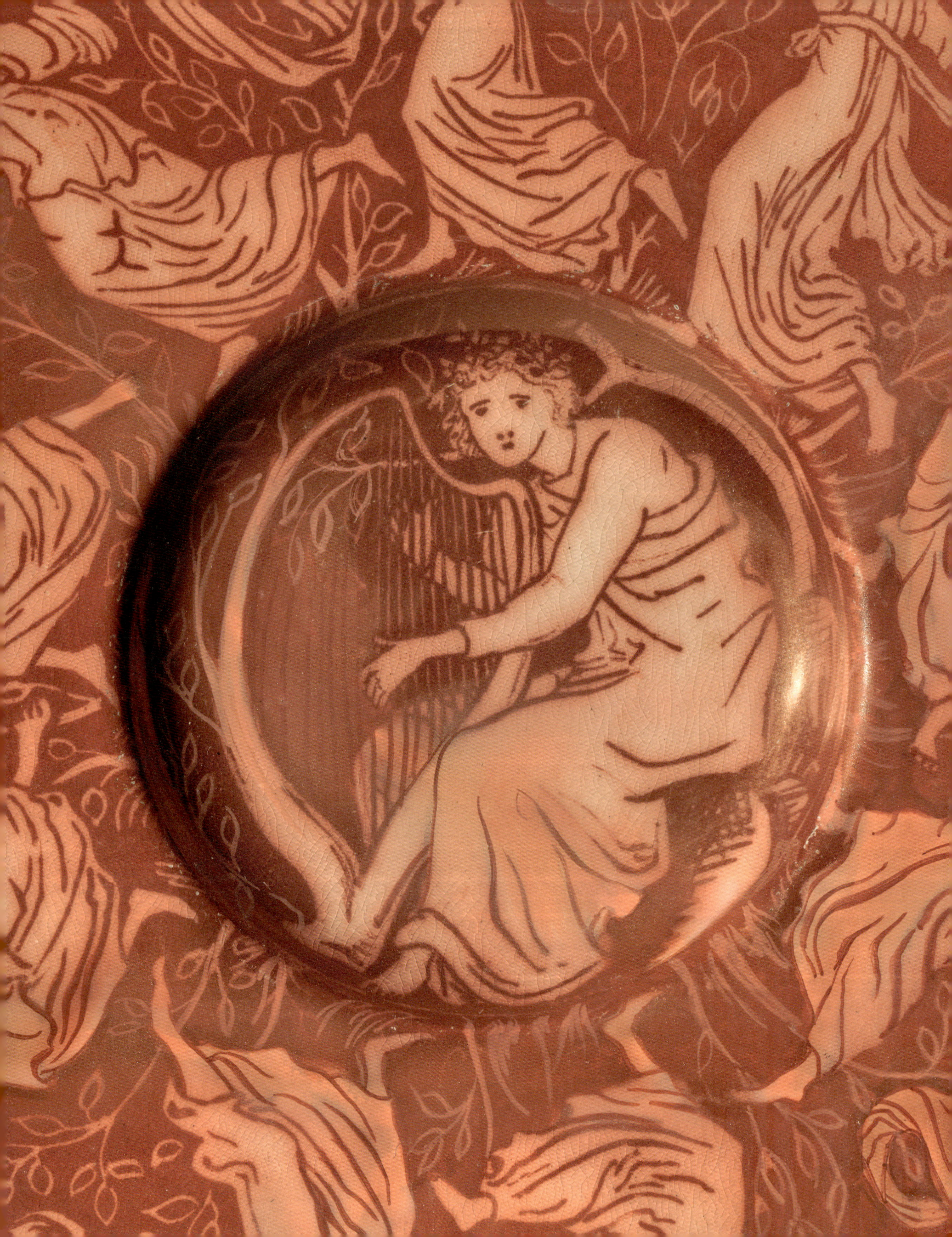

ENGLAND

Opposite: detail of no.**48**

45

Majolica tile

Stoke-on-Trent, Minton & Co., after a design by Augustus Pugin, 1851
Bequeathed by Peter Rose and Albert Gallichan, 2021, WA2021.26.

Dust-pressed buff earthenware body, pierced and moulded with foliate quatrefoil design. Decorated with coloured majolica lead glazes in orange, pale and dark blue and white.

22 × 22 cm (unframed)

CONDITION: minor chips to the edges.

PROVENANCE: unrecorded.

BIBLIOGRAPHY (including tiles of the same pattern): Atterbury and Wainwright 1994, p.149, fig.276; Atterbury 1995, p.382, no.137; Ribeyrol et al. 2023, p.53, fig.54.

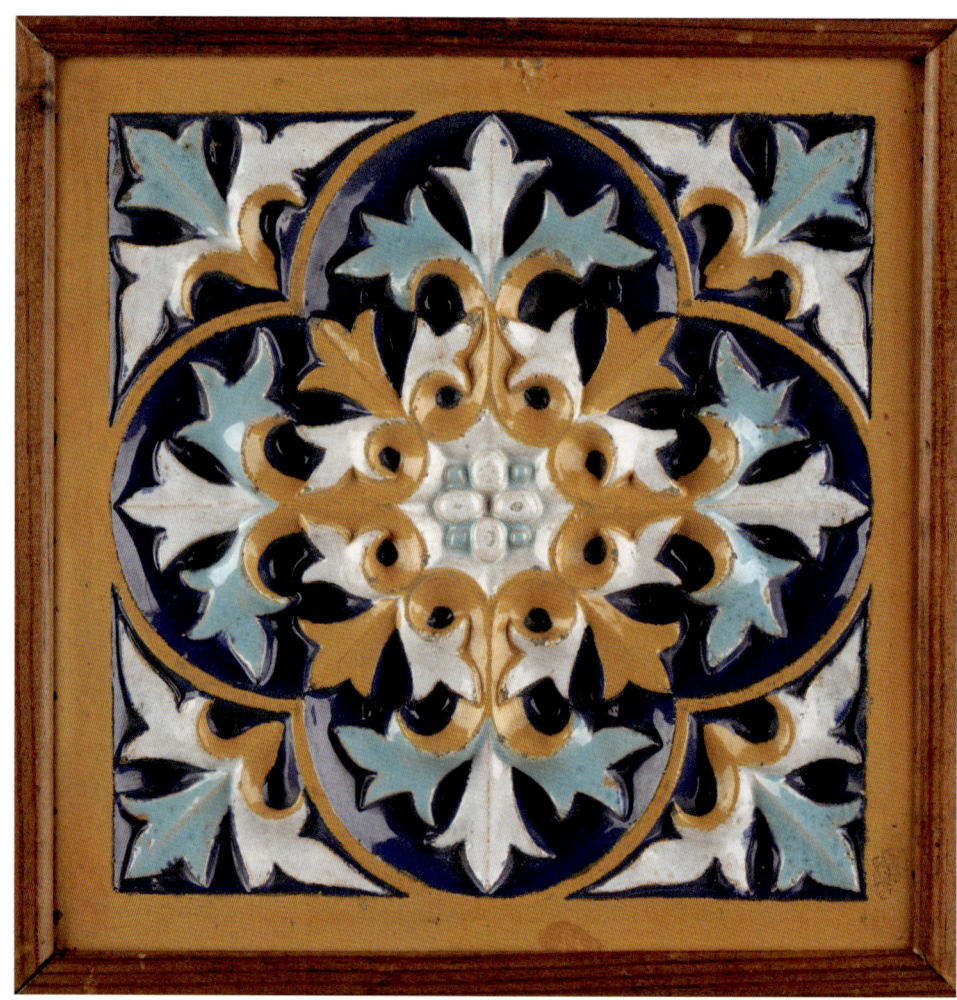

This majolica tile is probably from the celebrated *Great Stove* designed by Augustus Pugin (1812–1852), that formed the centrepiece of the Medieval Court at the Great Exhibition of 1851. Standing ten feet high by five feet wide and deep, the *Great Stove* was covered with tiles of five different designs in colourful majolica glazes that were supplied by Minton & Co. after Pugin's designs.[190] Those near to the top of the stove were pierced, as in this example, to allow the heat to escape. The metalwork elements of the stove were supplied by Hardman & Co. of Birmingham. The fate of the *Great Stove* is unclear, but it appears to have been dismantled after the Great Exhibition and the tiles dispersed. Examples of the same design and colouring are in the British Museum and V&A.[191]

Minton developed their so-called 'majolica' glazes in an attempt to emulate the market success of Italian and French Renaissance ceramics. First exhibited at the Great Exhibition in 1851, they were hugely popular. Unlike earlier maiolica, most nineteenth-century majolica was lead-glazed rather than tin-glazed, and this has led to some confusion between the terms. Minton initially called their new lead-glazed ceramics 'Palissy ware' after the sixteenth-century French potter, Bernard Palissy. This was to distinguish it from their tin-glazed 'majolica', which was emulating true maiolica. However, the name was soon dropped. The lead-rich glazes were extraordinarily colourful but highly toxic for the pottery workers and safety legislation limiting the lead content was introduced in the 1880s. Although Pugin designed many tiles for Minton & Co., his designs for the *Great Stove* are the only ones to use the new majolica glazes.

190 Pugin's designs are in the Minton archive, now in the City Archives of Stoke-on-Trent; illustrated in Jones 1993, p.179; Atterbury and Wainwright 1994, p.149, fig.275; Atterbury 1995, p.383, no.138.
191 British Museum, BEP1994,0502.1; V&A, 2768-1901.

46

Majolica tile

Stoke-on-Trent, Minton & Co., after a design by Augustus Pugin, 1851
Bequeathed by Peter Rose and Albert Gallichan, 2021, WA2021.27.

Dust-pressed buff earthenware body, pierced and
moulded with foliate quatrefoil design. Decorated
with coloured majolica lead glazes in brown, green,
yellow, pale blue, pink, white and orange.

21.5 × 21.5 cm (unframed)

CONDITION: minor chips to the edges and minor
wear.

PROVENANCE: unrecorded.

BIBLIOGRAPHY: see no.**45**.

Probably from Augustus Pugin's *Great
Stove*, exhibited at the Great Exhibition
of 1851; see no.**45** above. Another example
of the same design and colouring is in the
V&A.[192]

192   V&A, 2770-1901.

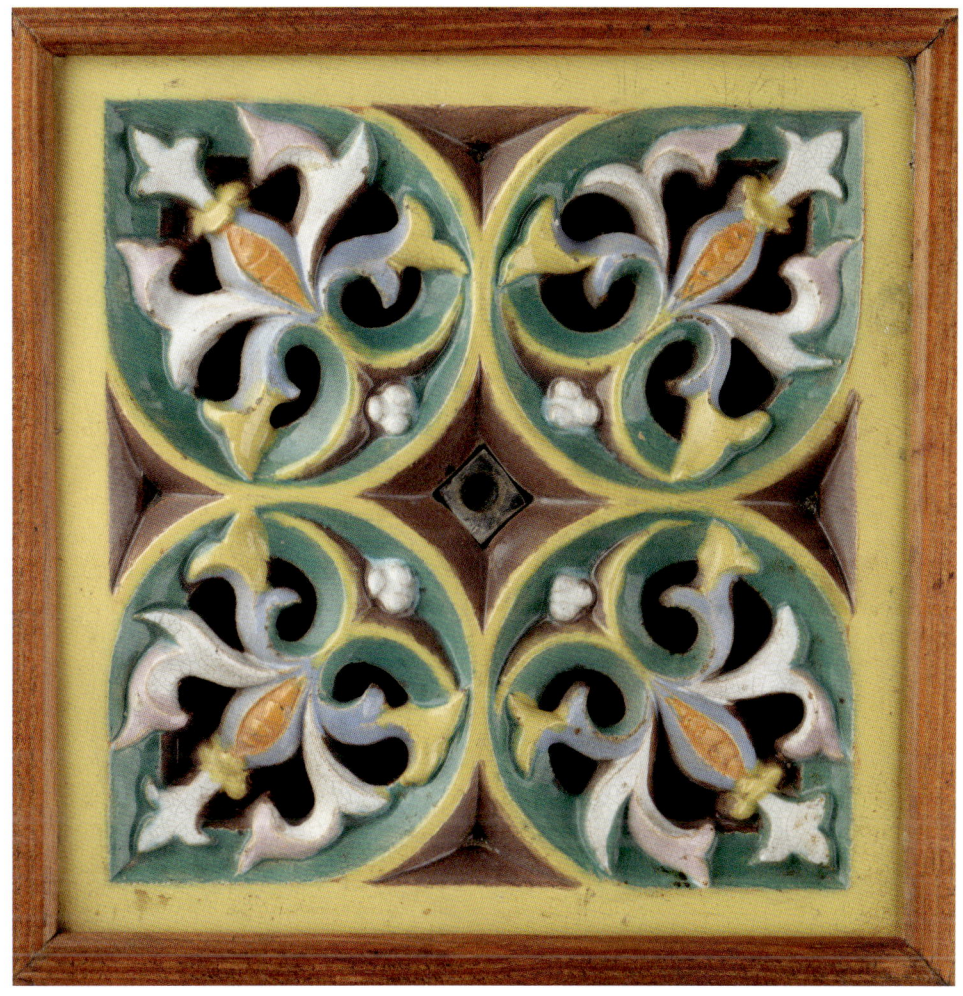

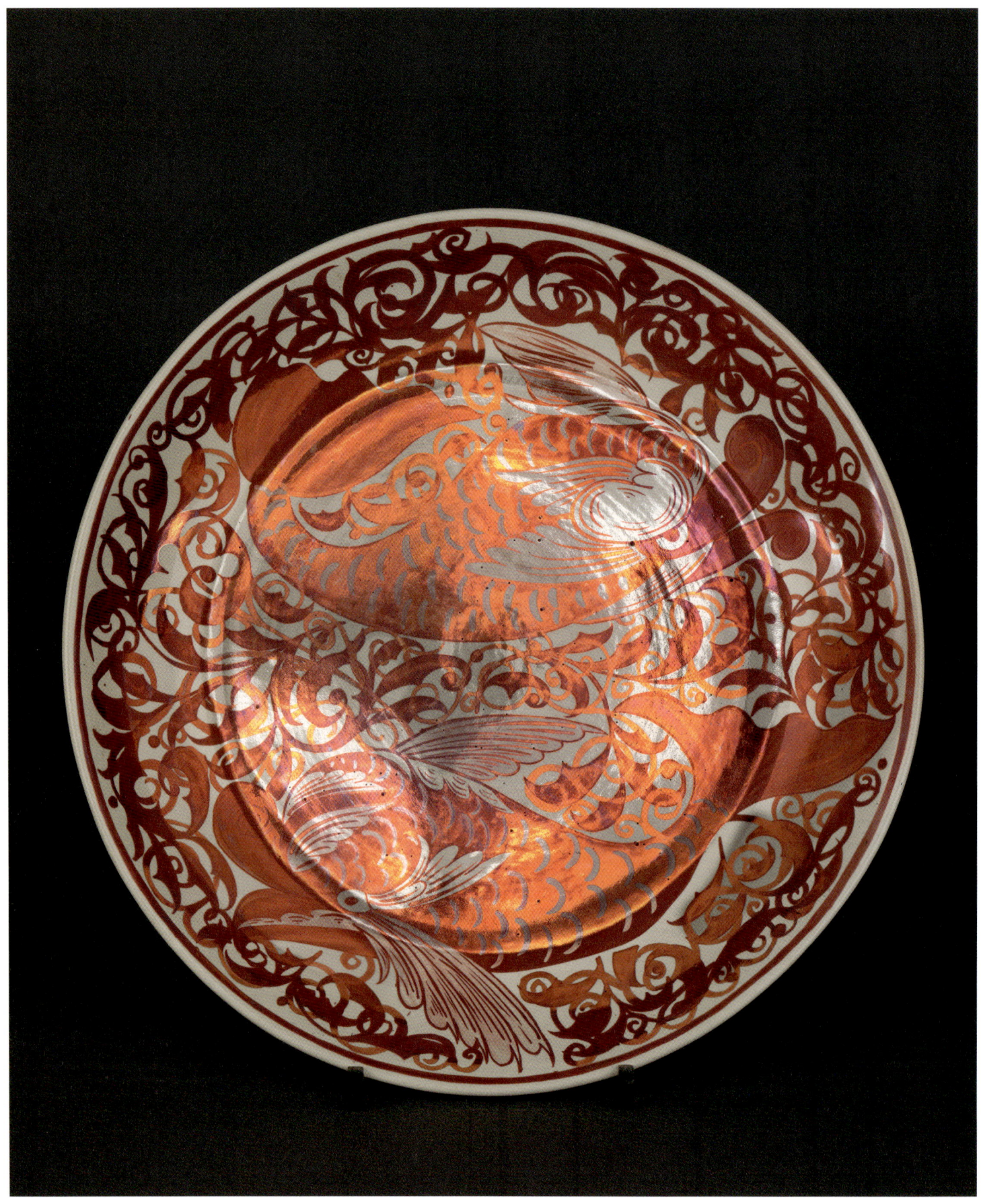

47

Dolphin dish

Chelsea, William De Morgan's Orange House Pottery, painted by Joe Juster, *c.*1880
Presented by the Thompson family, 2021, WA 2022.14.

Earthenware dish painted in ruby lustre on a cream background with two stylised dolphins facing opposite directions. The reverse painted in ruby lustre with concentric bands and radiating dashes; reverse impressed *O3* and decorator's mark *JJ* painted in lustre.

Diameter: 35.7 cm

CONDITION: good.

PROVENANCE: probably Reginald Campbell Thompson (1876–1941), nephew of William De Morgan; then by descent; presented by his grandchildren to the Museum.

William De Morgan was one of the most important ceramic artists and designers of the Arts and Crafts Movement. He initially trained as a fine artist, but his artistic direction changed after he met William Morris (1834–1896) in 1863. De Morgan's Orange House Pottery in Chelsea was in production from 1873 to 1882. The pottery then moved to a larger site at Merton Abbey, Surrey, close to Morris & Co.'s works. Between 1888 and 1898, De Morgan worked in partnership with Halsey Ricardo (1854–1928) at Sands End Pottery in Fulham. De Morgan remained at Sands End, in partnership with Frederick Passenger (1858–1938),

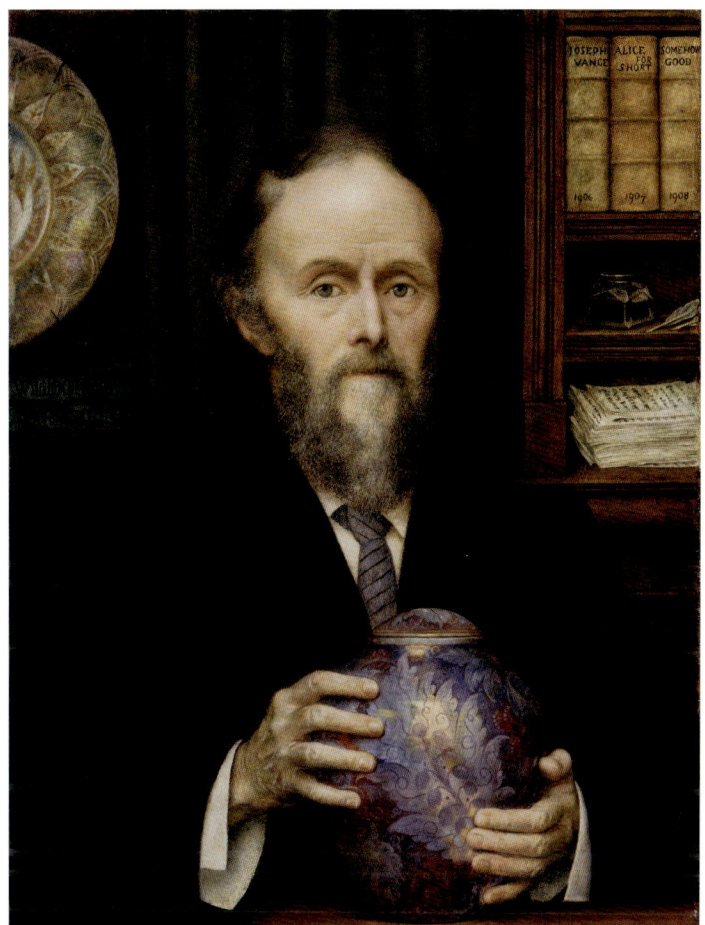

Fig.14 William De Morgan (1839–1917), by Evelyn De Morgan (1855–1919).
© National Portrait Gallery, London, NPG 6358

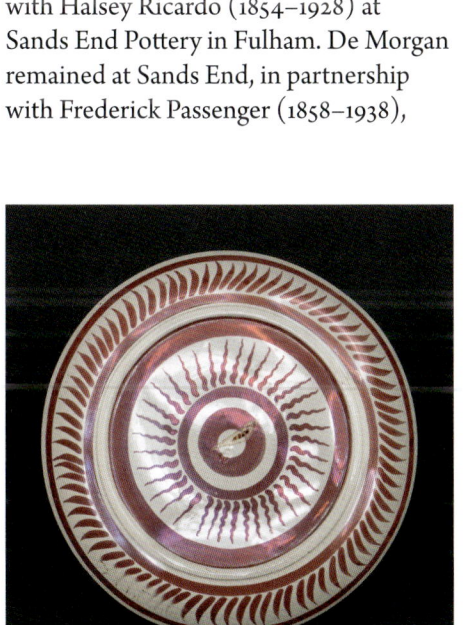

his brother Charles Passenger (active 1898–1911), and Frank Iles (active 1898–1911) until 1907. His partners continued production there until 1911. De Morgan's designs were often based on medieval, Renaissance, or Middle Eastern patterns, and he experimented with innovative glazes, lustres, and firing techniques. He is credited with rediscovering, for England, various lost lustre techniques. Later in life, De Morgan spent his winters in Florence and collaborated there with Ulisse Cantagalli, the two men perfecting their lustre techniques (see no.**14**). At

the height of his popularity, De Morgan employed over ten decorators in his workshop, but by the beginning of the twentieth century the popularity of his wares had begun to wane, and he left the pottery he founded in 1907, later making a new career as a successful novelist.

Joe Juster (active 1872–82) was the most skilful of the decorators at De Morgan's Chelsea factory.

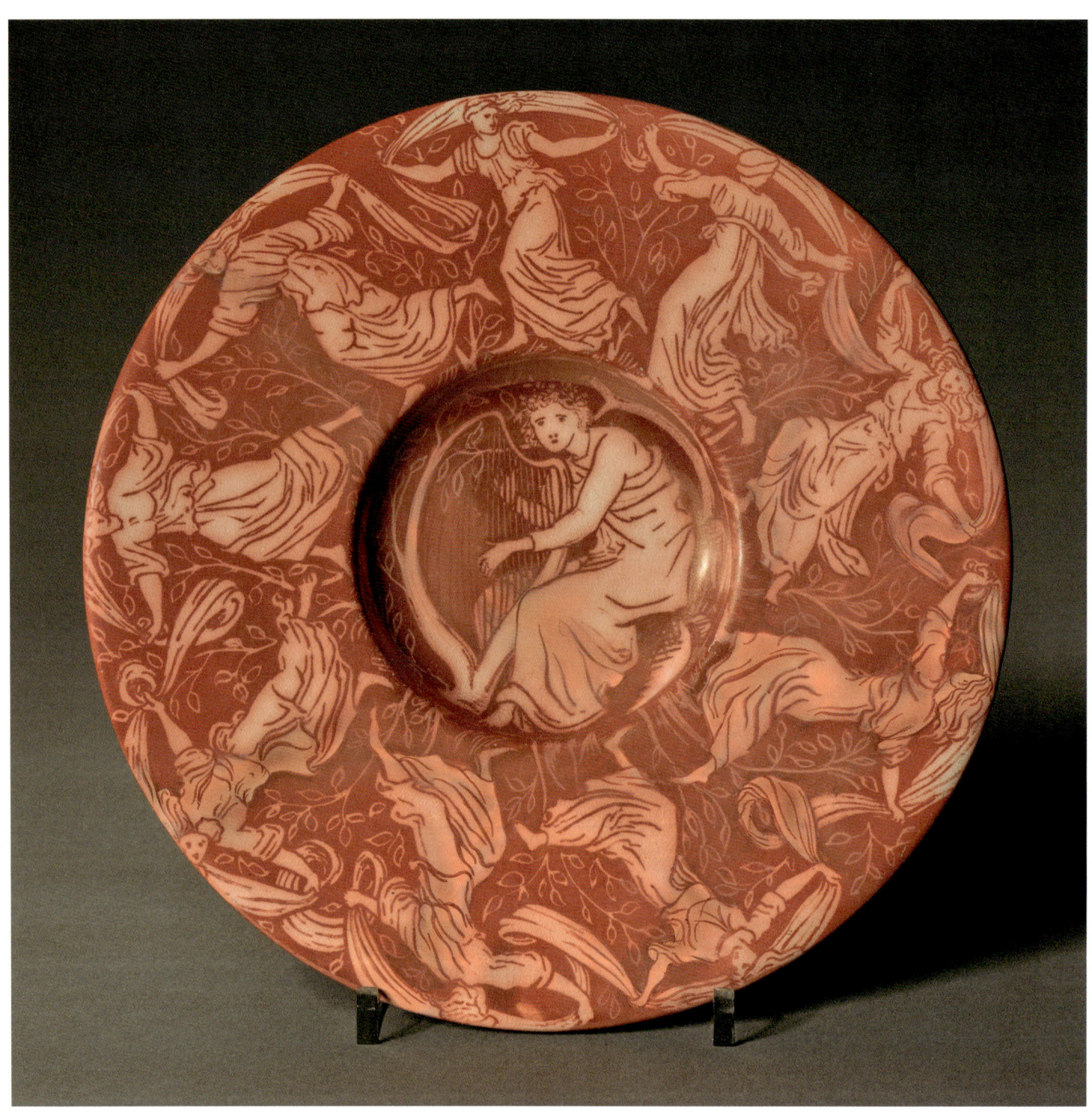

48

Dish, Orpheus and the Muses

Probably Chelsea, William De Morgan's Orange House Pottery, *c*.1880
Presented by the Thompson family, 2021, WA2022.15.

Earthenware dish with deep central well. Painted in ruby lustre with a seated figure of Orpheus playing a harp surrounded by a band of dancing Muses holding a sash, surrounded by branches and leaves. The reverse is painted in ruby lustre with pink concentric bands. Stamped on reverse: *JH DAVIS H.*

Diameter: 30 cm

CONDITION: good.

PROVENANCE: probably Reginald Campbell Thompson, nephew of William De Morgan; then by descent; presented by his grandchildren to the Museum.

BIBLIOGRAPHY: none.

The design for this dish was probably by Edward Burne-Jones (1833–1898). A dish with the same design but reversed is in the V&A.[193] The design on this plate was painted onto an earthenware blank made by J. H. and J. Davis, Trent Pottery, Hanley, Staffordshire.

193   V&A, CIRC.363-1961.

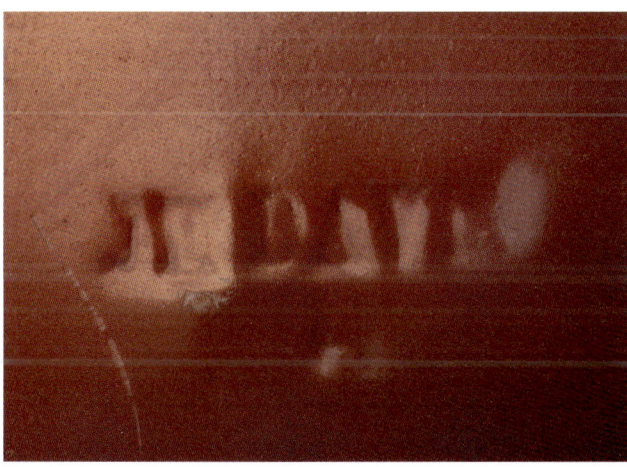

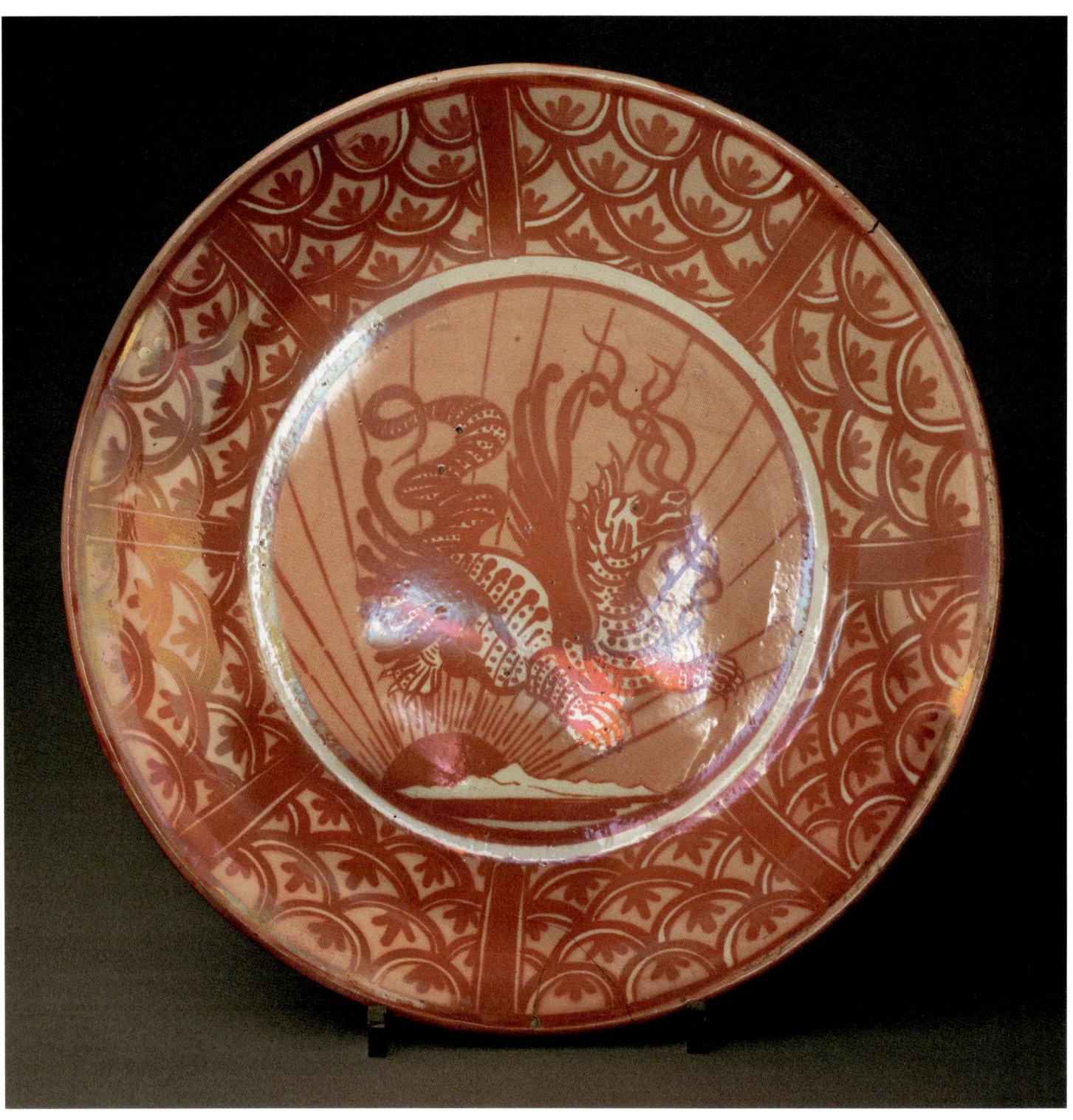

49

Sundragon dish

Probably Chelsea, William De Morgan's Orange House Pottery, *c.*1881
Presented by the Thompson family, 2021. WA2022.16.

Earthenware dish painted in ruby lustre on a pink
ground with a winged dragon flying in front of a
rising or setting sun. Surrounding border of scale
work. Reverse painted with a scale border in ruby
lustre on a pink ground; centre with a spiral scroll.
Unmarked.

Diameter: 33.5 cm

CONDITION: good.

PROVENANCE: probably Reginald Campbell
Thompson, nephew of William De Morgan; then
by descent; presented by his grandchildren to the
Museum.

A similar dragon in front of a rising or
setting sun, in a 1881 design for a dish
by De Morgan, in the V&A, was called
a 'Sundragon' by the artist (fig.15).[194]
The scale work border is derived from
sixteenth-century Gubbio maiolica.

194   V&A, E.1177-1917; Greenwood 1989, p.36.

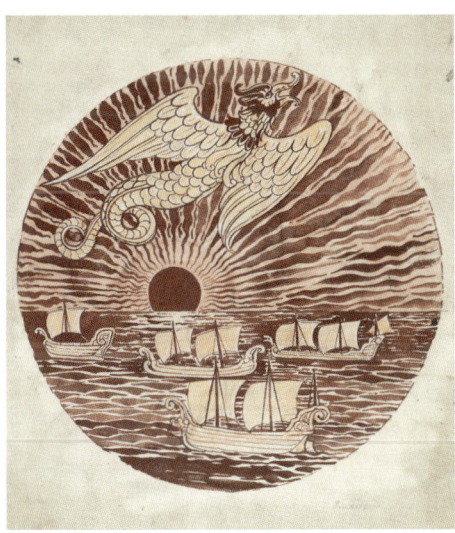

Fig.15 'Sundragon', dish design by William de
Morgan, 1881. © Victoria and Albert Museum,
London

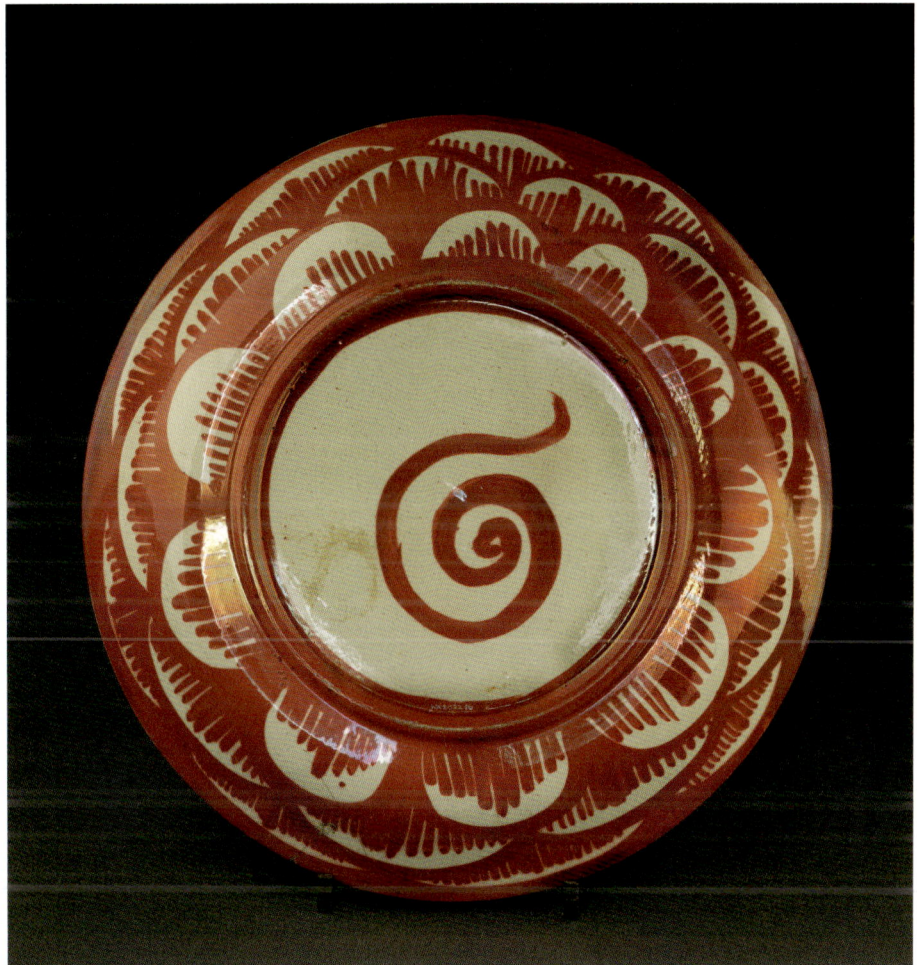

50

Dragon vase

Probably Chelsea, William De Morgan's Orange House Pottery, *c.*1880
Presented by the Thompson family, 2021, WA2022.17.

Onion-shaped earthenware vase with a tall neck.
Painted in ruby and pink lustre on a cream ground
with stylised flowers and buds and six dragons
around the lower body. Base covered with green
baize.

Height: 28 cm

CONDITION: good.

PROVENANCE: probably Reginald Campbell
Thompson, nephew of William De Morgan; then
by descent; presented by his grandchildren to the
Museum.

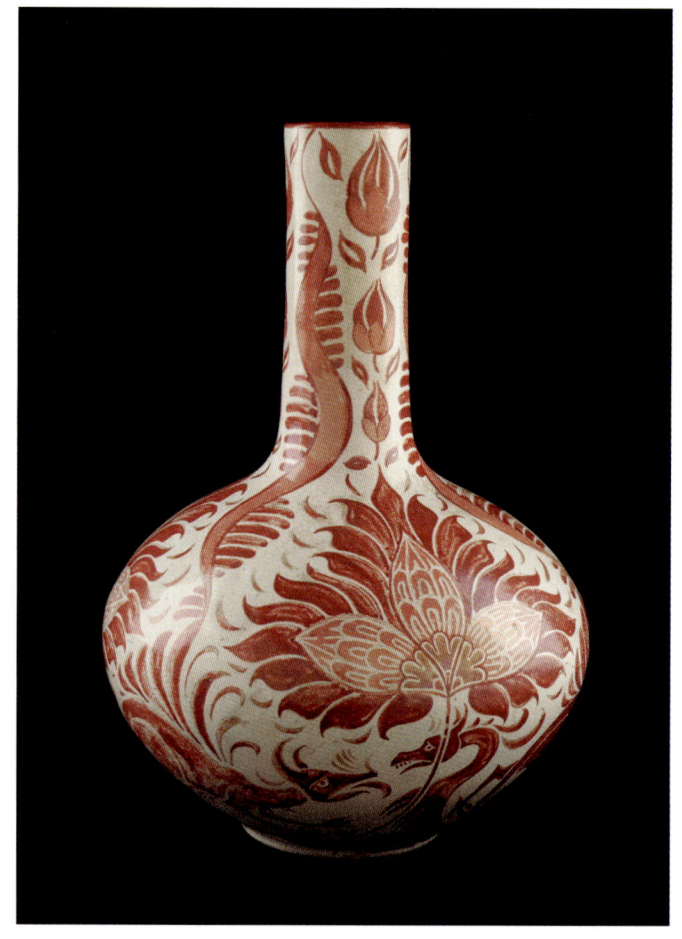

51

Vase

Made at one of William De Morgan's potteries, *c.*1880–90
Presented by the Thompson family, 2021, WA2022.21.

Double-gourd shaped earthenware body. Painted
in gold lustre on a cream ground with stylised
waterbirds. Unmarked.

Height: 14 cm; diameter: 8 cm

CONDITION: good.

PROVENANCE: probably Reginald Campbell
Thompson, nephew of William De Morgan; thence
by descent; presented by his grandchildren to the
Museum.

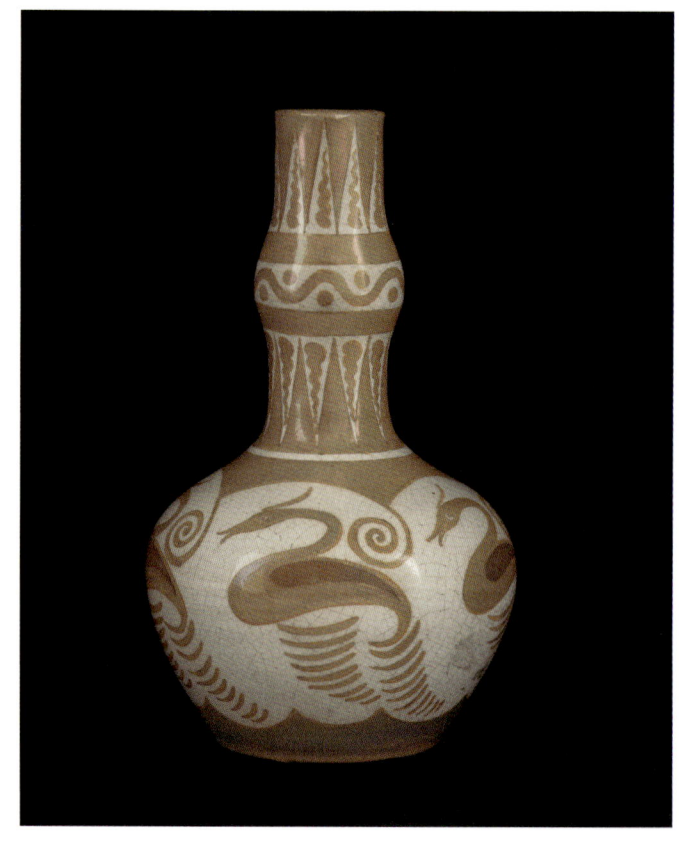

52

Running antelope dish

Decorated at one of William De Morgan's potteries, *c.*1880–90
Presented by Linda Lovelace Brownrigg in memory of her partner Philip Lewis, 2021, WA2022.25.

Circular dish painted in ruby lustre on a cream ground with a male and female antelope running against a foliate background. Reverse painted with concentric rings in ruby lustre and a foliate border on a cream ground. Reverse impressed: *20.*

Diameter: 36.2 cm

CONDITION: good.

PROVENANCE: Philip Lewis; Linda Lovelace Brownrigg.

BIBLIOGRAPHY: Greenwood 1989, p.38 (the design).

De Morgan's design for a dish with the same running antelope but a different background is in the V&A (fig.16).[195] Other running antelope dishes are in the British Museum and the De Morgan Foundation.[196] The blanks for these large dishes, known as 'rice dishes', were supplied by several firms including Wedgwood & Co. and Davis of Hanley, Staffordshire.[197]

195 V&A, E.1218-1917.
196 British Museum, BEP, 1928,0725.1.CR; De Morgan Foundation, C_WDM_0114.
197 Rudoe 1994, no.78.

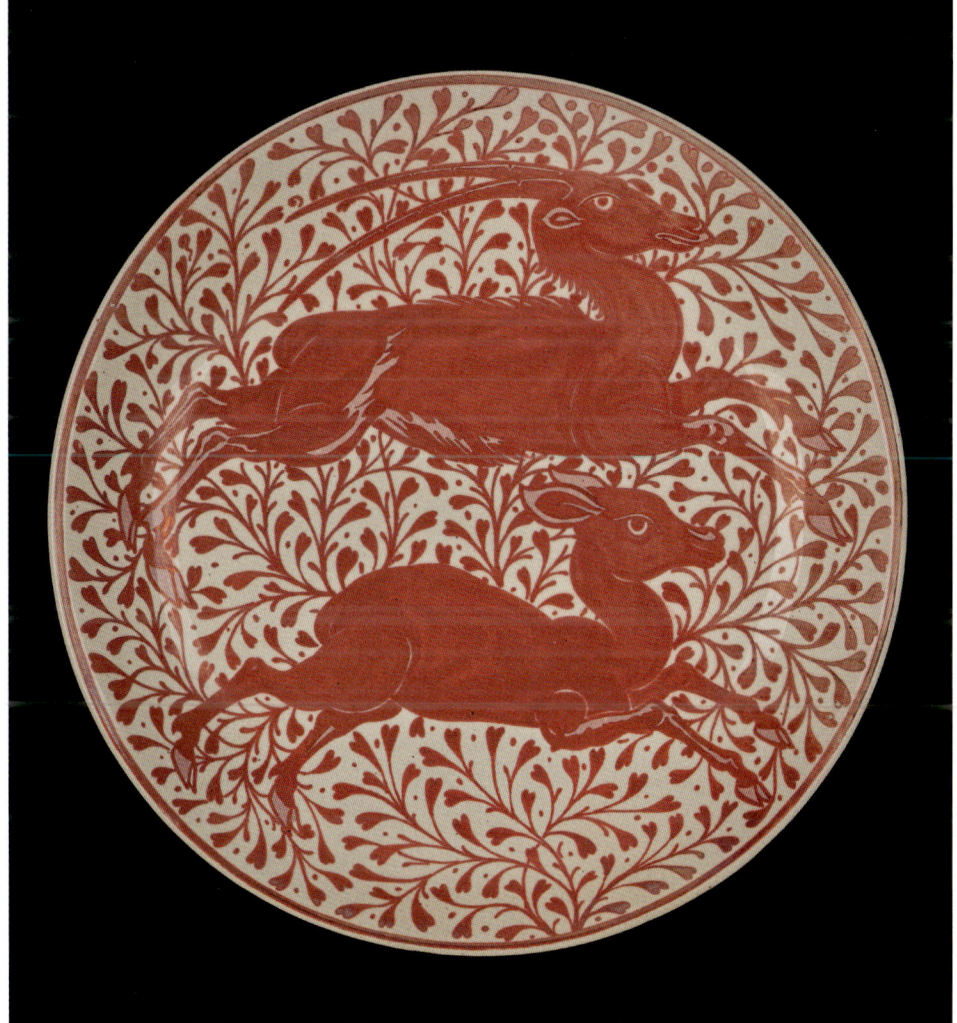

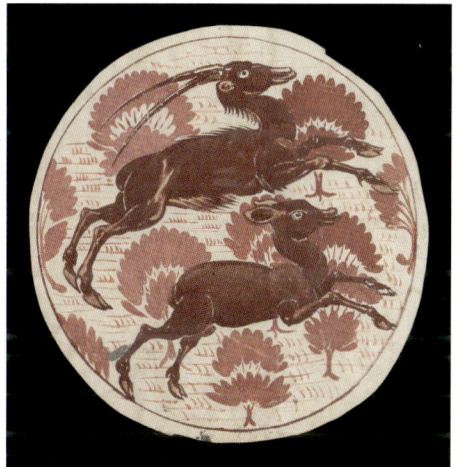

Fig.16 Design by William De Morgan. © Victoria and Albert Museum, London

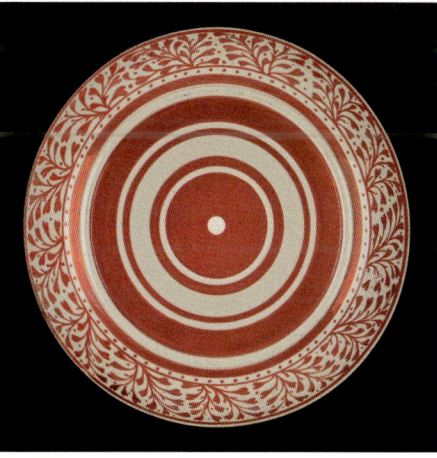

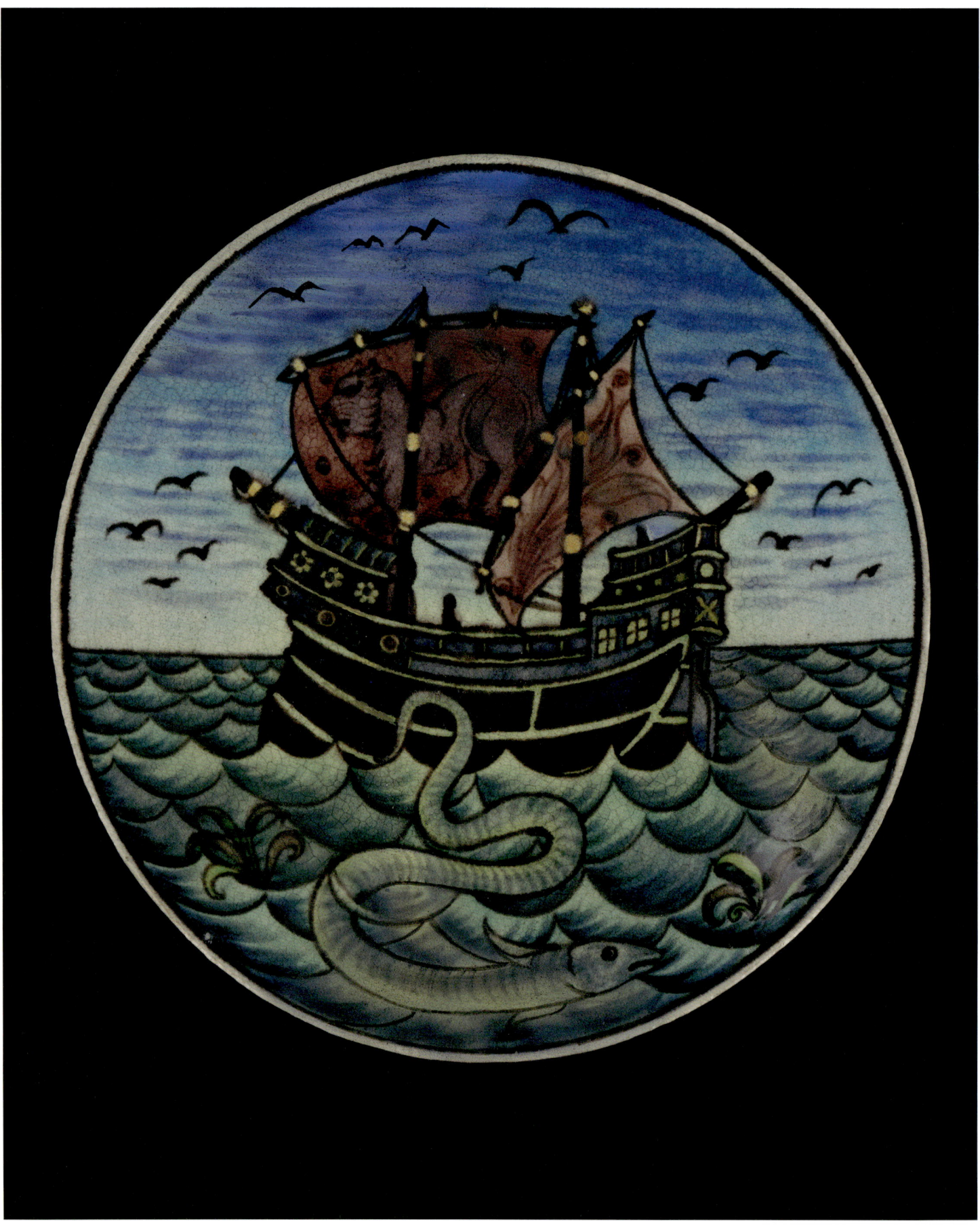

53

Ship dish

Fulham, William De Morgan's Sands End Pottery, painted by Charles Passenger, c.1888–1907
Presented by the Thompson family, 2021, WA2022.10.

Shallow earthenware dish on low foot painted in 'Persian' colours with a ship in full sail with a sea monster below. Reverse painted with concentric bands in blue and turquoise edged with black: Marked under foot in black: *DE MORGAN & CO FULHAM 1085 CP.*

Diameter: 21 cm

CONDITION: good.

PROVENANCE: probably Reginald Campbell Thompson, nephew of William De Morgan; thence by descent; presented by his grandchildren to the Museum.

De Morgan's design was inspired by the celebrated ship bowl (fig.17) in the South Kensington (now V&A) Museum, made in Malaga or Granada in the first half of the fifteenth century.[198]

The dish is marked under the foot with the initials of the decorator Charles Passenger. The brothers Frederick and Charles Passenger were two of De Morgan's most important and talented decorators. They first joined De Morgan in the 1870s and continued at the Pottery for nearly 40 years. They were partners with De Morgan from 1898 and remained at the pottery until 1911, four years after De Morgan had left. A similar dish, also decorated by Charles Passenger, is in the De Morgan Foundation collection.[199]

Apart from the pieces of De Morgan lustreware included here and the present plate, the generous gift from the Thompson family included other (unlustred) De Morgan pottery and tiles, all with the same interesting provenance to De Morgan's nephew.

198 V&A, 486-1864; Ray 2000, no.21.
199 De Morgan Foundation, C_WDM_0098.

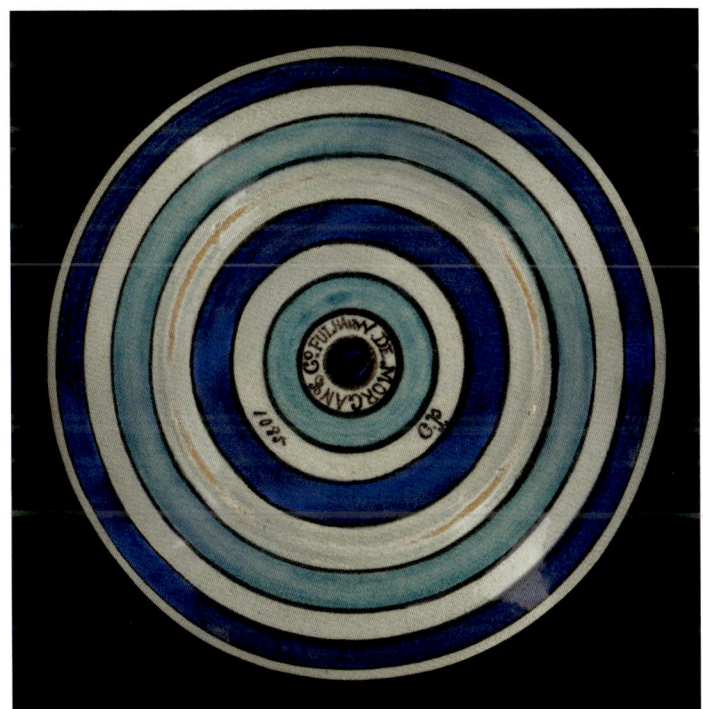

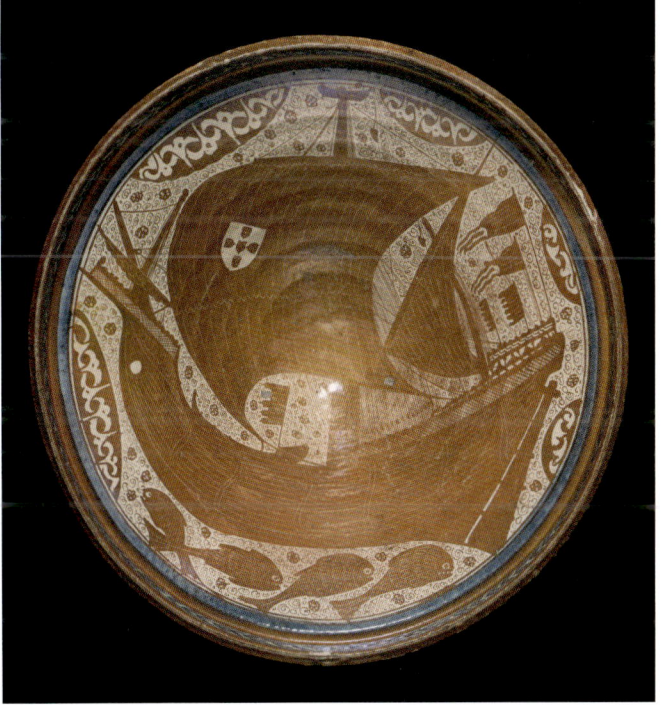

Fig.17 Lustred bowl, Spanish (Nasrid Kingdom, Malaga or Granada), c.1425–50. © Victoria and Albert Museum, London

54

Fish tazza

Fulham, decorated at William De Morgan's Sands End Pottery, *c.*1888–1907
Presented by Linda Lovelace Brownrigg, in memory of her partner Philip Lewis, 2021, WA2022.26.

Circular earthenware dish on low foot, painted in 'Persian' colours in the centre with three stylised fish and scrolls in green against a turquoise ground surrounding border of fin-like scrolls in green on cream ground. Reverse painted in turquoise, blue, beige and black with concentric bands. Base inscribed in black: *W.D.M. FULHAM CP*; stamped: *WEDGWOOD*.

Height: 7.6 cm; diameter: 22 cm

CONDITION: good.

PROVENANCE: Phillip Lewis; Linda Lovelace Brownrigg.

Painted by Charles Passenger on a Wedgwood blank (see no.**53**).

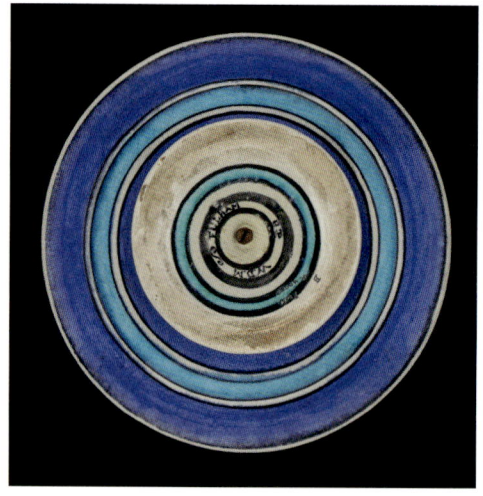

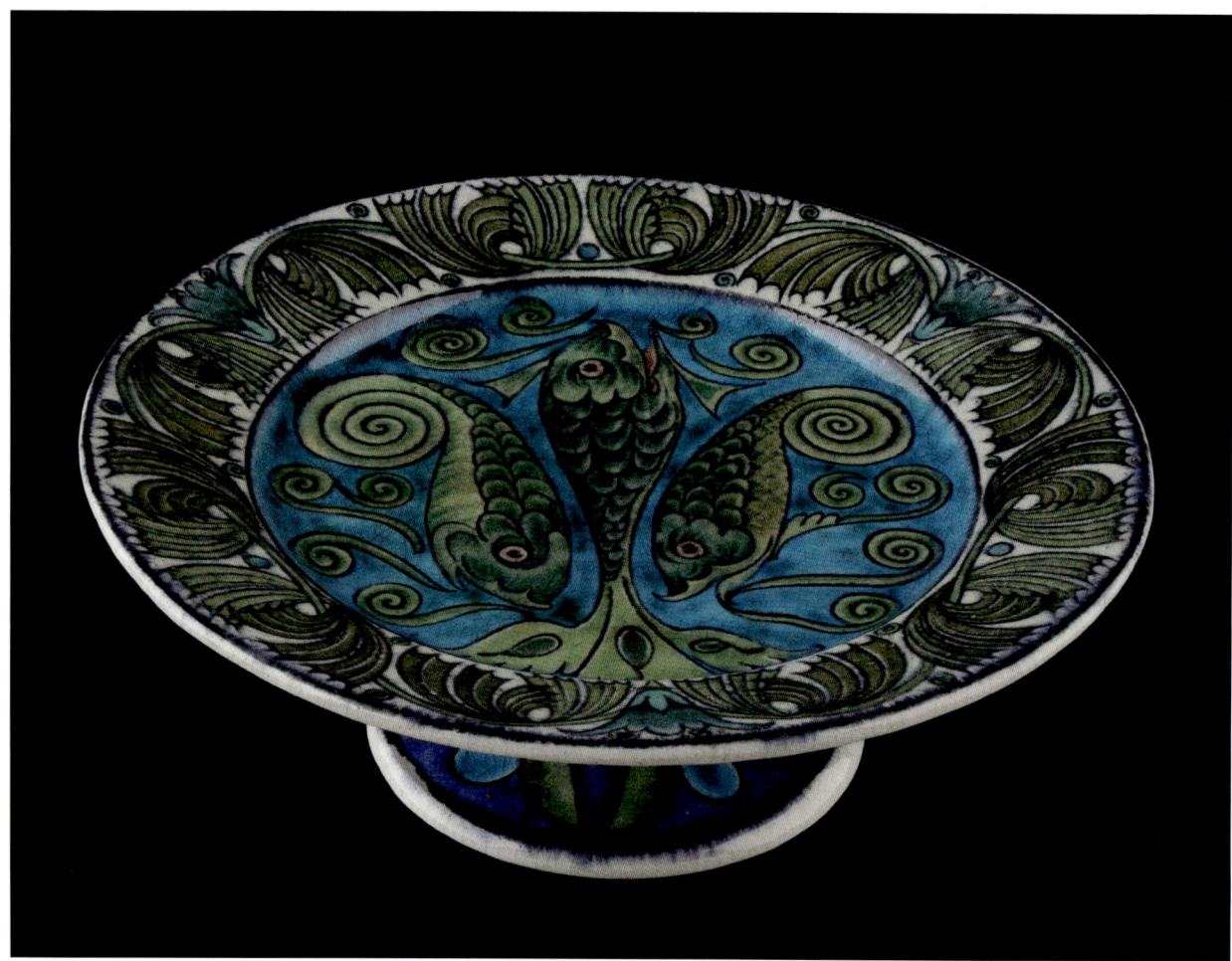

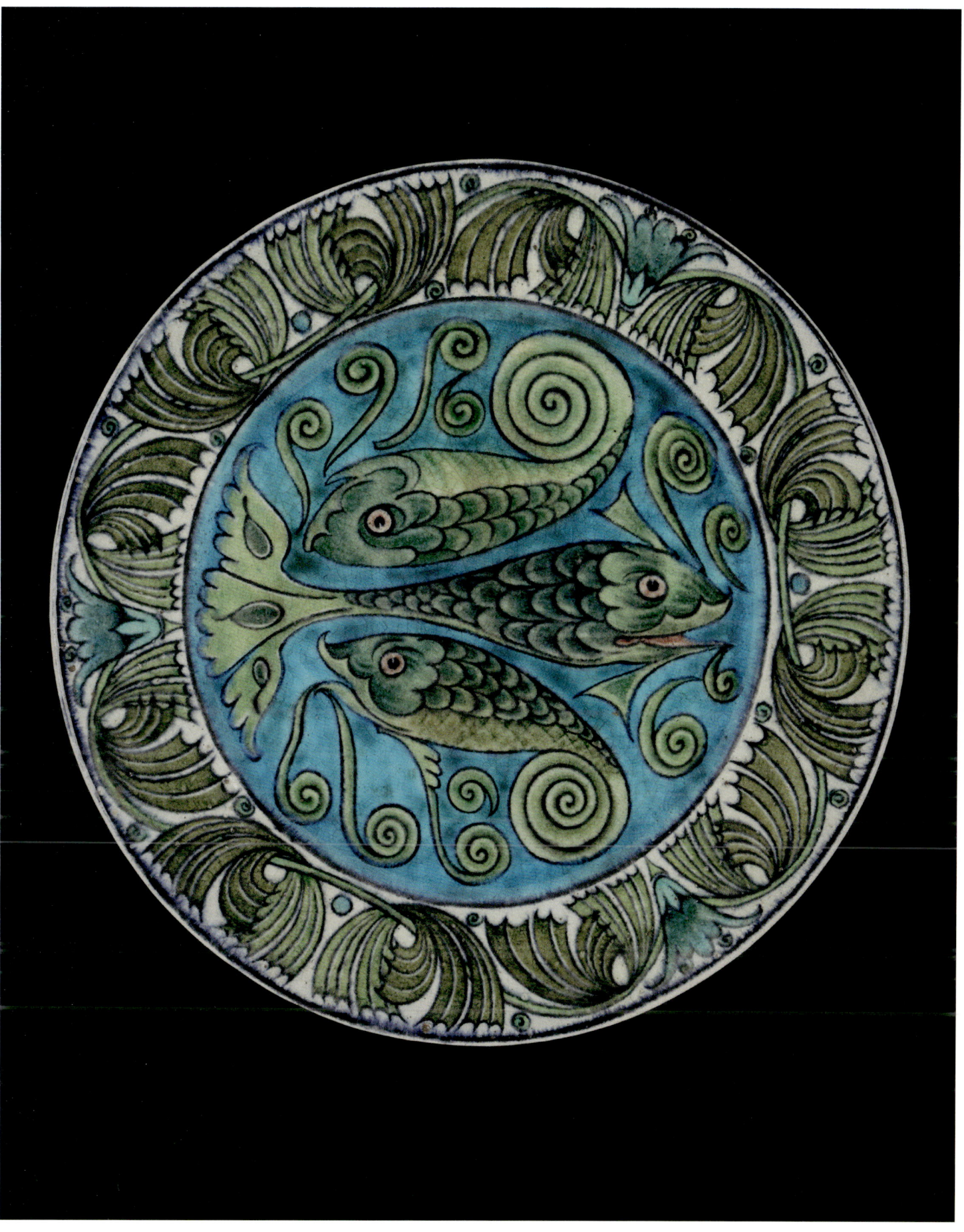

55

Tile, 'Raised Lion'

Fulham, made at William De Morgan's Sands End Pottery, *c*.1888–97
Presented by the Thompson family, 2021, WA2022.18.

Buff earthenware body moulded in shallow relief with a lion and lioness facing opposite directions, painted in olive green on a bright turquoise ground. Stamped on reverse with *W^M DE MORGAN SANDS END POTTERY FULHAM* around a Tudor rose.

15.8 × 15.7 cm

CONDITION: good.

PROVENANCE: probably Reginald Campbell Thompson, nephew of William De Morgan; thence by decent; presented by his grandchildren to the Museum, 2021.

BIBLIOGRAPHY: Catleugh 2002, p.140, pl.225, p.162, pl.258.

De Morgan's design for this tile is in the V&A.[200] Raised Lion pattern tiles are also in the V&A and De Morgan Foundation.[201]

200 V&A, E.1074-1917.
201 V&A, C.221-1976; De Morgan Foundation, C_WDM_T0012.

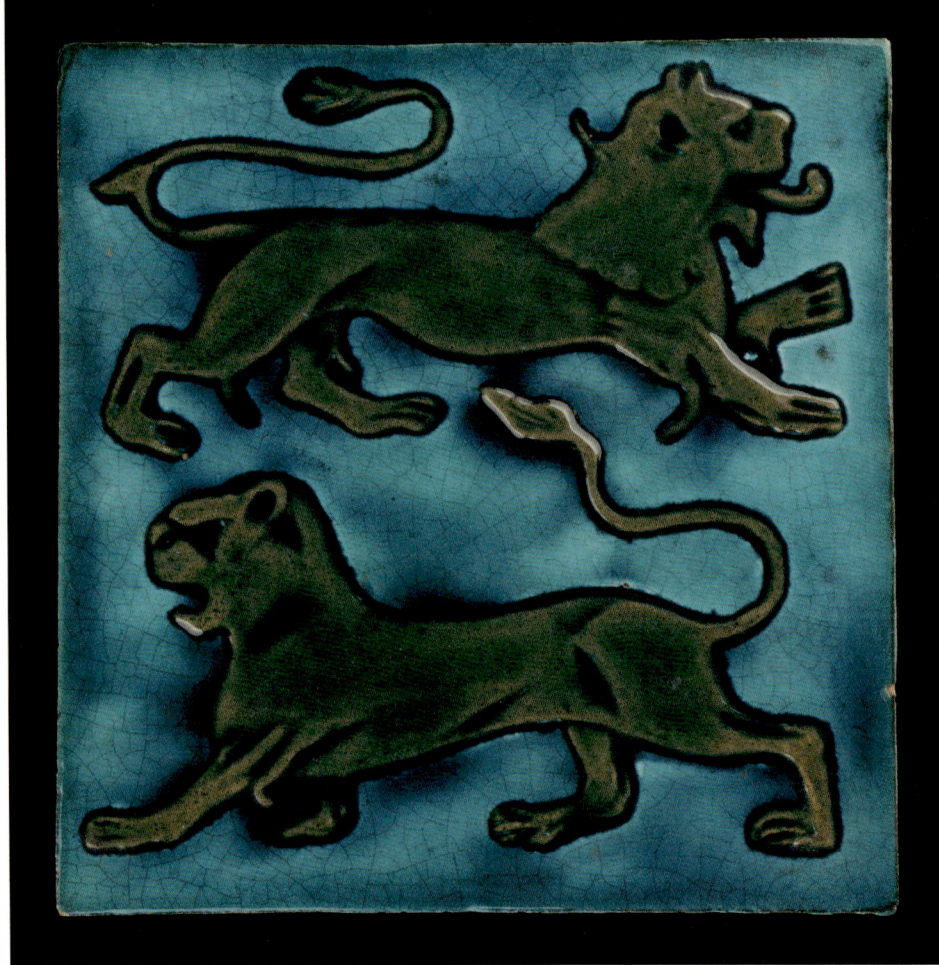

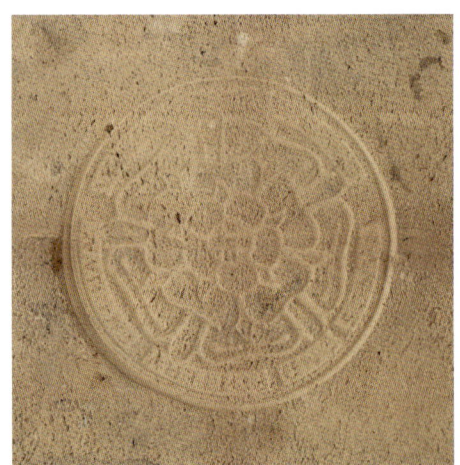

56

Vase

Lambeth, Doulton & Co. Ltd Studios, 1876
Bequeathed by Ian and Rita Smythe, 2023. WA2023.104.

Faience-style earthenware vase painted with coloured naturalistic poppies, cornflowers, and butterflies on buff ground. Egyptian-inspired zig-zag decoration on neck and foot. Impressed under foot: *Doulton Lambeth Faience 1876 W*

Height: 35.2 cm

CONDITION: good.

PROVENANCE: unrecorded.

Doulton established the first Art Pottery Studio at Lambeth in 1871. Students, mainly young women from the local school of art, incised and applied designs on stoneware, which was known as Doulton Lambeth ware. Their painted earthenware vases and plaques were known as Lambeth or Doulton Faience.[202]

202 The distinctive decoration has been attributed to John Bennett (1840–1907) by Jeffrey Davies. Bennett was Director of the Doulton Lambeth Faience Department from 1873 to 1877, before starting his own pottery in New York (1877–1883).

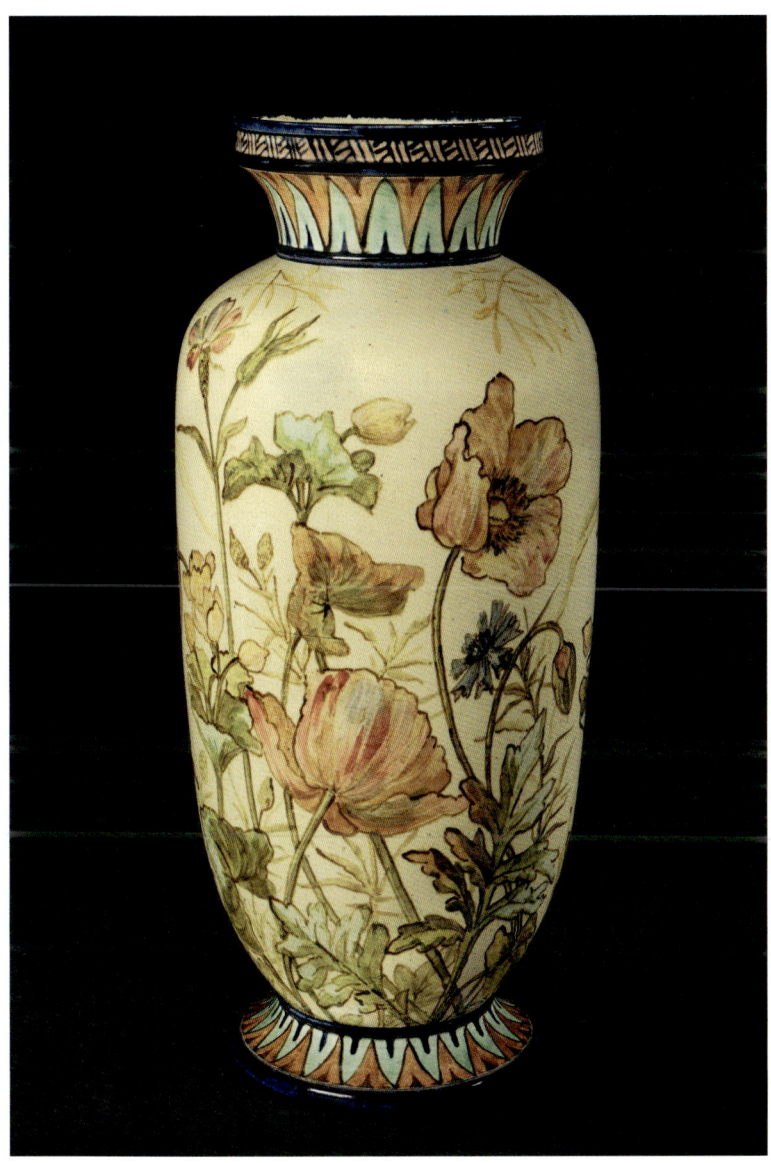

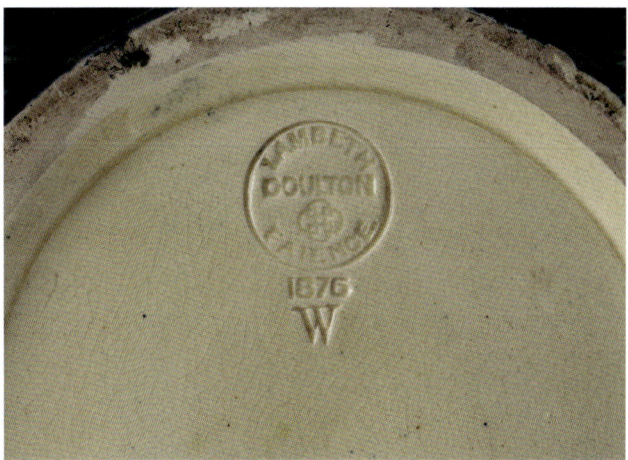

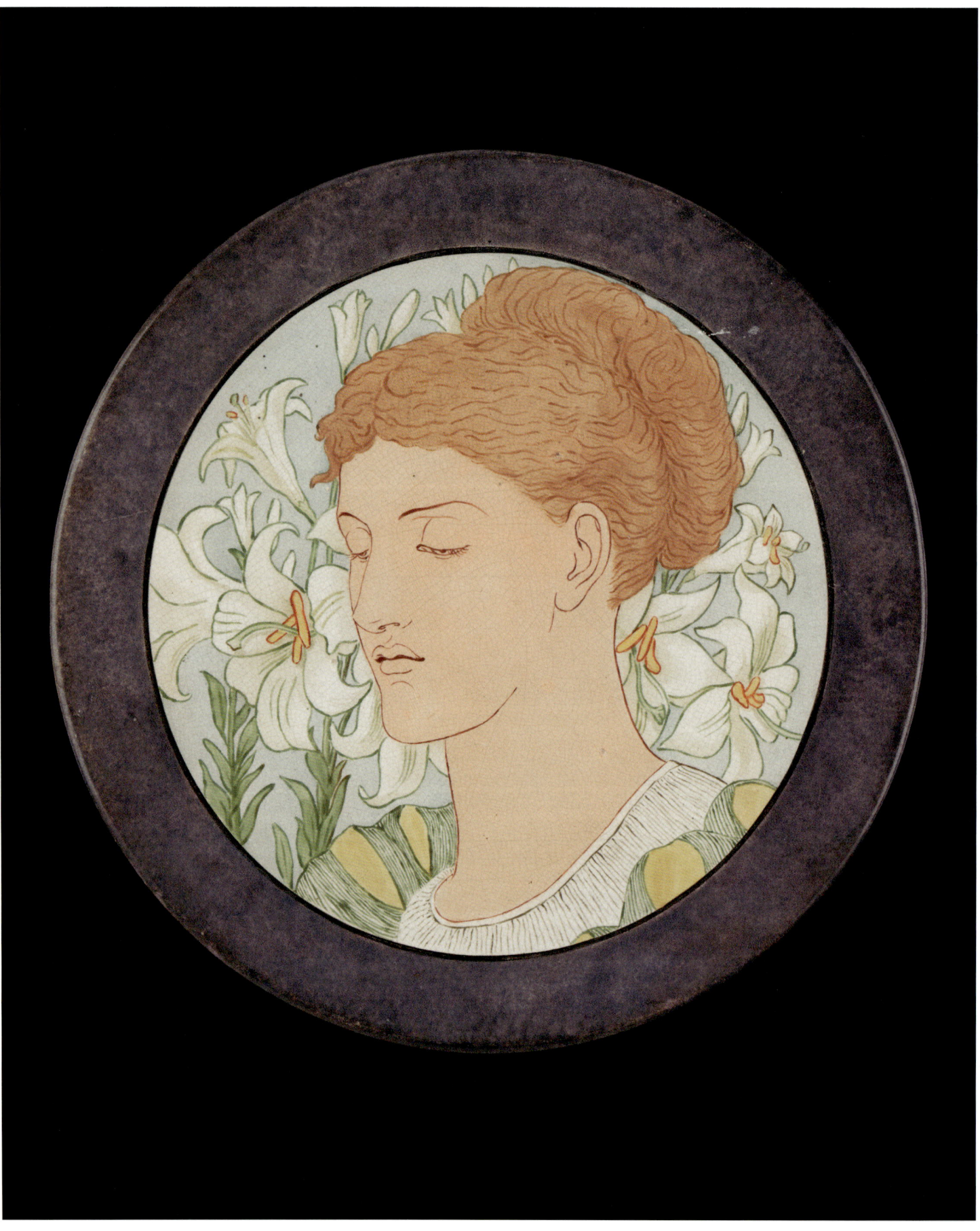

57

Plaque

Lambeth, Doulton & Co. Ltd Studios, *c.*1880
Bequeathed by Ian and Rita Smythe, 2023, WA2023.105.

Faience-style circular plaque with bust of a young
woman with red hair wearing Aesthetic dress,
surrounded by white lilies. Dark grey plain border.
Reverse painted: *Doulton & Co Lambeth.*

Diameter: 29 cm

CONDITION: good.

PROVENANCE: unrecorded .

Ian and Rita Smythe were London-based
antique dealers and collectors. As well as
the Ashmolean, the Victoria and Albert
Museum, the Potteries Museum, and the
Fitzwilliam Museum received objects
from their collection.[203]

203 Donnelly 2008 describes their collection.

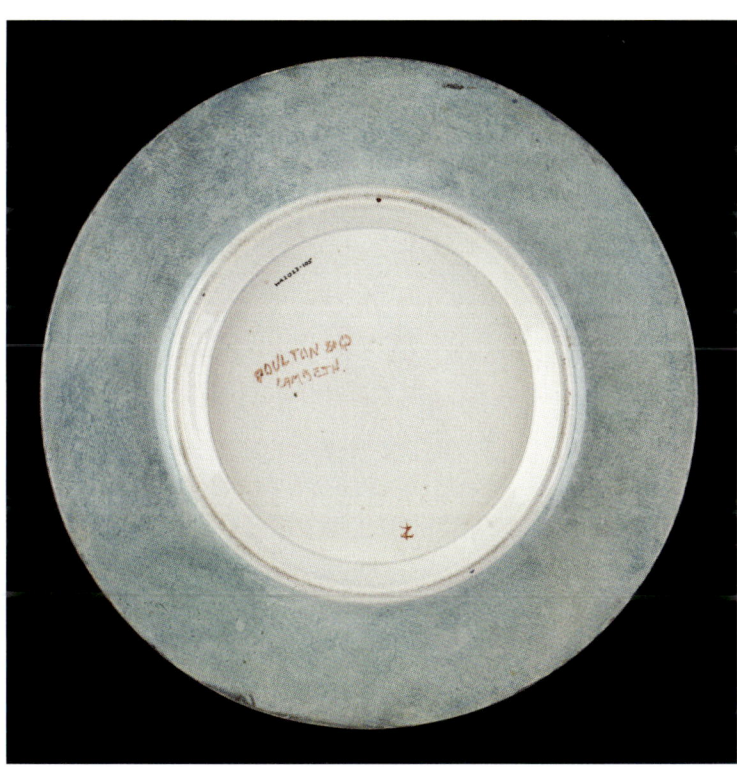

58

Large 'Anglo–Persian' vase

Leeds, Burmantofts Pottery, painted by Leonard King, *c.*1885–90
Bequeathed by Ian and Rita Smythe, 2023, WA2023.106.

Large earthenware onion-shaped vase with stylised flower and leaf decoration in dark blue, purple, cream, and green on a turquoise ground. Base stamped: *Burmantofts Faience 21;* painted monogram *LK* in black under base.

Height: 40.5 cm

CONDITION: good.

PROVENANCE: unrecorded.

Burmantofts Art Pottery, known as Burmantofts Faience, was produced between 1880 and 1904 as a response to the artistic ceramics made for middle-class markets by De Morgan, Doulton, and Minton. Burmantofts 'Anglo–Persian' wares have glazes of great clarity and brilliant colour due to the high quality of materials available to the pottery. A huge range of shapes and styles were made; they were retailed nationally, including at Harrods and Liberty, as well as internationally.

The pair to this vase, also from the Smythe collection, is in the V&A.[204]

204 V&A, C.218-2018.

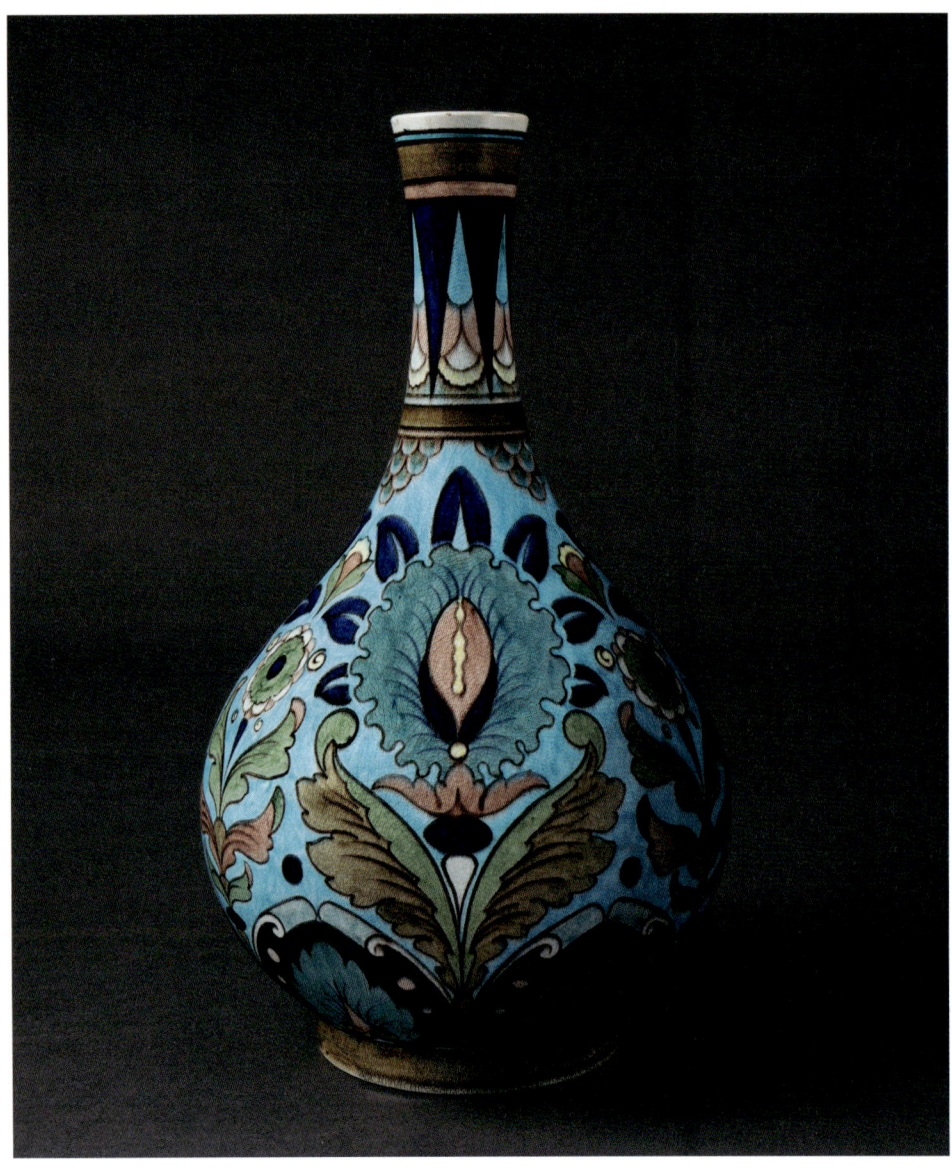

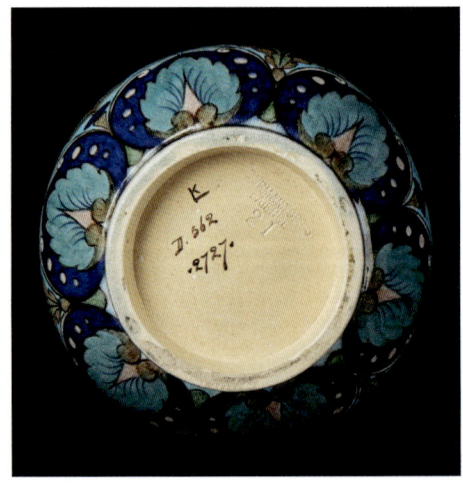

59

Large 'Parti-coloured' floral vase

Leeds, Burmantofts Pottery, designed by Joseph Walmsley, *c*.1900
Bequeathed by Ian and Rita Smythe, 2023, WA2023.107.

'Parti-coloured' baluster-shaped vase with incised and raised stylised artichokes and leaves in blue, green, and brown on a turquoise ground. Dark blue neck and foot. Base stamped: *2049 BURMANTOFTS FAIENCE ENGLAND*, with additional painted numbers.

Height: 34.6 cm

CONDITION: good.

PROVENANCE: unrecorded.

Further 'Parti-coloured' Burmantofts Faience ware, designed by Joseph Walmsley (1865–1956) and also from the Smythe collection, is in the V&A.[205]

205 V&A, C.215-2018, C.216-2018 and C.217-2018.

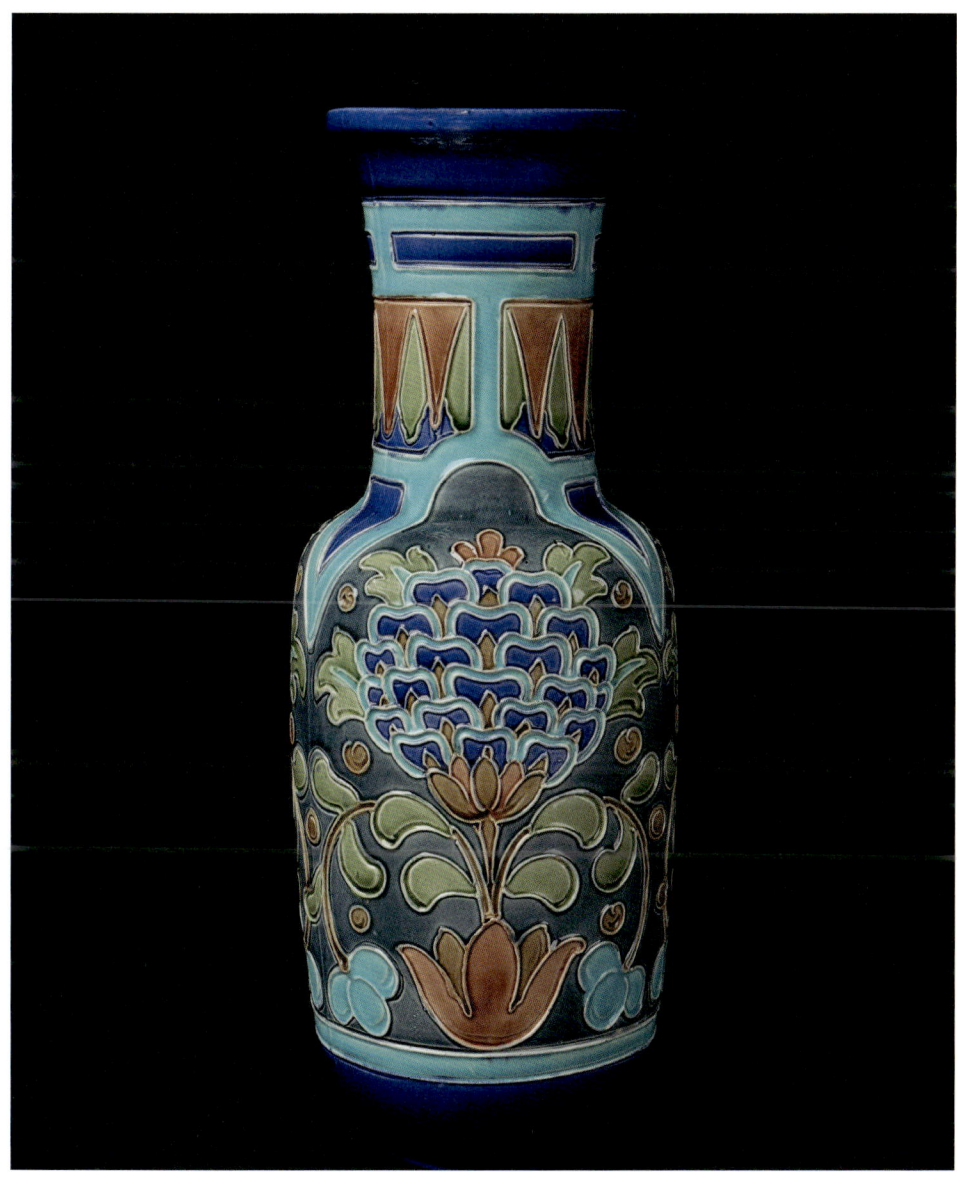

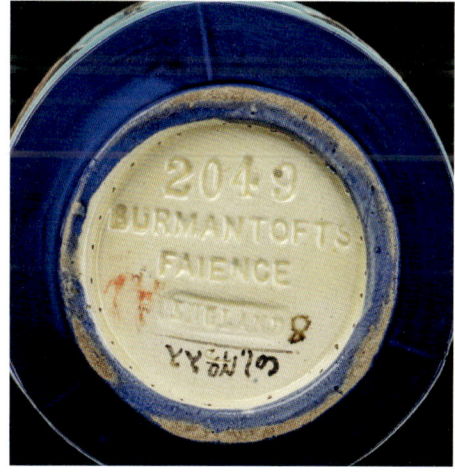

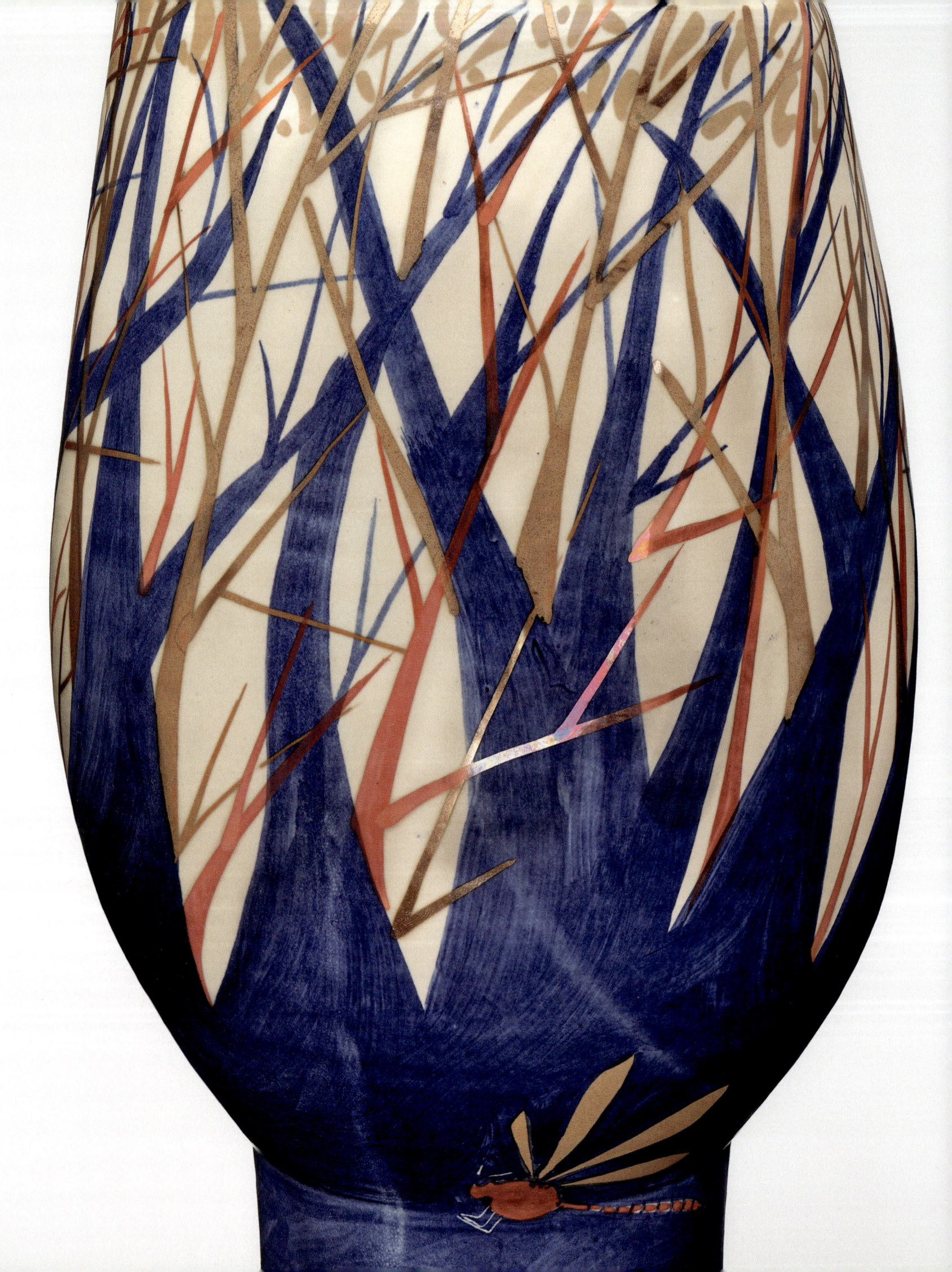

SPAIN

Opposite: detail of no.**60**

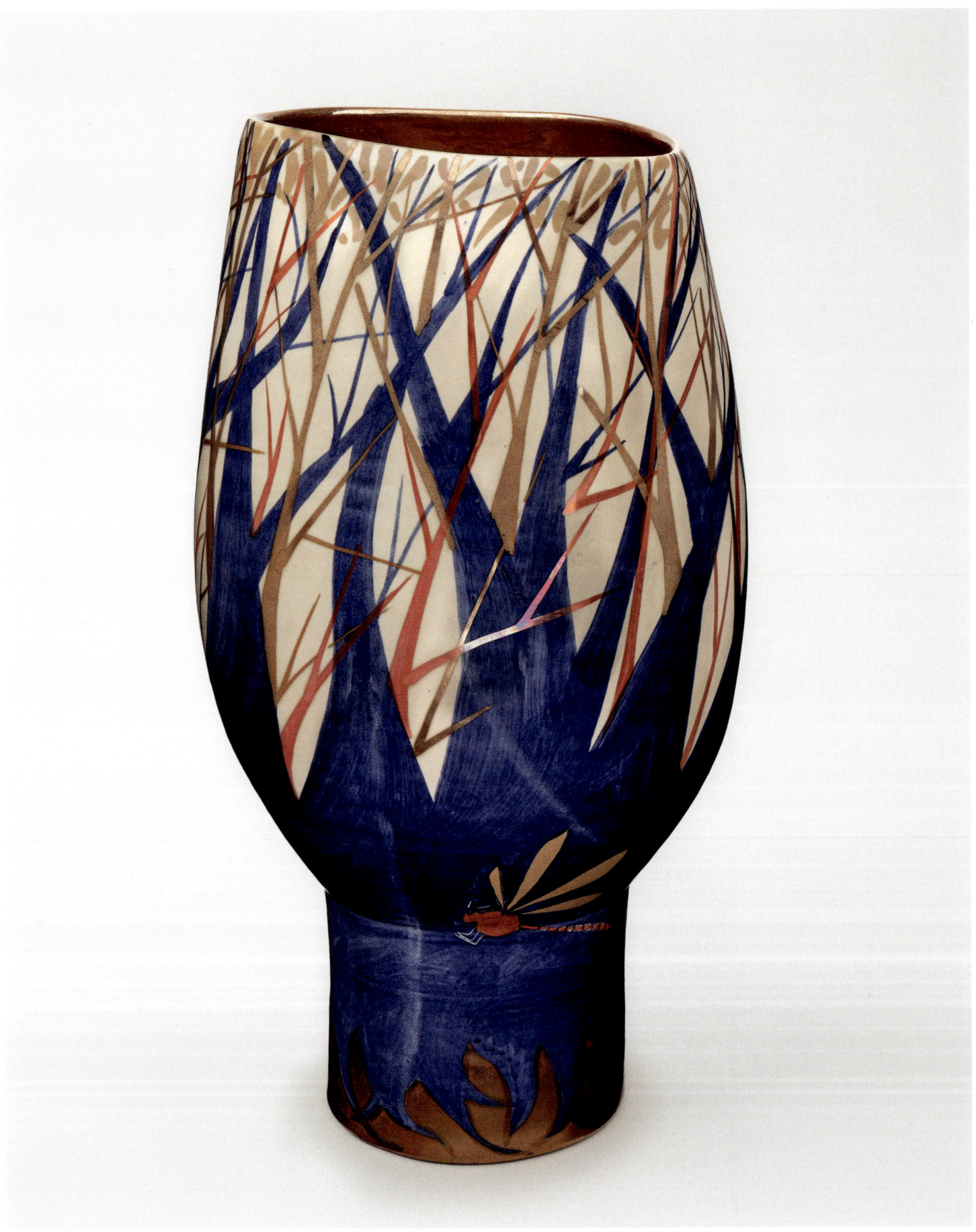

60

Vase with a design of branches and a flying insect

Manises, Arturo Mora Benavent, 2024
Presented by Timothy Wilson, WA2025.40.

Vase with one side flattened, on high foot. Maiolica, painted with a design of intersecting branches in blue and with a flying insect near the foot; painted in blue with red (copper) and golden (silver) lustre. Incised within the foot-ring with Mora's mark, representing an open hand, and painted in lustre with the same mark and inscription, *mora*.

Height: 33.5 cm

CONDITION: good.

PROVENANCE: Bought from the artist, 2025.

The wonderful tradition of lustred ceramics made by potters of Islamic faith in Spain, first of all in the Nasrid Kingdom (Malaga and probably also Granada) and subsequently in Manises near Valencia, has been brilliantly revived by Arturo Mora Benavent of Manises (b.1970), developing the work of his father Salvador Mora.[206] His family have been active as potters at Manises since the nineteenth century. He specialises in traditional reduction-fired lustre on a tin-lead glaze, and makes both virtuoso reproductions of fifteenth-century Manises lustreware and original pieces like this vase.[207] He has built a wood kiln for lustre firings (using rosemary to generate smoke), but this piece had all its firings in his main gas kiln.

206 For the suggestion that some of the Nasrid lustreware normally attributed to Malaga, including some of the 'Alhambra vases', may actually have been made within the Alhambra, see Conesa and Guzmán 2024.
207 Sannipoli 2018. Another expert exponent of reduction-fired lustre is Miguel Ruiz Jiménez of Granada, whose work includes reproductions of Nasrid lustreware.

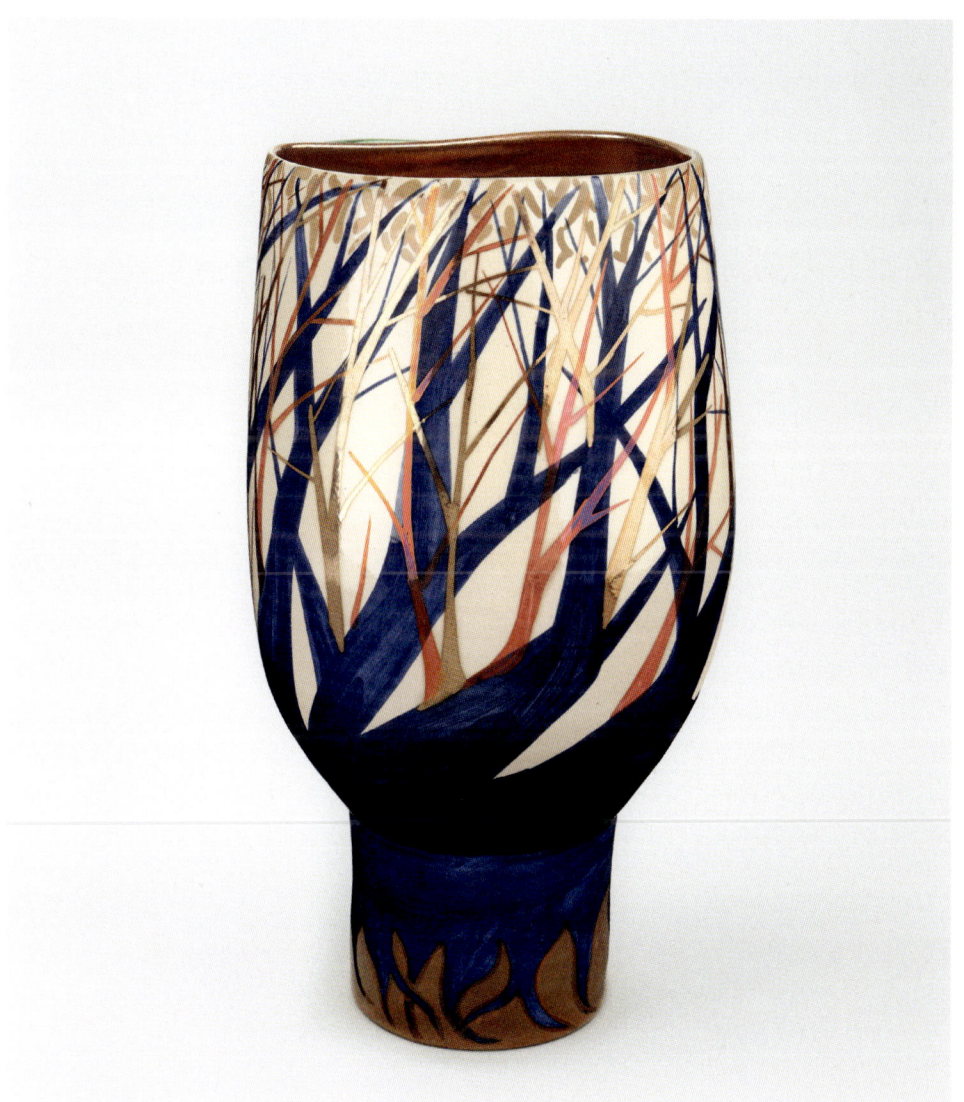

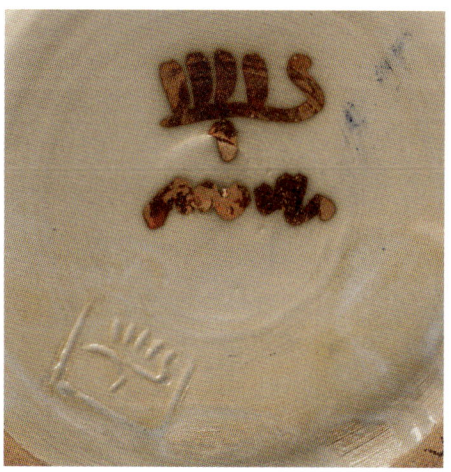

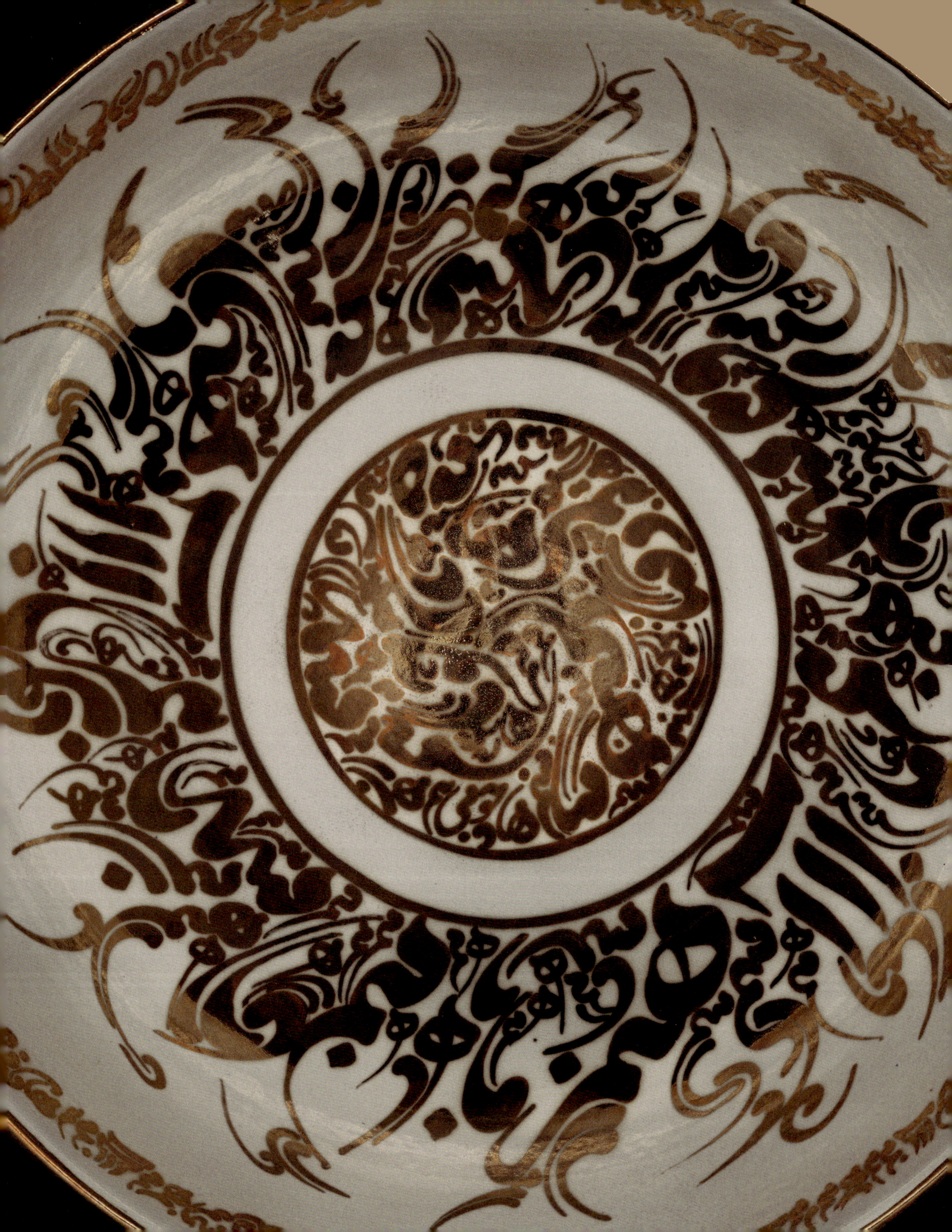

IRAN

Opposite: detail of no.**61**

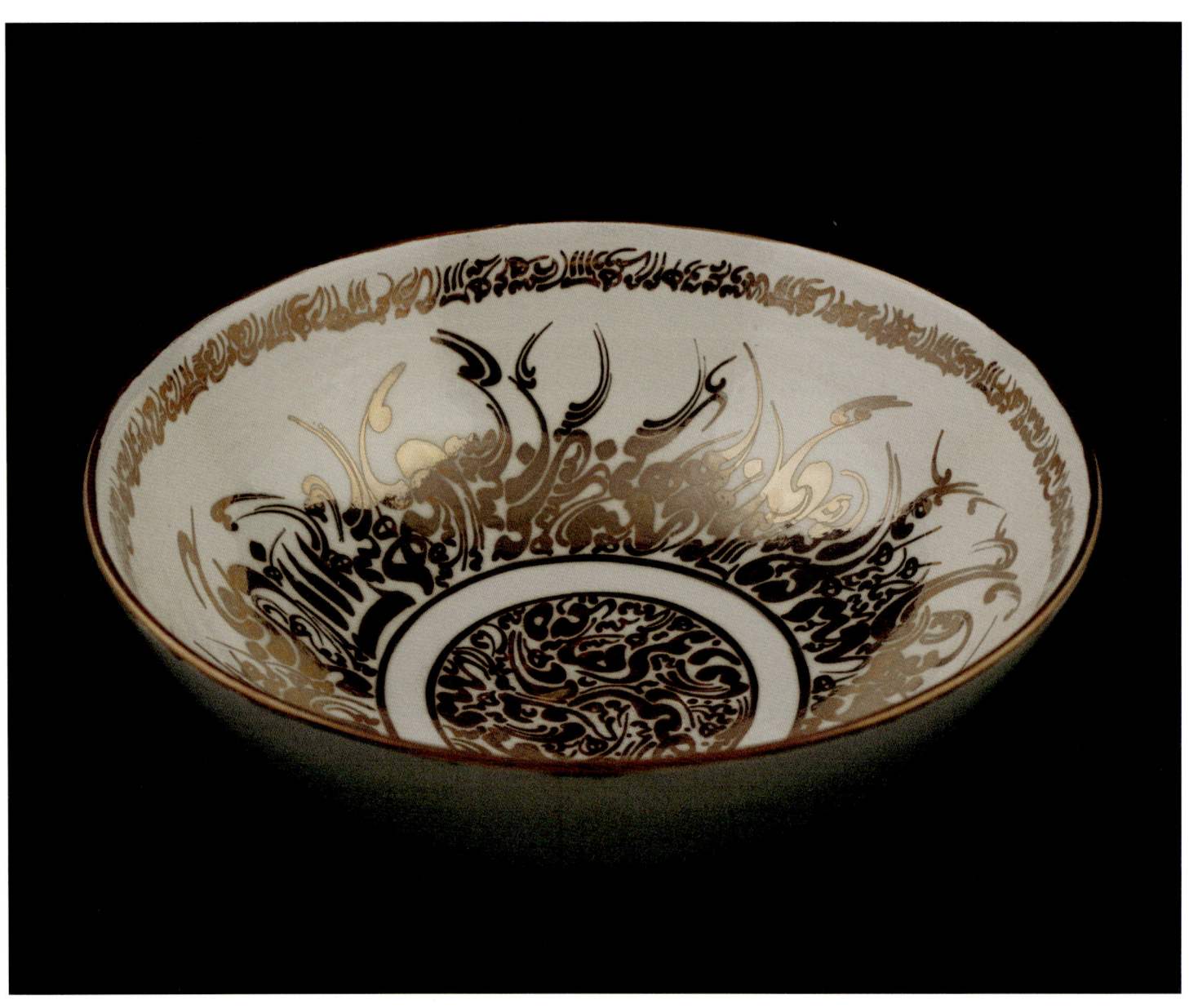

61

Bowl with pseudo-calligraphic lustred decoration

Manises, painted by Abbas Akbari in the workshop of Arturo Mora, 2019
Presented by Abbas Akbari, EA2020.162.

Signed in lustre on the base in Persian with the Islamic date 1398; and in Latin script, *A.A 2019*.

Diameter: 43 cm

CONDITION: good.

BIBLIOGRAPHY: Leoni 2021.

Abbas Akbari (b.1971) is one of Iran's leading contemporary ceramic artists and a witness to the centuries-old tradition of lustreware, which established his country's international artistic prestige centuries before being adopted across Europe.[208] This technique, first experimented on tin-glazed vessels in tenth-century Iraq, reached its technical and artistic peak in the city of Kashan in the twelfth century, resulting in a wealth of vessels and architectural decoration that were avidly acquired by European collectors from the second half of the nineteenth century onwards.

Working in this very city eight centuries later, Akbari is part of a group of contemporary artists who are now reviving this technique, infusing it with modern content and relevance whilst also looking at its global journey and legacy.

Made during a residency in Spain with fellow pottery artist and lustre virtuoso Arturo Mora (see no.**60**), this handsome bowl merges past and present. Its main decorative motif, three energetic pseudo-epigraphic bands, echoes Persian and Arabic inscriptions traditionally found on medieval lustre vessels but reinterpreted in contemporary form. The meaning and legibility of the words are here abandoned in favour of their visual quality and decorative impact, turning their fractured syllables into pure abstraction.

208   There is a biographical note in Sannipoli 2018.

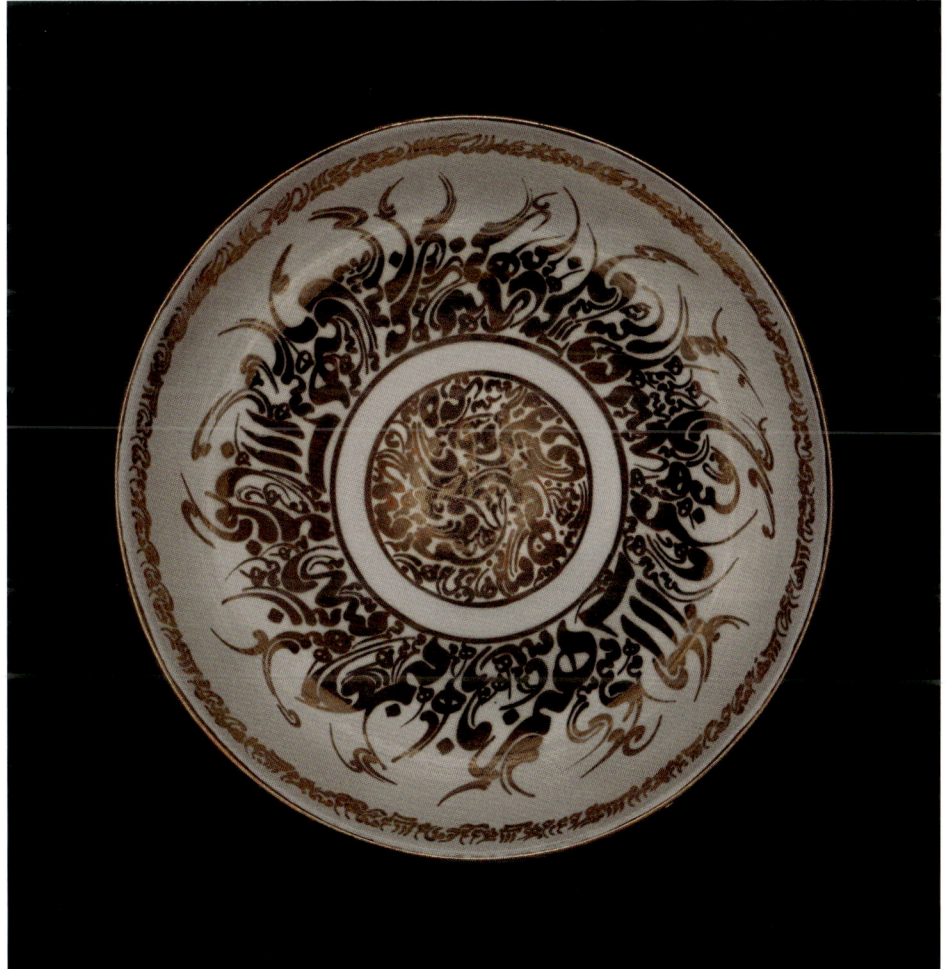

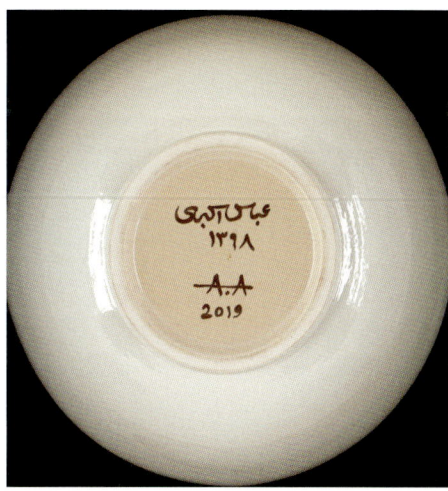

Concordance

No.**6** (detail)

Bibliography

Aix 1952. *Faïences de Moustiers* (exh. cat., Aix-en-Provence, 1952)

Alverà Bortolotto and Dumortier 1990. Alverà Bortolotto, Angelica and Claire Dumortier, 'Les majoliques "à la façon de Venise" de la première moitié du XVIe siècle', *Revue belge d'archéologie et d'histoire de l'art* 59 (1990), pp.55–74

Asioli Martini 2019. Asioli Martini, Giovanni, *'Sacro e profane'. L'animo e il corpo* (Imola, 2019)

Atterbury 1995. Atterbury, Paul (ed.), *A. W. N. Pugin: Master of the Gothic Revival* (New Haven, 1995)

Atterbury and Wainwright 1994. Atterbury, Paul and Clive Wainwright (eds), *Pugin: A Gothic Passion* (New Haven and London, 1994)

Ausenda 2000. Ausenda, Raffaella (ed.), *Musei e Gallerie di Milano. Museo d'Arti Applicate. Le ceramiche. Tomo primo* (Milan, 2000)

Baldassari 2018. Baldasssari, Monica (ed.), *Pisa, città della ceramica. Mille anni di economia e d'arte dalle importazioni mediterranee alle creazioni contemporanee* (Pisa, 2018)

Bandini 1996. Bandini, Giovanna, '"Delle impagliate" ossia annotazioni intorno alle maioliche da puerpera cinquecentesche', in Giovanna Bandini and Sara Piccolo Paci, *Da donna a madre. Vesti e ceramiche particolari per momenti speciali* (Florence, 1996), pp.59–109

Berti 1997–2003 . Berti, Fausto, *Storia della ceramica di Montelupo* (Montelupo, 1997–2003)

Bode 1898. Bode, Wilhelm, 'Altflorentiner Majoliken', *Jahrbuch der Königlich Preussischen Kunstsammlumgen* 19 (1898), pp.206–17

Bode 1911. Bode, Wilhelm, *Die Anfänge der Majolikakunst in Toskana* (Berlin, 1911)

Boerio 1867. Boerio, Giuseppe, *Dizionario del dialetto veneziano* (Venice, 1867)

Bojani 1991. Bojani, Gian Carlo, *Sotto il segno dell'ansa. Giulio Busti ceramiche* (exh. cat., Monte San Savino, 1991)

Bojani et al. 1985 . Bojani, Gian Carlo, Carmen Ravanelli Guidotti, and Angiolo Fanfani, *Museo Internazionale delle Ceramiche in Faenza. La donazione Galeazzo Cora. Ceramiche dal Medioevo al XIX secolo* (Milan, 1985)

Brown and Curnow 2015. Brown, Duncan and Celia Curnow, 'A Cargo of Grotesque Maiolica from a Shipwreck off the North-West Coast of Scotland', in Hugo Blake (ed.), *Gran Bretagna e Italia tra Mediterraneo e Atlantico: Livorno – 'un porto inglese'*, *Archeologia Postmedievale* 19 (Sassari, 2015), pp.185–200

Caiger-Smith 1991. Caiger-Smith, Alan, *Lustre Pottery* (London, 1991)

Calderwood 1845. Calderwood, David, *History of the Kirk of Scotland* (Edinburgh, 1845)

Cappellini 2022 . Cappellini, Patrizia, *Wilhelm von Bode e Elia Volpi. Fotografia e commercio d'arte fra Firenze e Berlino, 1892–1927* (Florence, 2022)

Caputo 2012. Caputo, Marinella (ed.), *The Rubboli Collection: Italian Lustre Pottery in Gualdo Tadino* (Passignano, 2012)

Cartier 2001. Cartier, Jean, *Céramiques de l'Oise* (Paris, 2001)

Catleugh 2002. Catleugh, Jon, *William De Morgan Tiles* (Shepton Beauchamp, 2002)

Chami 1963. Chami, Emile, 'L'art céramique du Beauvaisis au XVe et au XVIe siècle', *Cahiers de la céramique, du verre et des arts de feu* 30 (1963), pp.79–116

Chami 1968. Chami, Emile, 'La plat de la passion', *Bulletin du Groupe de recherches et d'études de la céramique du Beauvaisis* 2 (1968), pp.24–47

Chami 1973. Chami, Emile, 'La céramique du Beauvaisis du Moyen Age au XVIIIe siècle: la poterie vernissée au XVIe siècle', *Cahiers de la céramique, du verre et des arts de feu* 53 (1973), pp.28–31

Chompret et al. 1933–5. Chompret, Joseph, Jean Bloch, Jacques Guerin, and Paul Alfassa, *Répertoire de la faïence française* (Paris, 1933–5)

Collard-Moniotte 1988. Collard-Moniotte, Denise, *Catalogue des faïences de Moustiers* (Paris, 1988)

Conti et al. 1991. Conti, Giovanni, Giovanni Alinari, Fausto Berti, Mario Luccarelli, Carmen Ravanelli Guidotti, and Romualdo Luzi, *Zaffera et similia nella maiolica italiana* (Viterbo, [1991])

Conticelli 2007. Conticelli, Valentina, *'Guardaroba di cose rare e preziose'. Lo Studiolo di Francesco de'Medici. Arte, storia e significati* (La Spezia, 2007)

Cora 1964. Cora, Galeazzo, 'Sulla fabbrica di maioliche sorta in Pisa alla fine del'500', *Faenza* 50 (1964), pp.25–30

Cora 1973. Cora, Galeazzo, *Storia della maiolica di Firenze e del contado. Secoli XIV e XV* (Florence, 1973)

Cora and Fanfani 1986. Cora, Galeazzo and Angiolo Fanfani, *La porcellana dei Medici* (Milan, 1986)

Crainz 1986. Crainz, Franco, *La tazza da parto* (Rome, 1986)

Däubler 1994. Däubler, Claudia, 'La tazza da parto nella collezione Pringsheim', *Ceramic Antica* 4/6 (June 1994), pp.26–39

Deloche 1994. Deloche, Bernard, *Faïences de Lyon* (Plouguerneau, 1994)

Dethick 2008. Dethick, Janet Kinrade, *A History of the Dethick Family of Dethick 1200–1918* (Privately printed, 2008) [A copy of this is in the Derbyshire Record Office]

Donnelly 2008. Donnelly, Max, 'A Collection of British Art Pottery and *Fin-de-Siècle* Decorative Arts', *Magazine Antiques*, 173/6 (June 2008), pp.95–103

Drey 1991. Drey, R. E. A., '*Istoriato* Maiolica with Scenes from the Second Punic War: Livy's History of Rome as Source Material', in Wilson 1991, pp.51–61

Du Boulay 1984. Du Boulay, Anthony, *Christie's Pictorial History of Chinese Ceramics* (Oxford, 1984)

Dumortier 2002. Dumortier, Claire, *Céramique de la Renaissance à Anvers. De Venise à Delft* (Brussels, 2002)

Ekserdjian 2010. Ekserdjian, David, 'Colnaghi and the Hermitage Deal', in Jeremy Howard (ed.), *Colnaghi 250:1760–2010* (London, 2010)

Elliott 2000. Elliott, David, *Charles Fairfax Murray: The Unknown Pre-Raphaelite* (Lewes, 2000)

Falcioni et al. 2024. Falcioni, Anna, Walter Monacchi, and Vincenzo Mosconi, *Girolamo di Tommaso Galli ceramista. I documenti d'archivio* (Urbino, 2024)

Fantoni 1994. Fantoni, Marcello, *La corte del Granduca* (Rome, 1994)

Ferrazza 1994. Ferrazza, Roberta, *Palazzo Davanzati e le collezioni di Elia Volpi* (Florence, 1994)

Fiocco and Gherardi 1991. Fiocco, Carola and Gabriella Gherardi, *Museo del Vino di Torgiano. Ceramiche* (Perugia, 1991)

Franken and Laschitzer 1881. Franken, Daniel and Simon Laschitzer, *L'oeuvre gravé des van de Passe* (Amsterdam 1881)

Frescobaldi Malenchini and Rucellai 2011. Frescobaldi Malenchini, Livia and Oliva Rucellai, *Il risorgimento della maiolica italiana. Ginori e Cantagalli* (exh. cat., Museo Stibbert, Florence, 2011)

Gaimster 1999. Gaimster, David (ed.), *Maiolica in the North: The Archaeology of Tin-glazed Earthenware in North-West Europe c.1500–1600* (London, British Museum Occasional Papers no.122, 1999)

Gardelli 1993. Gardelli, Giuliana, 'San Crescentino e il drago, grande tavola in maiolica della galleria nazionale delle Marche. L'influenza di Raffaello nella iconografia ceramica', *Fimantiquari Arte Viva* 3 (1993), pp.39–45

Gardelli 1999. Gardelli, Giuliana, *Italika. Maiolica italiana del Rinascimento. Saggi e Studi* (Faenza, 1999)

Giguet 2002–3. Giguet, Bernard, 'Un nouveau fragment du plat de la passion', *Bulletin du Groupe de recherches et d'études de la céramique du Beauvaisis* 24 (2002–3), pp.22–4

Godefroy 1922. Godefroy, Maurice, *Exposition Coloniale de Marseille, 1922. Catalogue illustré de la section Mobilier et Céramique d'Art provençal* (exh. cat., Marseille, 1922)

Conesa and Guzmán 2024. Conesa, Jaumé Coll and Rafael López Guzmán (eds), *Cerámica nazarí. Proyección y contextos* (exh. cat., Alhambra, Granada, 2024)

Grandjean 2001. Grandjean, Gilles, *Trésors du musée de la Céramique* (Rouen, 2001)

Greenwood 1989. Greenwood, Martin, *The Designs of William De Morgan* (Ilminster, 1989)

Guasti 1902. Guasti, Gaetano, *Di Cafaggiolo e d'altre fabbriche di ceramiche in Toscana secondo studi e documenti in parte raccolti da Comm. Gaetano Milanesi* (Florence, 1902)

Guillemé Brulon 1997. Guillemé Brulon, Dorothée, *Histoire de la faïence française. Lyon et Nevers. Sources et rayonnement* (Paris, 1997)

Hamilton 1997. Hamilton, Mark, *Rare Spirit: a life of William De Morgan, 1839–1917* (London, 1997)

Hildyard 2025. Hildyard, Robin, 'Pots That Tell a Story: The Jonathan Horne Collection of Early Stonewares Acquired by the Ashmolean', *Oxford Ceramics Group Newsletter* 61 (February 2025), pp.18–24

Holcroft 1988. Holcroft, Alison, 'Francesco Xanto Avelli and Petrarch', *Journal of the Warburg and Courtauld Institutes* 51/1 (1988), pp.225–34

Hollein et al. 2022. Hollein, Lilli, Rainald Franz, and Timothy Wilson (eds), *Tin-Glaze and Image Culture: The MAK Maiolica Collection in its Wider Context. Catalogue by Timothy Wilson with contributions by Rainald Franz, Michael Göbl, Nikolaus Hofer, and with the collaboration of Alena Volk* (Vienna and Stuttgart, 2022)

Honey 1952. Honey, William Bowyer, *European Ceramic Art from the End of the Middle Ages to about 1815: A Dictionary of Factories, Artists, Technical terms, et cetera* (London, 1952)

Hurst 1991. Hurst, John G., 'Italian Pottery Imported into Britain and Ireland', in Wilson 1991, pp.212–31

Ivanova 2019. Ivanova, Elena, *Mayolika Urbino XVI–XVII bekov. Katalog kollektsiy* (Saint Petersburg, 2019)

Jones 1993. Jones, Joan, *Minton: The First Two Hundred Years of Design and Production* (Shrewsbury, 1993)

Julien 1991. Julien, Louis, *L'art de la faïence à Moustiers* (Aix-en-Provence, 1991)

Kaucher 2024. Kaucher, Greta, *Le Peintre du Marsyas de Milan. La majolique historiée à Urbino en 1530* (Paris, 2024)

Kube 1976. Kube, Alfred N., *Italian Majolica XV–XVIII Centuries: State Hermitage Collection* (Moscow, 1976)

Ladis 1989. Ladis, Andrew, *Italian Renaissance Maiolica from Southern Collections* (exh. cat., Georgia Museum of Art, Athens, Georgia, 1989)

Lefevre 2004. Lefevre, Michel, 'Le plat dit "de la passion"', *Bulletin du Groupe de recherches et d'études de la céramique du Beauvaisis* 25 (2004)

Leoni 2021. Leoni, Francesca, '"A Close Connection with Time": A Contemporary Lustre Bowl by Abbas Akbari', *Ashmolean Magazine* 81 (spring 2021), pp.24–5

Leprince 2009. Leprince, Camille, *Feu et talent. D'Urbino à Nevers, le décor historié aux XVIe et XVIIe siècles* (exh. cat., Maison Vandermeersch, Paris, 2009)

Leprince 2020. Leprince, Camille, *Festons de faïence. Rouen XVIe–XVIIIe siècles* (Paris, 2002)

Leprince and Raccanello 2016. 'The Transfer of the *Istoriato* Tradition from Italy to France', *The French Porcelain Society Journal* 6 (2016), pp.1–27

Lessmann 1979. Lessmann, Johanna, *Herzog Anton Ulrich-Museum Braunschweig, Italienische Majolika, Katalog der Sammlung* (Braunschweig, 1979)

Lingard 1837–9. Lingard, John, *A History of England* (London, 1837–9)

Luber 2023. Luber, Diana, *Islam in Europe* (exh. cat., Sam Fogg Gallery, London, 2023)

Mallet 1978. Mallet, J. V. G., 'Pottery and Porcelain at Erddig', *Apollo* 108 (July 1978), pp.40–45

Mallet 2004. Mallet, J. V. G., 'Compendiario Grotesque: The Evidence of Two Basins at Waddesdon Manor', in S. Glaser (ed.), *Italienische Fayencen der Renaissance. Ihre Spuren in internationalen Museumssammlungen* (Nuremberg, 2004), pp.181–97

Mallet 2007. Mallet, J. V. G., with contributions by Giovanna Hendel and Elisa Paola Sani, *Xanto: Pottery-painter, Poet, Man of the Italian Renaissance* (exh. cat., Wallace Collection, London, 2007)

Mallet 2024. Mallet, J. V. G., 'Two "A" Marked Porcelain Saucers enter the Ashmolean', *Oxford Ceramics Group Newsletter* 59 (June 2024), pp.26–33

Marini 2024. Marini, Marino, *Maiolica and Ceramics in the Museo Nazionale del Bargello* (Turin, 2024)

Marini 2024B. Marini, Marino, 'Xanto: *disiecta membra* della raccolta di Stefano Bardini', *Faenza* 110/2 (2024), pp.116–26

Massey 2024. Massey, Roger, 'The Anthony du Boulay Vauxhall Vase: A Masterpiece of Eighteenth-century English Blue and White Porcelain', *Oxford Ceramics Group Newsletter* 60 (October 2024), pp.3–7

Maternati-Baldouy 1997. Maternati-Baldouy, Danielle, *Faïences et porcelaines de Marseille XVIIe et XVIIIe siècles. Collections du musée de Faïence de Marseille* (Marseille, 1997)

Molinier 1888. Molinier, Emile, *La Céramique Italienne au XVe siècle* (Paris, 1888)

Mompeut 1980. Mompeut, Jacques, *Les faïences de Moustiers du XVIIe siècle à nos jours* (Aix-en-Provence, 1980)

Moore Valeri 1984. Moore Valeri, Anna, 'Florentine "Zaffera a Rilievo" Maiolica: A New Look at the "Oriental Influence"', *Archeologia Medievale* 11 (1984), pp.477–500

Moskowitz 2015. Moskowitz, Anita F., *Stefano Bardini, 'Principe degli Antiquari'. Prolegomenon to a Biography* (Florence, 2015)

Musacchio 1999. Musacchio, Jacqueline Marie, *The Art and Ritual of Childbirth in Renaissance Italy* (New Haven and London, 1999)

Niemeyer Chini 2009. Niemeyer Chini, Valerie, *Stefano Bardini e Wilhelm Bode. Mercanti e Connaisseur fra Ottocento e Novecento* (Florence, 2009)

Norman 1997. Norman, Geraldine, *The Hermitage: Biography of a Great Museum* (London, 1997)

Nyon 1957. *Trésors du Grand Siècle* (exh. cat., Château de Nyon, 1957)

Odom and Salmond 2009. Odom, Anne and Wendy Salmond, *Treasures into Tractors: The Selling of Russia's Cultural Heritage, 1918–1938* (Seattle, 2009)

Paolinelli and Wilson 2024. Paolinelli, Claudio and Timothy Wilson, *Maioliche roveresche. Ceramiche del Ducato di Urbino nell'epoca dei Della Rovere* (Urbino and Genoa, 2024)

Paris 1932. *La faïence française de 1525 à 1820* (exh. cat., Pavillon de Marsan, Musée du Louvre, Paris, 1932)

Perale 2021. Perale, Riccardo, *Maioliche da farmacia nelle Serenissima* (Venice, 2021)

Perlès 2014. Perlès, Christophe, *Céramiques Anciennes. La faïence de Rouen, 1700–1750* (Paris, 2014)

Perlès 2016. Perlès, Christophe (ed.), *French Faïence: The Sidney R. Knafel Collection* (Le Kremlin-Bicêtre, 2016)

Pesante 2018. Pesante, Luca, 'Luca Baldi da Urbino', in Claudio Giardini and Claudio Paolinelli (eds), *La ceramica nello scaffale. Scritti di storia dell'arte ceramica per l'apertura della Biblioteca 'G. Bojani' a Fano* (Fano, 2018), pp.147–52

Pescara 1989. *Le maioliche cinquecentesche di Castelli. Una grande stagione artistica ritrovata* (Pescara, 1989)

Piccolpasso 2007. Piccolpasso, Cipriano, *The Three Books of the Potter's Art*, Ronald Lightbown and Alan CaigerSmith (eds), with an introduction by Rowan Watson (Vendin-le-Vieil, 2007)

Poole 1995. Poole, Julia, *Italian Maiolica and Incised Slipware in the Fitzwilliam Museum, Cambridge* (Cambridge, 1995)

Raccanello 2018. Raccanello, Justin, *Chiaroscuro Iridiscente: The Experimental Lustre Glaze of Ulisse Cantagalli* (exh. cat., Shapero Rare Books, London, 2018)

Rackham 1904. Rackham, Bernard, 'Italian Maiolica and other Pottery', in *Catalogue of the Art Collection, Volume I, 8 Cadogan Square, S.W.* [Cook Collection] (London, 1904)

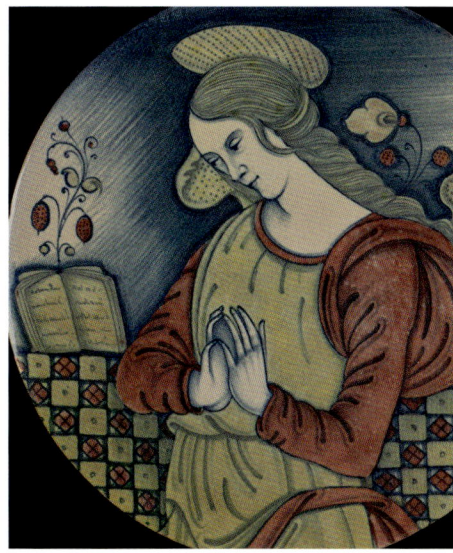

No.**16** (detail)

Rackham 1957. Rackham, Bernard, 'Xanto and "F. R.": An Insoluble Problem?', *Faenza* 43 (1957), pp.99–111

Rasmussen 1989. Rasmussen, Jörg, *The Robert Lehman Collection: 10: Italian Majolica* (New York, 1989)

Ravanelli Guidotti 1990. Ravanelli Guidotti, Carmen, *Museo Internazionale delle Ceramiche in Faenza. La Donazione Angiolo Fanfani. Ceramiche dal Medioevo al XX secolo* (Faenza, 1990)

Ravanelli Guidotti 1997–8. Ravanelli Guidotti, Carmen, *Magnificenza alla corte dei Medici. Arte a Firenze alla fine del Cinquecento* (exh. cat., Palazzo Pitti, Florence, 1997–8)

Ray 1968. Ray, Anthony, *English Delftware in the Robert Hall Warren Collection, Ashmolean Museum, Oxford* (London, 1968)

Ray 2000. Ray, Anthony, *Spanish Pottery 1248–1898* (London, V&A, 2000)

Reitlinger 1961–70. Reitlinger, Gerald, *The Economics of Taste* (London, 1961–70)

Ribeyrol et al. 2023. Ribeyrol, Charlotte, Matthew Winterbottom, and Madeline Hewitson (eds), *Colour Revolution: Victorian Art, Fashion & Design* (exh. cat., Ashmolean Museum, Oxford, 2023)

Rosen 2009. Rosen, Jean, *La faïence de Nevers 1585–1900* (Dijon, 2009)

Rouen 1999. *Peintures et sculptures de faïence: Rouen XVIII siècle* (exh. cat., Musées Rouen, 1999)

Rudoe 1994. Rudoe, Judy, *Decorative Arts 1850–1950: A Catalogue of the British Museum Collection* (London, 1994)

Sani 2007. Sani, Elisa Paola, 'List of Works By or Attributable to Francesco Xanto Avelli', in Mallet 2007, pp.190–201

Sani 2019. Sani, Elisa Paola, 'Una saliera derutese per i Reali d'Inghilterra', in Giulio Busti, Mauro Cesaretti, and Franco Cocchi (eds), *La maiolica italiana del rinascimento. Studi e ricerche* (Assisi/Turnhout, 2019), pp.107–14

Sani et al. 2017. Sani, Elisa, Matthew Reeves, and Justin Raccanello, *Maiolica before Raphael* (exh. cat., Sam Fogg Gallery, London, 2017)

Sannipoli 2008. Sannipoli, Ettore (ed.), *Omaggio a Alan Caiger-Smith maestro del lustro con opere di nove ceramisti umbri ed un tributo a Alan Peascod* (Gubbio, 2008)

Sannipoli 2018. Sannipoli, Ettore (ed.), *Cinque paesi una visione* (exh. cat., Gubbio, 2018)

Sfeir-Fakhri 2003. Sfeir-Fakhri, Liliane, 'Gironimo Tomasi, les dernières recherches', in Jean Rosen (ed.), *Majoliques européennes. Reflets de l'estampe lyonnaise* (Dijon, 2013), pp.102–5.

Simões 1946. Simões, João Dos Santos, 'Panneaux de majolique au Portugal', *Faenza* 32 (1946), pp.76–87

Spallanzani 1994. Spallanzani, Marco, *Ceramiche alla Corte dei Medici nel Cinquecento* (Modena, 1994)

Spallanzani 2024. Spallanzani, Marco, 'Niccolò Sisti alla corte dei Medici, un bicchiere di vetro tra Pisa e Firenze, 1584', in his *Otto studi sul vetro a Firenze secoli XIV–XVIII* (Florence, 2024), pp.79–83

Teodori and Celani 2017. Teodori, Brunella and Jennifer Celani (eds), *1915–1956–2016. Dall'asta al museo. Elio Volpi e Palazzo Davanzati nel collezionismo pubblico e privato del Novecento* (Florence, 2017)

Thornton and Wilson 2009. *Italian Renaissance Ceramics: A Catalogue of the British Museum Collection* (London, 2009)

Triolo 1996. Triolo, Julia, 'The Armorial Maiolica of Francesco Xanto Avelli', PhD thesis, Pennsylvania State University, Michigan, University Microfilms no. 9628192

Triolo 2023. Triolo, Julia, 'Archival Documents, 1530 to 1542, that Shed Light on the Life, Social Status, and Professional Milieu of the Italian Renaissance Maiolica Painter Francesco Xanto Avelli da Rovigo, "fictilium vasorum pictoris egregii" in Urbino', *Faenza* 109/2 (2023), pp.8–25

Tucker 2002. Tucker, Paul, '"Responsible Outsider": Charles Fairfax Murray and the South Kensington Museum", *Journal of the History of Collections* 14/1 (May 2002), pp.115–37

Tucker 2017. Tucker, Paul, *A Connoisseur and His Clients: The Correspondence of Charles Fairfax Murray with Frederic Burton, Wilhelm Bode and Julius Meyer (1867–1914)* (London, 2017)

Vasseur 1995. Vasseur, Roland, 'Les énigmes du plat de la passion de Beauvais: une nouvelle hypothèse de datation et d'interpretation', *Bulletin du groupe d'étude des Monuments et Oeuvres d'Art de l'Oise et du Beauvaisis* 65–6 (1995), pp.117–24

Vergnet-Ruiz 1956. Vergnet-Ruiz, Jean, 'Céramique de Beauvais et du Beauvaisis', *Positions de thésis des élèves de l'Ecole du Louvre* (1956), pp.82–92.

Vergnet-Ruiz 1964. Vergnet-Ruiz, Jean, 'Le plat de la Passion', *Revue de Louvre et de Musées de France* 2 (1964), pp.78–82

Vignon 2018. Vignon, Charlotte, *Masterpieces of French Faience: Selections from the Sidney R. Knafel Collection* (exh. cat., The Frick Collection, New York, 2018)

Wainwright 2002. Wainwright, Clive, 'The Making of the South Kensington Museum, IV: Relationships with the Trade: Webb and Bardini', in Charlotte Gere (ed.), *Journal of the History of Collections* 14/1 (May 2002), pp.63–78

Walker 1974. Walker, John, *Self-Portrait with Donors* (Boston, 1974)

Wallis 1903. Wallis, Henry, *Oak-Leaf Jars: A Fifteenth Century Italian Ware Showing Moresco Influence* (London, 1903)

Watson 1986. Watson, Wendy M., *Italian Renaissance Maiolica from the William A. Clark Collection* (London, 1986)

Williams and Wilson 1989. Williams, David and Timothy Wilson, 'A fragment of Italian Maiolica from Merstham', *Surrey Archaeological Collections* 79 (1989), pp.207–8

Wilson 1987. Wilson, Timothy, *Ceramic Art of the Italian Renaissance* (exh. cat., British Museum, London, 1987)

Wilson 1991. Wilson, Timothy (ed.), *Italian Renaissance Pottery: Papers Written in Association with a Colloquium at the British Museum* (London, 1991)

Wilson 1994. Wilson, Timothy, 'Alfred Pringsheim and his Collection of Italian Maiolica', in O. von Falke, *Italian Maiolica of the Pringsheim Collection* III (Ferrara, 1994) pp.79–99

Wilson 1996. Wilson, Timothy, *Italian Maiolica of the Renaissance* (catalogue of the Paolo Sprovieri Collection, Milan, 1996)

Wilson 2002. Wilson, Timothy, 'A Victorian Artist as Ceramic-Collector: The Letters of Henry Wallis', *Journal of the History of Collections* 14/1 (May 2002), pp.139–59; 14/2, pp.231–69

Wilson 2003. Wilson, Timothy, 'Gironimo Tomasi et le plat marqué *1582 leon* du British Museum', in Jean Rosen (ed.), *Majoliques européennes. Reflets de l'estampe lyonnaise* (Dijon, 2013), pp.86–101

Wilson 2004. Wilson, Timothy, 'The Maiolica-Painter Francesco Durantino: Mobility and Collaboration in Urbino *istoriato*', in Silvia Glaser (ed.), *Italienische Fayencen der Renaissance. Ihre Spuren in internationalen Museumssammlungen. Wissenschaftliche*

Beibände zum Anzeiger des germanischen Nationalmuseums, Band 22 (Nuremberg, 2004), pp.111–45

Wilson 2007. Wilson, Timothy, 'A Personality to be Reckoned With: Some Aspects of the Impact of Xanto on the Work of Nicola da Urbino', *Faenza* 93/4–6 (2007), pp.251–68

Wilson 2017. Wilson, Timothy, *Italian Maiolica and Europe* (Oxford, 2017)

Wilson 2018. Wilson, Timothy, *The Golden Age of Italian Maiolica Painting: Catalogue of a Private Collection* (Turin, 2018)

Wilson 2019. Wilson, Timothy, 'From Seville to Southwark: Tiles and Tile Pictures in Sixteenth-century Europe', *Oxford Ceramics Group Newsletter* 45 (September 2019), pp.3–9

Wilson and Sani 2006–7. Wilson, Timothy and Elisa Paola Sani (with the collaboration for vol. II of Carola Fiocco, Gabriella Gherardi, Marino Marini, and Claudio Paolinelli), *Le maioliche rinascimentali nelle collezioni della Fondazione Cassa di Risparmio di Perugia* (Perugia, 2006–7)

Winterbottom 2018. Winterbottom, Matthew, 'New Acquisition', *Ashmolean Magazine* 75 (spring 2018), pp.27–8

Winterbottom 2019. Winterbottom, Matthew, 'New Acquisition: Early Twentieth-century Florentine Bowl', *Ashmolean Magazine* 78 (autumn 2019), pp.22–3

Winterbottom 2023. Winterbottom, Matthew, 'Ye Bat Friend – A Portrait of WC', *Ashmolean Magazine* 86 (autumn 2023), pp.27–8

Index

References are to pages unless otherwise indicated. Museums are indexed under the place where they are located.
The notes have been indexed selectively.

Overleaf: detail of no.**2**

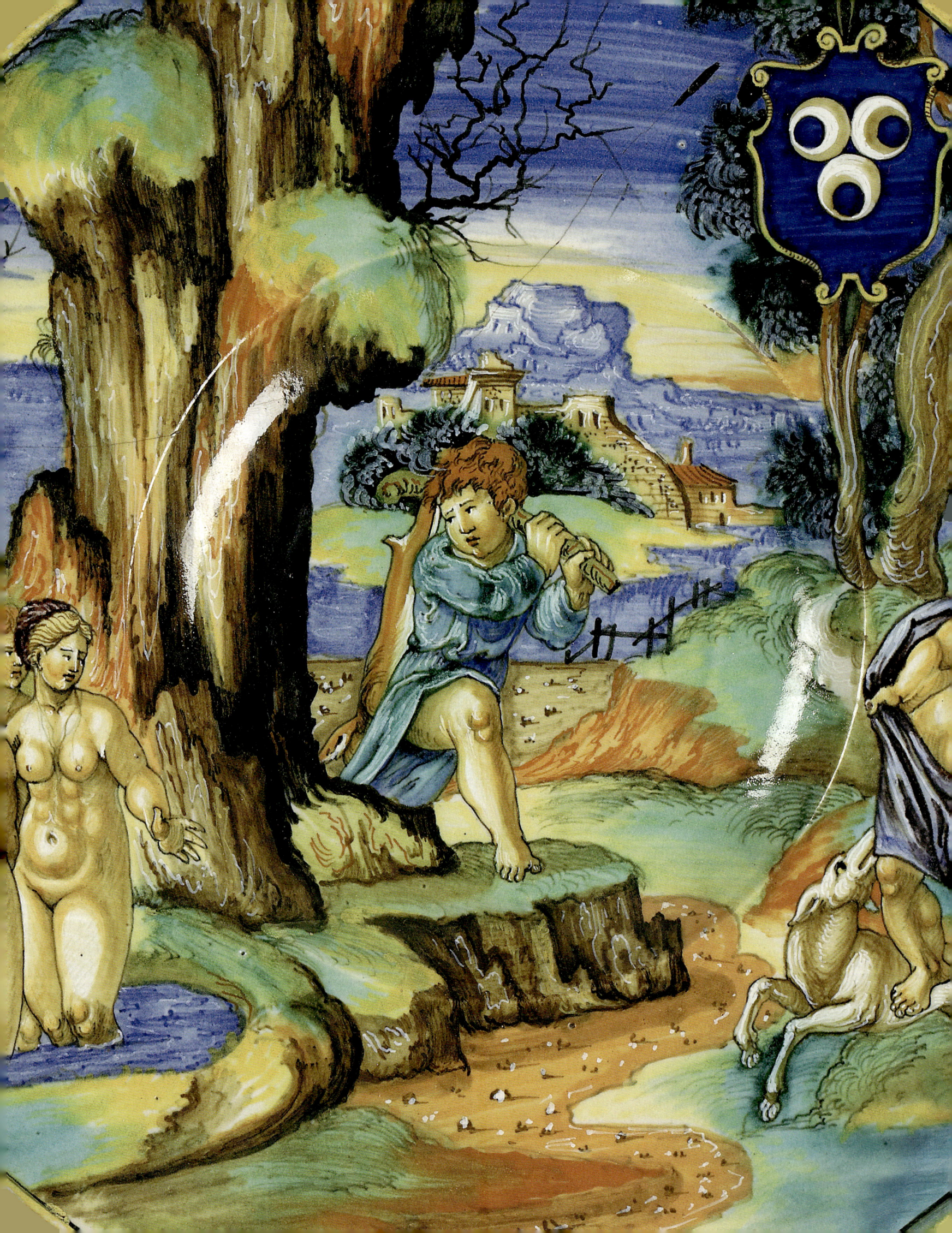

e tutto questo fa quel ase disopra doue entra il pal del
rochetto B e gli pali de gli mulini C. c. D. impero eb uolta
do il rochetto tira lasse ase co quel torco che e nella
sua gamba tirado tira ambe dua i pali e rispegendo
si puoi fa dar la uolta al macinello di tutta dua li
mulini come qui si uede

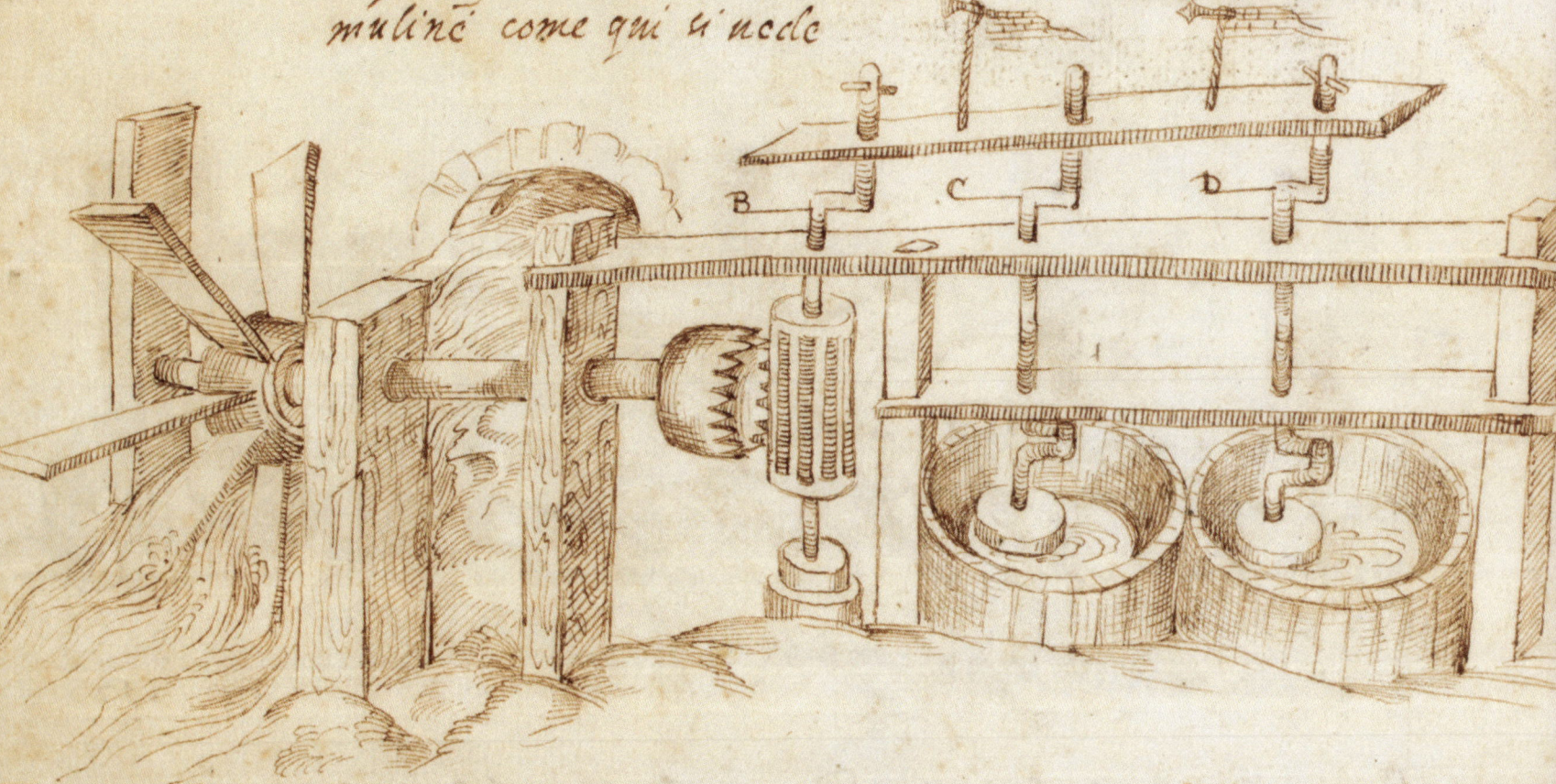

Ora mi resta mostrarui luso de gli mulini di Vinegia et
no e molto diferete dal nro. eglino hano di piu una
Rota di asse graue fitta nel palo del macinello ell
macinate sta impie di altro no uie questo anco in
tendo farui uedere niscuno no mi biasmi se io homeso
al Mulino ui buo uestito di una ueste co maniche a Comie